TYRONE

The Irish Revolution, 1912–23

Tyrone

Fergal McCluskey

FOUR COURTS PRESS

This book was set in 10.5 on 12.5 point Ehrhardt by
Mark Heslington Ltd, Scarborough, North Yorkshire for
FOUR COURTS PRESS
7 Malpas Street, Dublin 8, Ireland
www.fourcourtspress.ie
and in North America for
FOUR COURTS PRESS
c/o ISBS, 920 N.E. 58th Avenue, Suite 300, Portland, OR 97213.

A catalogue record for this title
is available from the British Library.

ISBN 978-1-84682-299-5 hbk
ISBN 978-1-84682-300-8 pbk

Printed in Great Britain
by Antony Rowe Ltd, Chippenham, Wilts.

Contents

Illustrations

Credits

Illustrations 1, 4, 9, 10: Linen Hall Library (Belfast) Postcard Collection; 2, 3, 30, 31: Cooper Collection (D1422) PRONI; 5, 30: PRONI; 6: National Museums Northern Ireland; 13: Independent Archive, National Library of Ireland; 14: Gerald MacAtasney; 15: McGarrity collection, Villanova University; 16: Fearghal O'Donnell; 17: *Ulster Herald*; 18: *Clogher Record*; 21, 23: Dr Éamon Phoenix; 22: © National Portrait Gallery, London; 24: Solo Syndication/Associated Newspapers Ltd; 26: Bertie Foley; 27, 28: Liam Ó Duibhir; 29: Louis O'Kane papers, CÓFLA; cover image courtesy of James Langton.

MAPS

Abbreviations

Adj.	Adjutant
AFIL	All for Ireland League
AG	Adjutant General
AOH	Ancient Order of Hibernians
ASU	Active Service Unit
ATIRA	Anti-Treaty IRA
BMH	Bureau of Military History
CAB	Cabinet Records, TNA
CBS	Crime Branch Special
CI	County Inspector, RIC/RUC
CO	Colonial Office, TNA
CÓFLA	Cardinal Tomás Ó Fiaich Memorial Library & Archive, Armagh
CS	Chief of Staff
CSORP	Chief Secretary's Office Registered Papers
DD	*Dungannon Democrat*
DÉ	Dáil Éireann
DÉLG	Dáil Éireann Local Government
DF	Department of Finance
DI	District Inspector, RIC/RUC
DIB	*Dictionary of Irish biography*
DN	*Dungannon News*
DORA	Defence of the Realm Act(s)
DORR	Defence of Realm Regulations
DT	Department of the Taoiseach
FJ	*Freeman's Journal*
GAA	Gaelic Athletic Association
GHQ	General Headquarters
GOIA	Government of Ireland Act
GOC	General Officer Commanding
HA	Home Affairs, PRONI
HO	Home Office, TNA
IF	*Irish Freedom*
IFS	Irish Free State
IG	Inspector General, RIC
IHS	*Irish Historical Studies*
II	*Irish Independent*
IMA	Irish Military Archives
IN	*Irish News*

INL	Irish Nation League
IPP	Irish Parliamentary Party
IRA	Irish Republican Army
IRB	Irish Republican Brotherhood
IT	*Irish Times*
ITGWU	Irish Transport and General Workers' Union
IV	*Irish Volunteer*
IVF	Irish Volunteer Force
JP	Justice of the Peace
KC	King's Counsel
LGB	Local Government Board
MHA	Ministry of Home Affairs
MP	Member of Parliament
MSP	Military Service Pension
NAI	National Archives of Ireland
NCO	Non-Commissioned Officer
ND	Northern Division
NEBB	Northeast Boundary Bureau
NI	Northern Ireland
NL	*Belfast Newsletter*
NLI	National Library of Ireland
NVF	National Volunteer Force
O/C	Officer Commanding
PR	Proportional Representation
Précis	Précis Report Crime Branch Special, RIC
PRONI	Public Records Office of Northern Ireland
QM	Quartermaster
QMG	Quartermaster General
RDC	Rural District Council
RIC	Royal Irish Constabulary
ROIA	Restoration of Order in Ireland Act
RUC	Royal Ulster Constabulary
SF	Sinn Féin
SFSC	Sinn Féin Standing Committee
TC	*Tyrone Courier*
TCD	Trinity College Dublin
TD	Teachta Dála, member of Dáil Éireann
TNA	The National Archives, London
UCDAD	University College Dublin Archives Department
UDC	Urban District Council
UH	*Ulster Herald*
UIL	United Ireland League

USC	Ulster Special Constabulary
UUC	Ulster Unionist Council
UVF	Ulster Volunteer Force
UWU	Ulster Workers' Union
WO	War Office, TNA
WS	Witness Statement to Bureau of Military History

Editors' note: The *IHS* convention has been followed when referring to Derry for the city and bishopric, and Londonderry for the county and parliamentary constituencies.

Acknowledgments

The novel research on this book was carried out during my time as an IRCHSS postdoctoral fellow at NUI Galway. I owe a sincere debt of gratitude to Gearóid Ó Tuathaigh who was incredibly generous with his time, not only as my supervisor at Galway but also as this book neared publication, when his help was significant. I would also like to thank Fearghal McGarry and Marie Coleman of QUB for all their help and advice. I had originally planned to write a monograph on the period 1918–25 as a follow up to my first book, but my editors, Daithí Ó Corráin and Mary Ann Lyons, convinced me of the merits of this series. I have to thank Daithí, in particular, who spent a lot of his time editing and helping me to condense voluminous material and numerous drafts into a single monograph. I am also grateful to Mike Brennan for his hard work on the maps. Ba mhaith liom mo bhuíochas a ghabháil den fhoireann go léir i gColáiste Feirste, go háirithe Diarmaid agus Séamus i Roinn na Staire agus Breandán a bhíodh riamh do mo spreagadh. Chudigh Dónal Ó Dálaigh agus Dara Mac Coille go mór liom agus mise ag cur na ngrianghraf le chéile. Several people read various drafts, including Brian Kelly, Fearghal Mac Ionnrachtaigh, Michael McCann and Patrick Smylie. I wish to thank the staff at all the archives listed in the bibliography. Many people helped to write this book by providing information and encouragement and I have to thank Gerard MacAtasney; Mother Begnignus Kelly (RIP); Bertie Foley; Róisín Kelly; Pat John Rafferty (RIP); Aidan Fee; Martin Molloy; Robert Stewart; Cathal Murtagh; Plunkett Nugent; Oweny McCaughey (RIP); Donal McAnallen and Liam Ó Duibhir. I apologize in advance to anyone I have left out. I owe a special debt of gratitude to my extended family and especially to my wife, Michelle, whose limitless patience and unconditional support made it possible to balance my writing with a full-time post in Coláiste Feirste. Tiomnaítear an leabhar seo do mo bhean chéile álainn mar sin de agus dár leanbh, Cara, nach raibh aithne go fóill agam uirthi agus mise á scríobh.

Foreword

Recent decades have seen an impressive increase in the volume of academic – and more popular – publications dealing with aspects of the Irish historical experience during the 'revolutionary era', 1912–23. Improved access to primary sources and an increase in the number of younger historians (from many countries) engaged in research on modern Irish history have been significant stimuli to the growing body of work and the range of fresh perspectives on this pivotal period. It must also be acknowledged that the protracted conflict in Northern Ireland during the final third of the last century – and the appeal to historical precedent and pedigree by the main parties to the conflict – undoubtedly gave a frequently dark topicality and urgency to some of the research. Indeed, the violence of the conflict cast a shadow of interpretative anxiety – on moral and ethical as well as ideological grounds – on a number of important publications, provoking controversy and recrimination that resonated well beyond the boundaries of academic debate. It is reasonable to expect that the decade of centenary commemorations will see a continuing flow of academic – and other – publications on all aspects of the revolutionary era in Ireland.

The litany of pivotal events in Irish history, bounded at one end by the introduction of the third home rule bill in April 1912 and, on the other, by the close of the Irish Civil War in May 1923, needs no recital here. New research in recent years on many aspects of this eventful period – key episodes, movements, actors and the global canvas against which events in Ireland have to be considered – has forced historians and members of the general public (sensitized to the new research through the media of television, the higher journalism and the wider public debate in civil society) to reconsider long-established, dominant narratives and historical myths, nationalist and unionist.

Among the most valuable of the new publications of recent years has been the crop of local studies of the revolutionary decade, notably at county level, with monographs now published on Clare, Cork, Longford and Sligo, together with a heavier crop of articles and book chapters concerned with aspects of the revolutionary period at a county or indeed sub-county level. What has been missing until now from this mosaic of local studies has been a closely researched study of one of the six counties in Ulster that came to constitute Northern Ireland under the Government of Ireland Act of 1920. This deficit has now been rectified by the publication of Fergal McCluskey's important monograph on Tyrone.

Earlier studies at county level have dealt with counties where nationalists were in the majority, in some instances overwhelmingly so; unionist sentiment and electoral strength was a minor theme, and the narrative of political change in the revolutionary period revolved around the dynamics of the rivalry between 'varieties' of Irish nationalism. Tyrone stands in a different category. Notoriously described by an exasperated Asquith as '... that most damnable creation of the perverted ingenuity of man', County Tyrone was pivotal in the prolonged 'Ulster crisis' that climaxed with partition in 1920, in time becoming a 'settled' structure with the winding up of the Boundary Commission in 1925.

Tyrone and Fermanagh, on a county basis, had nationalist majorities in 1920. This did not prevent their incorporation into the firmly unionist-dominated Northern Ireland. How this happened is a central theme of McCluskey's study. Geo-cultural factors, the salience of religion, class and gender, and issues of leadership, are all key elements of the story. The dynamics of competition (and conflict) between various factions of Irish nationalism are carefully identified. But it was the resources available to unionism that would ultimately prove decisive. Though in a slight minority at county level, Tyrone unionists proved cohesive and single-minded in their determination not to surrender or be sundered from their position within the provincial hegemon of Ulster unionism. The military resources at their disposal were considerable. But McCluskey also emphasizes the wider considerations of empire (related to security and sentiment) that ensured that Ulster (including Tyrone) unionists would enjoy the decisive support of influential sections of the Tory elite in Britain – in government and in the higher reaches of the military and political establishments – at crucial moments throughout the revolutionary decade.

Whether an alternative outcome may be imagined – for example, a class-based challenge to the two bourgeois-led confessional blocks within Tyrone politics and society – is a question to which different readers will make their own responses. But Fergal McCluskey has provided a rich body of evidence that demands careful consideration in any assessment of the political options present in Tyrone during the turbulent years 1912–23. This original and important study advances our knowledge, and ought to enhance our understanding of the political conflict in Tyrone in these years and of the complex and troubled legacy bequeathed to later generations.

Gearóid Ó Tuathaigh,
Professor Emeritus in History,
National University of Ireland, Galway
December 2013

The Irish Revolution, 1912–23 series

Since the turn of the century, a growing number of scholars have been actively researching this seminal period in modern Irish history. More recently, propelled by the increasing availability of new archival material, this endeavour has intensified. This series brings together for the first time the various strands of this exciting and fresh scholarship within a nuanced interpretative framework, making available concise, accessible, scholarly studies of the Irish Revolution experience at a local level to a wide audience.

The approach adopted is both thematic and chronological, addressing the key developments and major issues that occurred at a county level during the tumultuous 1912–23 period. Beginning with an overview of the social, economic and political milieu in the county in 1912, each volume assesses the strength of the home rule movement and levels of labour and feminist activism. The genesis and organization of paramilitarism from 1913 are traced; responses to the outbreak of the First World War and its impact on politics at a county level are explored; and the significance of the 1916 Rising is assessed. The varying fortunes of constitutional and separatist nationalism are examined. The local experience of the War of Independence, reaction to the Truce and the Anglo-Irish Treaty and the course and consequences of the Civil War are subject to detailed examination and analysis. The result is a compelling account of life in Ireland in this formative era.

Mary Ann Lyons
Department of History
NUI Maynooth

Daithí Ó Corráin
Department of History
St Patrick's College, Drumcondra

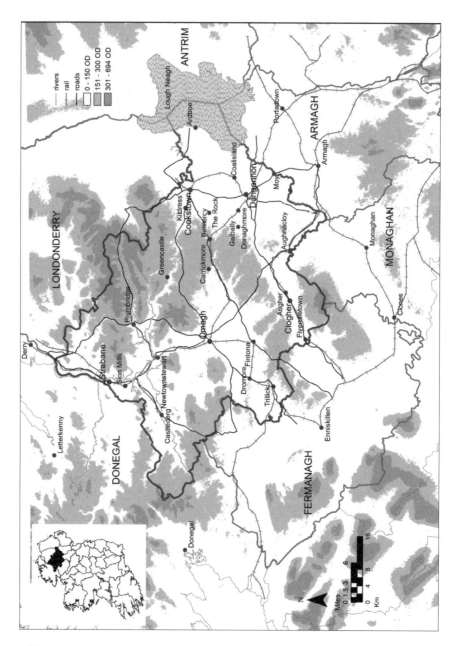

1 Places mentioned in the text

1 County Tyrone in 1912

Sitting at the political crossroads of Ireland, County Tyrone was at the centre of the conflict between nationalism and unionism, and the evolution of partition; its fate shaped that of Ireland itself. The collapse of the Buckingham Palace Conference of July 1914 called to negotiate a partitionist settlement to the home rule controversy led H.H. Asquith, the Liberal Party prime minister to describe Tyrone as 'that most damnable creation of the perverted ingenuity of man'.[1] Although the revolutionary period that followed pulsated with demands for freedom and equality, Tyrone's fate hinged on the vexed question of partition. The 'pivot counties' of Fermanagh and Tyrone loomed large in deliberations over the boundary line that would ultimately divide Ireland. Tyrone witnessed an intense battle between constitutional nationalism and republicanism. The county's abandonment to unionist rule posed serious questions regarding the all-Ireland demand. Tyrone was also home to deeply entrenched and formidable traditions of unionism and Orangeism. Hence, Edward Carson insisted on an 'irreducible minimum' of six counties in any future unionist regime, as the abandonment of Tyrone jeopardized the entire project.[2]

On an imperial scale, Tyrone weighed heavily on the minds of statesmen tasked with solving the Irish question in line with Britain's global interests, not alone in 1914 but after the war's end also. The Easter Rising and Sinn Féin's (SF) mandate for self-determination may have transformed Irish politics, but the highly problematic political allegiances in Tyrone persisted. The county was central to competing republican and unionist territorial demands and, prior to the Anglo-Irish Treaty of December 1921, the British cabinet resolved that if negotiations with SF broke down it should be on the principle of upholding the Empire rather than coercing border nationalists into a unionist administration.[3] In February 1922 Churchill famously captured the intractability of conflicting aspirations in west Ulster: 'The whole map of Europe has been changed ... but as the deluge subsides and the waters fall short we see the dreary steeples of Fermanagh and Tyrone emerging once again.'[4]

Tyrone represented a border zone between nationalist and unionist Ireland. Of a total population of 142,665 in 1911, Catholics comprised a slender majority of 55.4 per cent or just over 10,000.[5] Any treatment of Tyrone must acknowledge the area's colonial past. The Flight of the Earls (1607) symbolized the final collapse of the Gaelic order. After the Ulster Plantation (1609), Tyrone, seat of the O'Neills, became one of Ireland's most colonized areas with three areas of planter settlement. The first ran between Lough Neagh and the Sperrin foothills, centring on Scottish settlement in Cookstown. On the western border with Donegal, the area around Strabane and Newtownstewart represented an additional area of Scottish settlement. By 1911 most of the county's Presbyterian population, 18.6 per cent of the total, lived in the Cookstown and Strabane Rural District Councils (RDCs). The largest planter area from the southwest tip of Lough Neagh across the Clogher Valley contained the majority of Tyrone's Anglicans, 22.7 per cent of the population. Therefore, Tyrone represented 'a contact zone between the two major units of British settlement': Ulster-Scots and Ulster Anglo-Irish.[6] In contemporaneous maps compiled by Irish nationalists, Ulster unionists and British civil servants, orange and green symbolized this geo-political topography; the former represented settlers and the latter natives. As Michael Laffan remarks, 'by and large, religious maps and contour maps coincided; brown hills represented green Catholics, green valleys represented orange Protestants'.[7]

This colonial history left an indelible mark on the Tyrone psyche. The terms nationalist and unionist have been selected over religious labels because, even as late as July 1913, the RIC estimated that five per cent of the Protestant population favoured home rule, predominantly among the Presbyterian tenantry.[8] In general, two opposing social pyramids, one orange and one green, occupied the same geographical territory. This cleavage, whether expressed through religion, nationality or ethnicity, dominated local politics. Kevin O'Shiel, the prominent Omagh nationalist, moderate Sinn Féiner and Irish Free State judge, described how, growing up, a

> kind of involuntary or unconscious 'apartheid' existed … sanctioned by the custom of circumstances and accepted as inevitable … And, whilst undoubtedly this 'apartheid' originated from and had its roots in the Protestant Ascendancy… a large section of the Catholic population adhered to it as firmly as the most bigoted Orangeman.[9]

The privileged position occupied by local unionists, whether granted by plantation, providence or preferment, explained their pre-eminence in the two major sectors of the local economy – land and linen. In 1911 sixty-four per cent of adult males were engaged in some form of agriculture, with labourers and farm servants accounting for a quarter of the agricultural population.[10] Just over three-quarters of the population lived on agricultural holdings. This marked Tyrone out as something of a transition zone between the four more eastern counties, excluding Belfast, which all had figures close to sixty per cent, and the rural west – Cavan, Donegal, Fermanagh and Monaghan – which registered figures of over eighty per cent. Tyrone's agricultural population was also relatively poor with fifty-eight per cent living on land valued at £15 or less, a percentage point lower than the national average. In Ulster this was only surpassed by Monaghan, Cavan and impoverished Donegal.[11]

Class and social status represented key indicators of leadership within Tyrone

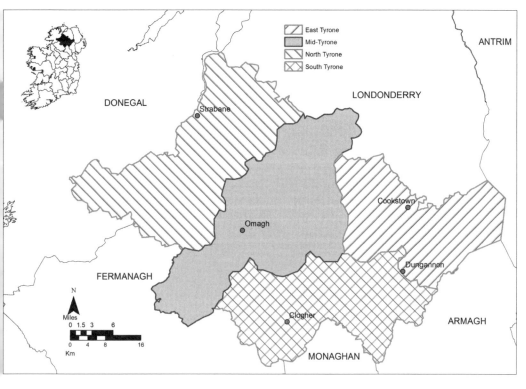

2 Parliamentary constituencies, pre-1918

unionism. Political influence rested with the local aristocracy, particularly the well-connected Abercorn and Ranfurly families, who summered in Ireland but wintered in London and fulfilled several roles in imperial administration. Many Ulster unionists, particularly Belfast's commercial and professional élite, favoured a less aristocratic, provincial movement with greater independence from British Toryism.[12] Factory owners and the professional middle class swelled the ranks of the Ulster Unionist Council (UUC) established in 1905 under the presidency of the 2nd duke of Abercorn. The UUC had 200 delegates from across the nine Ulster counties, including 100 constituency members and 50 Orangemen. The council's creation formalized trends towards a distinct Ulster unionist organization, on separate, but friendly, terms with existing bodies in southern Ireland and Britain. The UUC helped consolidate unionism in Ulster and silence alternative voices such the Independent Orange Order and trade unionism. It also embodied Belfast's virtual domination of Ulster unionist politics.[13] Landlord acquiescence altered the complexion of the Tyrone squirearchy, if not its ultimate character. Indeed, Hugh de Fellenberg Montgomery, the leading landlord and UUC delegate, acknowledged that

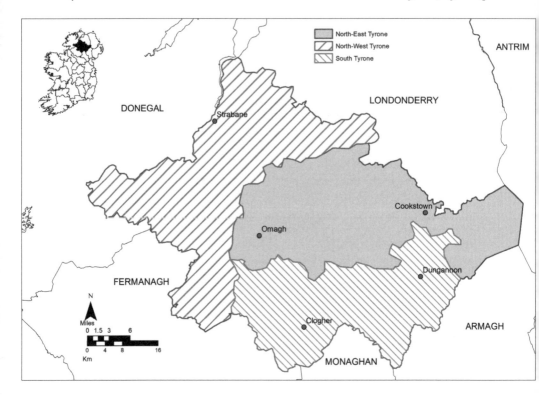

3 Parliamentary constituencies, post-1918

although William Coote, Ballygawley Presbyterian, factory owner and MP for South Tyrone, was 'not altogether an admirable person', he had to be included in the local leadership since he 'represents the Unionist and Orange democracy here.'[14] As in any broad-based consensus, local unionism contained heterogeneous elements. While Coote, who led the South Tyrone Ulster Volunteer Force (UVF), was an unreconstructed bigot, his superior officer, Ambroise St Quentin Ricardo, the English-born manager of Herdman's Mill at Sion Mills, a village to the south of Strabane on the western border with Donegal, supported the local feis and adopted a more tolerant, though no less unionist, attitude.

If the landed interest still dominated, local employers represented the new blood necessary in any popular movement. By 1911 twenty per cent of adult males were engaged in industry, mainly along the western shores of Lough Neagh. Coote's Woollen Mill, near Ballygawley, a small village thirteen miles south-west of Dungannon, was an exception, as it lay in the largely rural Omagh Union. In addition, competition for employment partly explains the strength of the rival Orange Order and Ancient Order of Hibernians (AOH). Formed in 1795, the Orange Order spread rapidly among the Anglican lower class who

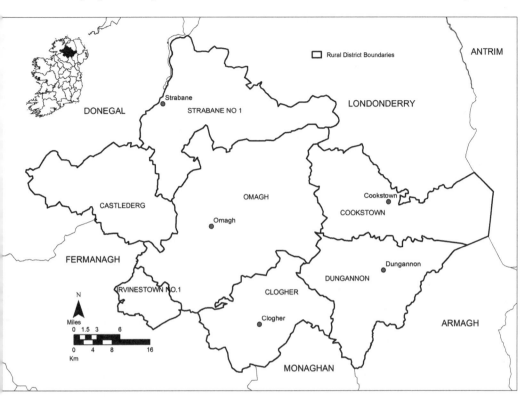

4 Local government divisions

pledged 'the maintenance of "Protestant Ascendancy" against the Catholic and republican.'[15] The Order's fortunes declined in the nineteenth century. In response to the challenge of the Land League, however, many unionist landlords joined the Order to promote a broad-based unionist movement opposed to home rule in 1885–6. This led to significant growth of Orangeism in the late Victorian period. By the time of the third home rule crisis Tyrone was 'probably the most densely organized county, over a third of adult male Protestants were Orangemen in 1912'.[16] The Order represented the centrifugal element in a cross-class unionist identity and the seed-bed of loyalist militancy.

On the nationalist side, Ribbonmen, a secret Catholic society, flourished in rural Tyrone in the nineteenth century and later emerged in the guise of the AOH. The Catholic lower classes subscribed to a Ribbon identity that mirrored Orange sectarianism. Both espoused an aggressive form of popular ideology masked by religious observance; both indulged their passion for band parades and the regalia of the sash and party song; both had their big day at the field, the Orangemen on 12 July and the Hibernians on 15 August (the Feast of the

Assumption or what the Hibernians called 'Lady Day'). From a political perspective, both also engaged in the sectarian faction fighting that punctuated the summer and reached its zenith at local and Westminster elections.

By 1911 the AOH had eighty divisions and formed the backbone of the constitutional movement in Tyrone.[17] This expansion took place under the stewardship of Belfast's Joseph Devlin, the national president of the Board of Erin (the governing body of the Irish AOH) from July 1905 and leader of northern constitutionalism. While the unionist upper and middle class sought to harness popular Orangeism, the Catholic middle class and clergy endeavoured to control the Hibernians in their struggle with unionism for mastery of local government and parliamentary representation. The removal of a clerical ban, the strong support of Bishop Patrick O'Donnell of Raphoe and a designation as a friendly society added further respectability to the AOH.[18] By 1912 it had replaced the United Irish League (UIL) as the main nationalist organization in Tyrone. The UIL, which emerged as a radical agrarian movement in Mayo in 1898, spread rapidly across the country, shedding its radicalism in the process. By the time of the Ulster crisis it represented the rather tame constituency organization of the Irish Parliamentary Party (IPP), where priests and members of Tyrone's small Catholic professional and mercantile class plotted the downfall of unionist local government.

In the 1885 general election, the Conservatives and Unionists gained sixteen and the Nationalists seventeen seats in Ulster. The Liberal Party in Ulster was obliterated, due partly to the enfranchisement of agricultural labourers and the resulting upsurge in popular Orangeism and nationalism, but also due to profound divisions within Ulster liberalism itself. The emergence of opposing unionist and nationalist blocs was consolidated when William Gladstone introduced the first home rule bill in 1886. The first home rule crisis convinced Ulster Liberals such as Tyrone's Hugh de Fellenberg Montgomery to throw in his lot with unionism. It also persuaded them that in the words of James Hamilton, the future second duke of Abercorn, 'a union of liberals and conservatives' was needed 'to stem the nationalist tide'.[19] The second home rule crisis of 1893 similarly bound all shades of unionism together. It also demonstrated close relations between the British Conservative Party and the landed unionist élite. By the time of the third home rule crisis in 1912, the unionist position had evolved, particularly after the formation of the UUC. From 1886 onwards the IPP was locked into an alliance with the Liberal Party.

At a county level, local government provided the arena for organized unionist and nationalist rivalry with control of Tyrone County Council the prize. Under the Local Government (Ireland) Act 1898, local elections took place every three years. The measure effectively ended the political dominance of the landlord class. Nationalists won nearly seventy-five per cent of county council seats in 1899. Even in Ulster, nationalists 'were only 6 per cent short of the unionist total and in the board of guardian elections more nationalists were returned than unionists.'[20] Despite Tyrone's nationalist majority, unionists maintained control of local government. The electoral boundaries drawn up in 1898 by Tory officials favoured northern unionists. Of the seven Rural District Councils in Tyrone, unionists secured a majority on Castlederg, Clogher, Cookstown and Dungannon, even though all had a nationalist majority population.[21] Of the four urban districts, Omagh, Strabane, Dungannon and Cookstown, only the latter had a majority unionist population, yet nationalists only controlled Strabane Urban District Council (UDC).[22] As RDC chairmen became ex officio members of the county council, this guaranteed a unionist majority, and with it control of local government appointments. Interestingly, when the nationalists wrested control of Omagh UDC, 'whole streets and terraces of working-class houses sprang up with mushroom-like suddenness' in the town's southern ward, into which poured nationalist labourers, thereby securing future nationalist control of Omagh town council.[23]

Throughout the period, unionist-controlled bodies appointed employees on a sectarian basis. Prior to the introduction of proportional representation (PR) in 1919, only five nationalists appeared on Tyrone County Council's salaried list. Through gerrymandering, Dungannon UDC returned a unionist majority, which employed just two nationalist refuse collectors.[24] This pattern persisted throughout the county. William Miller, Newtownstewart JP, Orange delegate to the UUC and local UVF adjutant, requested that the 3rd duke of Abercorn return from England in order to secure the election of Andrew Young as rate collector as he was 'a good unionist ... secretary of the Killeter Unionist Association and a section leader in the UVF and thus deserves support'.[25] Only rate payers held the parliamentary and local government franchise. Therefore rate collectors proved invaluable at the revision sessions, where unionist and nationalist election agents and solicitors contested objections to the local voters' list before sizeable crowds, in those 'cinemaless days' when revision sessions 'provided a species of public entertainment'.[26]

An examination of Tyrone's four parliamentary constituencies reveals a further level of regional and political variation. In 1912 the county had four parliamentary seats. Typically, the East and Mid-Tyrone constituencies returned a constitutional Nationalist candidate; South Tyrone a Unionist; while an agreed Liberal candidate represented North Tyrone. East Tyrone had an extremely slim nationalist majority and electoral contests were notoriously tight with a handful of votes enough to separate nationalist victor from unionist opponent. In 1906 Tom Kettle took the seat for the IPP by a mere eighteen votes. The area included the linen towns of Dungannon, Cookstown and Coalisland, and was a hub of sectarian tension, where orange and green competed for employment and electoral advantage. This division was evident in the local press. The *Tyrone Courier*, printed in Dungannon (population 3,830), and *Mid-Ulster Mail*, printed in Cookstown (population 3,685), adopted a pronounced Orange-Tory tone, while the *Dungannon News* reflected the liberal unionist perspective until its absorption by the *Courier* in early 1914. When William Archer Redmond, son of the IPP leader, won the East Tyrone seat in December 1910 by 140 votes, the *Courier* applauded the fact that only fourteen 'of the resident Protestant voters' failed to vote and proclaimed that 'in East Tyrone, no Protestant ever votes for the Nationalist'.[27] The ardently Devlinite, *Dungannon Democrat*, came into circulation in 1913 at the height of the home rule crisis. The Dungannon area formed the western tip of Ulster's linen triangle which extended eastwards to industrial Belfast. The Dungannon and Cookstown Poor Law Unions, in essence the East Tyrone parliamentary constituency, were home to forty-three of Tyrone's fifty-one leading manufacturers. Most notable were the two large mills in Cookstown – Gunning's and Adair's – and the two major concerns in Dungannon – Dickson's and Stevenson's – all owned by leading unionists.

The same area also had an established working-class Irish Republican Brotherhood (IRB) tradition which, since its foundation in 1858, sought an independent democratic Irish republic, rejected constitutional nationalism and adopted a consciously non-sectarian outlook. It faced considerable opposition from middle-class nationalism, both clerical and lay.[28] Indeed, James 'Dundee' Devlin from Ardboe, Tyrone county centre, warned members 'against telling anything in connection with the movement to priests', who 'were traitors in political matters'.[29] The IRB produced such revolutionary notables as Dungannon's Tom Clarke, the lead signatory of the 1916 Proclamation. The Dungannon–Coalisland nexus represented the core territory of Mid-Ulster Fenianism, which fanned out in a crescent along the south and west shores of Lough Neagh and was supported by some local artisans, labourers, small farmers and factory workers. The Tyrone IRB was involved in nascent trade unionism; activism that continued into the revolutionary period.[30] In 1913 the RIC reported that the IRB in North Armagh and East Tyrone had sent 'trifling sums' to help Jim Larkin during the Lockout.[31] The police reflected the typical class prejudice of Edwardian Ireland, continually dismissing Tyrone republicans due to their low social status.[32] Dungannon IRB members such as John 'Jack' McElvogue, the town centre, successively and successfully stood in the urban council's nationalist west ward 'to explode the old theory that it was only men with money, whether they had brains or not, were fit to look after the affairs of the town'.[33] This influential local IRB tradition championed the Irish Volunteer movement early on and continued that backing after the Redmondite split. In due course the Tyrone IRA also drew the bulk of its members and support from this community, despite majority support for SF among Tyrone nationalists by 1919.

IRB influence extended westward into the Sperrin Mountains and the small remnant of Gaeltacht Thír Eoghain. The Mid-Tyrone constituency had a more secure nationalist majority than East Tyrone. Its urban hub was the county town of Omagh, with a population of 4,836, which acted as an agricultural market town and administration centre but with little manufacturing. It was also the headquarters of the RIC in the county, which comprised thirty-five barracks and 247 officers under the command of W.J. Millar, the County Inspector (CI).[34] Omagh was also a garrison town with the military depot of the Royal Inniskilling Fusiliers. Although the officer corps was overwhelmingly unionist, typically, two-thirds of the soldiers were nationalist 'townees' and agricultural labourers who enlisted for economic reasons. Omagh had two influential newspapers. The Hibernian *Ulster Herald* was founded in 1901 on John Street and was owned by Michael Lynch, a leading constitutionalist and JP. The unionist *Tyrone Constitution,* the county's oldest paper, was 'rather rabid on the subject of Home Rule', as its editor, Philip Cruickshank, was also county secretary of the UVF.[35]

Mid-Tyrone exhibited the factionalism and underlying class tensions within Tyrone nationalism. It witnessed a struggle between the IPP's popular Hibernian wing, which followed the lead of Joe Devlin and John Dillon, and the more conservative, middle-class element centred on the Murnaghan family, which gravitated towards Tim Healy and the Catholic Church. In 1892, due to insecurity surrounding the North and South Tyrone constituencies, the Dillonites offered the Liberal Party both seats in return for nomination rights. This led to the 'Omagh Scandal' of 1895 when Healy accused Dillon of 'selling Tyrone Nationalists to the Liberals'.[36] The division between conservative Healyites and the popular Dillonite majority endured after the IPP's official reunification in 1900.[37] George Murnaghan senior (Mid-Tyrone MP, 1895–1910) was a self-made man who returned from St Louis, US, and took an active role in local commerce and politics. He was chairman of Omagh RDC from 1899 until 1924, and of Omagh Board of Guardians.[38] At the beginning of the twentieth century Healyites fought the AOH for control of local constitutionalism. Devlin's dual appointments as UIL national secretary and Board of Erin president allowed the local Hibernians to gain the upper hand.[39] Nominally, the struggle concerned the democratic selection of IPP election candidates. In reality, however, Devlin employed the Hibernians to cement centralized control against Healyite factionalism. At the January 1910 general election, the IPP nominated John Valentine, with local AOH support, over Murnaghan, who stood as an independent nationalist. This ensured a unionist victory. However, the seat was recaptured by Richard McGhee of the IPP in December 1910. The Murnaghanites and their clerical supporters were aggrieved that a 'crowd of nobodies' selected the nationalist candidate for Mid-Tyrone.[40] Kevin O'Shiel, whose father was Murnaghan's election agent, described the working-class area of Brook Street in Omagh as

a vile squalid lane reeking with foul smells and inhabited largely by
slatterns and down and outs and good for naughts, all mainly in rags.
Respectable people would not venture down that ill-lit street at night
because of the drunken orgies of its disorderly inhabitants ... It was
mainly, but not wholly, Catholic, I regret to say.[41]

O'Shiel's memoir of his early days in Omagh is a highly entertaining account,
which exposes, quite unconsciously, the petty class snobbery of the
Murnaghanites and an element among Tyrone's small Catholic professional
class. Ironically, the Murnaghanites played a major role in SF's successful
struggle against the IPP after the Easter Rising. Apart from a shared enthusiasm
for the Irish language, the Healyite bourgeoisie and the traditional republican
community were unlikely allies during the SF revolution.

North Tyrone normally elected a Liberal home ruler in line with the deal that
provoked the 'Omagh Scandal'. Strabane, with its population of 5,107 in 1911,
was the largest town in the constituency and conjoined Lifford in County
Donegal. The town had a large nationalist majority and an IRB cell. Throughout
the period local nationalists and republicans had a close affiliation with Donegal.
Strabane was the hub for what the Donegal CI labelled a cluster of 200 Sinn
Féiners.[42] Indeed, the area was closely associated with East Donegal, operating
in the hinterland of Derry city. At the 1895 general election, Charles Hemphill,
the Liberal candidate and solicitor-general, wrested the seat from the possession
of the Hamilton family. James Hamilton, duke of Abercorn and Irish Masonic
grandmaster, not only sat in the House of Lords but also chaired Tyrone County
Council. He subsequently sponsored the UVF's 1st (North) Tyrone Battalion.
His Baronscourt estate, three miles south of Newtownstewart, was the centre of
UVF activity during the Ulster crisis. Indeed, unionists from the forty per cent
Protestant East Donegal constituency had a close affinity to their brethren across
the Tyrone border. Donegal's 3,000 Ulster Volunteers perfected their training at
Baronscourt in June 1914.[43] The local UVF leadership centred on Baronscourt
and Sion Mills, with Ambroise Ricardo and his brother-in-law, E.C. Herman,
the unsuccessful unionist candidate in the 1910 North Tyrone by-election,
leading the local battalion. When the time came for the Ulster Covenanters to
abandon Donegal, the most forceful opposition from within the six counties
came from Ricardo.

The North Tyrone constituency area was predominantly agricultural but
there were four manufacturing concerns, particularly Herdman's in Sion Mills
and two sizeable garment factories in Strabane, satellites of Derry city's established shirt trade. A succession of Liberal government officials succeeded
Hemphill in North Tyrone. The most controversial was Redmond John Barry,
who served as solicitor and then attorney-general. His nomination provoked
equal resentment among local unionists and Healyites, who felt disenfranchised

5 Police and British army distribution, 1921–2.
† Each district headquarters area also contained Ulster Special Constabulary (USC) (A &
B Class)
* RIC/USC A Class only

by the selection of a Liberal. Another Liberal and privy counsellor, T.W. Russell,
succeeded Barry in a by-election in 1911. However, Russell already had an established, if chequered, connection with Tyrone politics, as he had held the
neighbouring South Tyrone seat until 1910.

South Tyrone, by contrast, which traversed the majority unionist Clogher
Valley, regularly returned a Unionist MP. The chain of small rural villages that
comprise the area is immortalized in the local rhyme: 'Augher, Clogher,
Fivemiletown, Sixmilecross and seven mile round'. Between 1886 and 1910 the
seat was held by T.W. Russell, a liberal unionist and ardent land reform
campaigner, who tended to pursue an independent political course. Relying on
tenant-right rhetoric as well as Presbyterian and nationalist cross-voting, he
achieved several significant by-election victories over official Unionist candi-

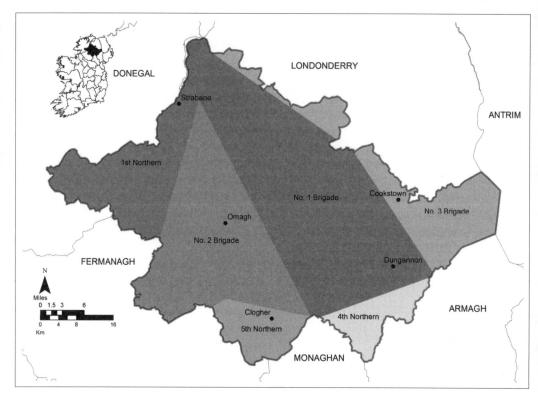

6 IRA battalion and Northern Divisional areas, 1922

dates. By January 1910 Russell had become a Liberal home ruler and was defeated by Andrew Horner, a Limavady Presbyterian and unionist KC. Like any political bloc, Tyrone unionism represented a diverse grouping. At his peak, Russell argued that Presbyterian tenantry supported the union due to 'specific material grievances' rather than 'the strength of the Orange Order or the ingrained sectarianism of the Belfast merchants and artisans'.[44] Yet plebeian loyalism and Orange sectarianism arguably represented the dominant element within Tyrone unionism. The real importance of Russell's defeat, however, was that it signalled the triumph of the UUC, which had vanquished heterogeneous and relatively progressive currents in early twentieth-century unionism such as the Russellites and the Independent Orange Order. By the 1910 election, this had been practically achieved and unionism faced the impending home rule crisis in robust shape. Belfast's Old Town Hall would face little dissent from Tyrone unionists. The unionist leadership could rely on the loyalty of their supporters, an advantage their IPP rivals did not enjoy.

Throughout the 1912–23 period British party rivalry and the pursuit of high office profoundly influenced Tyrone politics. Conservative opposition to home rule centred on the fundamental issue of empire. Every unionist, British and Irish, who rebelled against home rule between 1909 and 1914 thought imperially. When the late king's godson, James Hamilton, duke of Abercorn, urged Omagh's Apprentice Boys to 'die if necessary' in opposing home rule, he spoke not only as scion of the local aristocracy, but as a leading Ulster unionist, a former member of Arthur Balfour's 1905 Tory administration and future Northern Ireland (NI) governor-general.[45] This influence in British élite circles provided Ulster unionism with a significant advantage over its Irish nationalist rival. In effect, unionist leaders operated at every level of politics. Within Tyrone, they occupied the premier position in a colonial hierarchy and simultaneously they operated at the very apex of British society. Their standing emerged from an historical process which saw Ireland, as a colony, experience increasing integration into the metropolitan centre. Perhaps more significantly, pressure from the democracy in Britain itself affected Irish policy.[46] In this respect, constitutional innovation driven by democratic pressure within Britain often challenged Irish unionism, particularly when the Liberal government sought to implement wide-ranging social reforms prior to the Ulster crisis. Similarly, as the Irish revolution progressed, the burden of British public opinion caused as much, if not more, disquiet to Lloyd George and his cabinet than the military efforts of the IRA.

If, in unionist terms, the realm of imperial governance remained the preserve of aristocrats, then the formation of the UUC witnessed the broadening of unionist representation at a British level. The distinction between imperial and national politics is vague because both British and imperial executive authority resided at Westminster. Moreover, Ireland's entanglement in British national politics meant that 'perhaps a quarter of Conservative MPs after 1906 were either Irish Unionists, Southern Irish gentry sitting for mainland constituencies, or married into Southern Unionist families'.[47] This process bridged the gap between the national and provincial (that is, Belfast) and also between Belfast and parochial or grass roots level (that is, Tyrone). Some agents such as the duke of Abercorn and the earl of Ranfurly operated at every level. It is problematic, therefore, to speak about the British and imperial political establishment and Ulster unionism as distinct. Indeed, well into the 1920s the Irish unionist tail still effectively wagged the Tory bulldog, especially in terms of the die-hard element within the Conservative Party.[48]

Revolutions involve the overthrow of an existing government in favour of a new system, typically by forceful means. The Irish revolution owed its origins to the events of 1912, but it did not begin until Easter Week 1916. The proclamation demanded a republican form of government for the whole of Ireland. Secular and inclusive, it identified British involvement as the primary cause of national disunity. It also encompassed an extension in democratic rights and an appeal for greater social equality; it was revolutionary. These popular demands for access to political power and, ultimately, national self-determination, conditioned élite policy as the powerful sought to maintain their position. Both British political parties maintained that an Irish settlement could not jeopardize fundamental, global interests. Nevertheless, in the period covered by this study much of the population of Ireland and Britain sought the very democratic ideals that tend to interfere with the unfettered exercise of such power. This book demonstrates that wider imperial considerations led to the eventual partition of Ireland and the blocking of an independent Republic as mandated in 1918, and that Tyrone played a pivotal role in determining the unsuccessful outcome of the Irish Revolution.

This study opens with a consideration of the state of unionism and nationalism in Tyrone between 1912 and the First World War. Unionist resistance to home rule eventually obliged the Liberal government and their Nationalist allies to accept some form of exclusion or partition to avert potential unionist rebellion. The strength and vitality of the UVF and the political connections of its aristocratic leadership meant that the abandonment of majority-nationalist Tyrone represented a step too far, even for the Belfast-dominated UUC that threw the three peripheral Ulster counties 'to the wolves with very little compunction'.[49] The campaign of unionist resistance and the IPP's reluctant acquiescence to partition shattered the apparent nationalist unanimity of 1910. Nationalist disharmony based on ideology, class interests and naked self-interest proliferated within this fractured consensus. Developments during the period from the outbreak of war, including the split in the Irish Volunteers, until the Easter Rising and its direct aftermath merely accentuated these divisions.

The Rising reinvigorated republicanism and expanded the remit of separatism in Tyrone from the traditional working-class Fenian network to more moderate, and indeed affluent, converts. These different strands of nationalist opinion took shelter under the SF umbrella between 1916 and the 1918. The conscription crisis of that year accelerated an existing process and by the December 1918 general election SF had displaced Devlinite Hibernianism as the voice of majority nationalist opinion. The separatists now had to reconcile rhetoric to reality and deal with the emerging issue of partition. Politically, SF attempted to form a counter-government. Nevertheless, the implementation of the 1920 Government of Ireland Act (GOIA) and the emerging struggle between the IRA and Ulster Special Constabulary (USC) in 1921 dominated events in the county, which led many ardent republicans to ignore the primacy of politics. This political myopia proved fatal after the Anglo-Irish Treaty facilitated the final consolidation of unionist control. While the IRA and the vast majority of SF cumainn opposed the Treaty, Tyrone became mired in the incongruous policy of Michael Collins, as discussed in chapter 8. The lack of decisive action presented the ideal opportunity for James Craig's government to suppress all nationalist opposition, Free State or republican, and consolidate unionist rule in a county that had consistently voted in favour of inclusion within a home rule parliament and then an Irish Republic.

2 No home rule and no surrender![1]

Opposition to home rule represented the glue that united unionists throughout Tyrone. The spectre of Irish self-government generated myriad fears: political, economic and religious. For unionist leaders it endangered not only their attachment to the empire and the British Conservative Party but also their control of local patronage. The business man and his factory hands feared the loss of economic prosperity under a Dublin parliament likely to erect tariffs. Protestants dreaded the Catholic Church's potential influence under an Irish legislature. The AOH represented a bogeyman for Orangemen, perhaps because it held a mirror up to their own prejudice. Most Tyrone unionists believed home rule would imperil their civil and religious liberties, and British citizenship, a position with powerful emotional resonance in Ulster and in Britain. Between the Parliament Act of 1911 and the outbreak of the First World War, unionists engaged in political defiance by re-establishing the Unionist Clubs movement and lobbying British political opinion, but, more importantly, they promoted militant action through the UVF. Resistance evolved from propagandizing in 1911 to the mass signing of the Covenant in 1912 to a quasi-military campaign in 1913 and 1914. Throughout, the driving ideology rested on global and local conceptions of empire; the notion of two nations in Ireland held little relevance.

Ulster unionism benefited from the inspirational leadership of Edward Carson, the efficacy of James Craig and the co-ordination of the UUC. The latter reformed the Unionist Clubs in 1912, spearheaded a propaganda campaign in Britain and formalized disparate local militancy through the 'forward policy' of the UVF.[2] Real power rested with the standing or executive committee of the UUC. Initially composed of twenty members, this body eventually included MPs and the most significant provincial unionists. Abercorn, Montgomery, Herdman, Gunning-Moore and Andrew Horner MP represented Tyrone. When the Carson–Craig leadership sought to initiate policy, or change course, the standing committee acted as a sounding board and transmitted decisions to the local level. Nonetheless, Belfast dominated Ulster unionism, as evidenced by the stance taken on partition. In January 1913 Carson proposed the exclusion of the nine counties of Ulster, a 'strategic thrust' to wreck home rule in its entirety.[3] By the autumn, with events escalating potentially beyond control, the Belfast leadership demanded the exclusion of the six 'Plantation' counties. Carson reluctantly agreed to this irreducible minimum, Tyrone included.[4]

Ulster unionism embraced the entire social pyramid from the agricultural labourer and mill hand at the base, to the ermine-clad peer and industrialist at its apex.[5] It also included women's associations. Four hundred women attended the inaugural meeting of the North Tyrone Women's Unionist Association in Newtownstewart in April 1907.[6] It sought 'to help the men's efforts by every means possible and suitable for women'.[7] The establishment of the Ulster Women's Unionist Council (UWUC) in January 1911 led to local clubs mushrooming across Ulster. Within a year there were thirty-two branches with over 40,000 members and by 1914 100,000 women had joined. Indeed, on Ulster Day signatories of the women's declaration outnumbered their male counterparts by 10,000.[8] In Tyrone unionist women's clubs were strongest in the urban centres. For example, the Dungannon club, chaired by Countess Ranfurly, claimed to have 440 members in early 1912.[9] Upper- and middle-class women had sufficient leisure time to become involved, and were either married or related to their male counterparts. Essentially, the women's clubs represented a subordinate extension of male activism.[10]

The UWUC concentrated solely on the issue of opposition to home rule and conspicuously avoided the suffragist question.[11] Carson may have envisaged female suffrage under the planned Ulster Provisional Government and female activism may have challenged the worst excesses of unionist chauvinism, but the women's clubs hardly constituted conduits to 'genuine liberation'.[12] Indeed, while the cream of local female society founded their unionist women's association, Gretta Cousins, the militant suffragette, treasurer and co-founder with Hanna Sheehy-Skeffington of the Irish Women's Franchise League, addressed a meeting in Dungannon.[13] She told her audience at George's Hall that 'they did not claim to be better than men, but they claimed to be their equals'.[14] Local suffragettes subsequently burned mail boxes and interfered with mails to protest against the treatment of prisoners in Belfast, as well as holding other local meetings, one of which nearly ended in a riot.[15] Notwithstanding this, the significance of female activism lay in its impressive scale within unionism, where both men and women realized the gravity of the home rule crisis and organized against it.

The third home rule bill emerged from a British constitutional crisis when the House of Lords opposed Lloyd George's People's Budget in 1909. This led to two general elections in 1910, which left John Redmond and the IPP holding the balance of power. The Liberals, in office since 1906, required Nationalist support for their reform programme; home rule was the price.[16] The context of the third home rule crisis differed decisively from its predecessors in 1886 and 1893 due to the passing of the Parliament Act in 1911. This limited the veto of the House of Lords to two years and opened the way for Irish self-government. The Parliament Act strengthened the resolve of both the Ulster Unionists and an outraged British Conservative Party under its new leader, Andrew Bonar Law, who had family connections with Ulster. Tory support for Ulster was a matter of political strategy. As A.C. Hepburn has commented, for many Conservatives 'the traditional values of the British Empire were being swept away by radicals' and 'Ulster, where militant loyalty cut across class barriers, was the ideal place for a defiant stand.'[17] In addition to the dubious argument that home rule lacked a popular mandate, the unionists protested that British subjects in Ulster could not be arbitrarily deprived of their citizenship, that the concession of Irish self-government threatened the empire, as well as Ulster's economic prosperity and that home rule would mean 'Rome Rule', leaving Protestants at the mercy of Catholic intolerance and political domination by the sectarian AOH. As the duke of Abercorn told a unionist audience at St Helens, Merseyside, in January 1912, the Ulster unionists' 'one object is to uphold the same religion as their forefathers held 250 years ago, to maintain loyalty and devotion to the Crown, and integrity to the Empire'.[18]

The year 1912 marked the real beginning of the third home rule crisis in Tyrone. Prior to this unionist opposition remained the preserve of career politicians and Orangemen. As late as October 1911 the RIC reported Carson's attendance at Omagh, 'with the view of stimulating interest in the Unionist Clubs, which at present is not so keen as the leaders would like to see it'.[19] In 1910 the UUC revived the Unionist Clubs, an organization originally established to counteract the second home rule bill in 1893, as the clubs held a 'much broader appeal than the Orange Order'.[20] But in Tyrone, as elsewhere, the clubs were largely indistinguishable from the Order.[21] In relation to the three peripheral counties of Donegal, Monaghan and Cavan, Terence Dooley has contested Buckland's claim that Ulster unionism has often been unfairly equated with Orangeism since prominent Orangemen, particularly local landlords, headed the Unionist clubs and later the UVF.[22] This was also very much the case in Tyrone. In April 1911 the unionist lawyer David Douglas Reid, the defeated candidate for East Tyrone in December 1910, suggested that the clubs sought to 'educate' British public opinion and that the 2,968 votes polled by him demonstrated the area's immunity from 'that species of animal known as the "rotten" Protestant'![23]

Over 1,000 Tyrone delegates from twenty-four re-established Unionist Clubs were present at Carson's introduction to his loyalist following at Craigavon House, home of James Craig, on 23 September 1911.[24] Backboned by the Orange Order, the Tyrone clubs were quickly revitalized. Neighbouring Derry clubs took a year longer to reach the same level of organization even though the county, 58.5 per cent Protestant, contained only 2,000 fewer inhabitants than Tyrone.[25] During the Craigavon meeting 18,000 Orangemen and club members from Armagh and Tyrone marched in military formation.[26] Their 'smart appearance' and orderly marching earned the praise of Ronald McNeill, the prolific journalist, Glens of Antrim landlord, UUC member and Unionist MP for a constituency in Kent, who believed the 'spirit of emulation naturally suggested to others to follow the example of the Tyrone Lodges.'[27] Indeed, as early as January 1911 eighty Tyrone Orangemen had 'declared their readiness to die in opposition' to home rule.[28] The Craigavon meeting further underlined a resolve that should propaganda fail, the rank and file would countenance more militant resistance.

Carson followed the Craigavon demonstration with a series of rallies throughout Ulster. In December 1911 he addressed a crowd of 15,000 at Omagh.[29] This strategy had the desired effect and within a month the RIC reported drilling at twenty-nine Orange halls involving over a thousand men.[30] By April 1912, when the third home rule bill made its parliamentary debut, drilling had spread throughout Tyrone and Armagh; the westerly counties, which had smaller unionist populations, gradually followed suit. By June, in neighbouring Donegal 'quiet and unobtrusive' drilling was reported in Raphoe, while in Fermanagh drilling was due 'to commence at once'.[31] Despite the enthusiasm for drilling from January 1912 onwards, it is unclear whether the Orangemen, who formed the mainstay of the UVF, contemplated actual rebellion. George Boyd, an instructor in Dungannon, claimed that 'the object of the drilling was to teach the members to march properly past Mr Bonar Law at … Belfast on Easter Tuesday.' Yet the same party had attempted to purchase a consignment of Martini Henri rifles.[32] Indeed, by May 1912 the earl of Ranfurly granted lands in Dungannon Park to construct a firing range.[33] The local constabulary appeared to mirror Asquith's policy of 'wait and see'. They compiled evidence of illegal drilling from unionist sources, praised the nationalist community's 'admirable' tolerance 'at the most irritating displays', but took little effective action in the belief (even as late as 1913) that the 'first fine flush of enthusiasm' would burn itself out.[34]

The controversy surrounding Winston Churchill's visit to Belfast on 8 February 1912 provided further evidence of growing militancy. Tyrone Orangemen had pledged 'to send contingents to Belfast if required'; in the event, they were not.[35] Churchill, who had proposed temporary exclusion by county plebiscite to the cabinet, had decided on the trip of his own volition.[36] The Ulster Liberals then sought assistance from Joseph Devlin, Nationalist MP for West Belfast, to arrange a large pro-home rule meeting. The UUC planned to deny the use of the Ulster Hall by occupying it, which provoked major security concerns and the meeting's relocation to rain-soaked Celtic Park in Devlin's constituency.[37] Unionist leaders felt 'grievously provoked' by the audacity of a home rule meeting in the great unionist citadel, where Churchill's father had proclaimed that Ulster would fight and Ulster would be right.[38] J.B. Armour, the Presbyterian minister and Ulster Liberal, wrote that 'the excitement in Belfast is growing with immense intensity, lunacy is in the ascendant. The Unionist Council is threatening to raise a riot and commit murder if Winston dares to speak in the Ulster Hall.'[39] The episode not only served to embolden Ulster unionists, but brought home to senior British figures the stridency of their opposition.

The imminent introduction of the home rule bill further stimulated drilling as did the carefully coordinated mass meeting at the Balmoral show grounds on 9 April 1912, attended by 300,000, at which Bonar Law pledged unconditional Tory support for Ulster. Two thousand Tyrone men drilled in a formation of 25,000 under the largest Union Jack ever produced.[40] The nationalist press dismissed this 'Balmoral Show' as 'a reproduction of the usual twelfth of July demonstration and nothing more' and deemed the speeches 'of the regulation kick the Pope order', with Carson's in particular 'indicative of the anger of defeat that has torn away the very thin veneer of gentlemanliness'.[41] By the summer of 1912, the aristocracy, most notably the Abercorn and Ranfurly families, lent respectability to unionist resistance by patronizing drilling, or in the case of Ranfurly's son, Lord Northland, joining the Orange Order. Nevertheless, nationalist editorials consistently exhibited a haughty mixture of nonchalance before the unionist threat and disdain at bigoted efforts to check liberal progress. Surprisingly, this complacency remained largely unshaken despite increased unionist militancy.

A clear majority of Tyrone Protestants signed the Ulster Solemn League and Covenant on 'Ulster Day', 28 September.[42] Yet people aligned themselves for different reasons – all Tyrone Orangemen were unionists, but not all unionists were Orangemen. Local unionist support had broadened considerably, partly due to propaganda arising from the McCann case and the Castledawson incident. The former was essentially a marital dispute that had been manipulated in the context of the Catholic Church's *Ne Temere* decree of April 1908 to raise concerns about the religious upbringing of children in mixed marriages.[43] That Devlin denounced the case as a 'political dodge' and Armour as 'political scoundrelism [sic] in the name of religion' did little to reassure moderate northern Protestants, particularly liberal Presbyterians, fearful of the influence of Catholic Church.[44]

Much of the initial unionist propaganda portraying home rule as a 'Catholic sectarian tyranny' was aimed at Scottish Presbyterians and English Non-conformists. The Presbyterian Convention of February 1912 specifically directed its resolutions to Scottish kin, whom, it was felt, unwittingly accepted nationalist propaganda that unionism was the preserve of the Episcopalian 'Ascendancy' and 'its populist tool, the Orange Order'.[45] The same month William Coote told Edinburgh unionists that 'words could hardly describe the power of the priest over the ordinary Roman Catholic people' and that 'fair and square British law' was 'the only thing' that kept the priests 'back from gobbling up the country and driving out the Protestant population'.[46]

In Tyrone, fears of Rome rule and interference with civil and religious liberties were stoked by Anketell Moutray, Aughnacloy Unionist Club president and deputy grand master of the Orange Order, who exposed (or more likely engineered) the case of Mary Moore of Feddan, near Clogher. She claimed that her father, the local curate and a Catholic missionary, who believed she was 'living in sin' and 'as bad as those who are on the streets', unsuccessfully attempted to abduct her.[47] The case drew the attention of Horner, and, interestingly, the loyalist hardliner, Fred Crawford, who referred it to English non-conformist newspapers.[48] Moutray claimed that, although Moore's testimony represented the only evidence, had the priests managed to get her from the house 'all was clear sailing, with a clear course to a lock-up Roman Catholic institution not subject to Government inspection, but which should be'.[49] The Moore controversy had served its purpose and quietly dissipated as the propaganda campaign subsided after the mass enthusiasm of 'Ulster Day', to be replaced by the militancy of the UVF.

Although the sensationalism and lurid details may have repelled as many British Non-conformists as they convinced, 'Rome Rule' propaganda clearly affected Irish Presbyterians. Home rule appeared to guarantee that the Catholic Church would increase its already considerable influence over Irish education. Added to this, many Ulster Presbyterians feared a Dublin government dominated by the AOH. The Hibernians were the *bête noire* of unionist demonology. In December 1911 Horner warned Carson's Omagh rally that the AOH's 'avowed objects were complete separation, and, as a means to that end, the expulsion of all Unionists – the British garrison – from the country.'[50] The incident at Castledawson, a small village outside Magherafelt, on 29 June 1912 apparently confirmed unionist paranoia. The episode lasted for only a few minutes, after a 'general melee' between rival adult males broke out when a drunken Hibernian, returning from a demonstration in Maghera, 'seized a small Union Jack carried by a boy' from a Belfast Presbyterian Sunday School excursion.[51] Although no women or children were injured, deliberately exaggerated reports provoked unionist fury within the tinderbox atmosphere so carefully cultivated by the UUC in Belfast.[52] The Castledawson episode represented a spectacular nationalist reverse. Hibernians had called the Maghera meeting to oppose a proposal by Thomas Agar-Robartes, a Liberal backbencher, that the majority unionist counties be excluded from home rule. After the amendment's defeat, nationalist leaders advised the cancellation of the meeting. Nevertheless, local Hibernians, spurred on by 'publicans who had laid in a quantity of whisky', went ahead, with the result that 'the Orange party' gained 'a cry for which they were longing – a better cry than even the McCann case.'[53] In many respects, the Castledawson mêlée was no more remarkable than the innumerable riots that peppered communal life across rural Ulster. The context in which Castledawson took place, however, elevated it above the mundane.

News of Castledawson landed in Belfast like kindling on an Eleventh night bonfire. It was exploited by unionist leaders 'in a manner which appeared to give licence to retaliation', thereby justifying the Belfast shipyard expulsions of July 1912.[54] Devlin told the House of Commons that over 2,000 Catholics and some

500 Protestants were driven from their place of work 'owing to the reign of terror', a figure in line with police estimates.[55] There are several interesting aspects to these expulsions. First, they signposted the disproportionate nature of unionist reprisals in the summer of 1920, a pattern whereby loyalists held the city's entire Catholic population responsible for specific actions by nationalists or republicans elsewhere in Ireland. Second, they provided the opportunity to expel Protestant trade unionists and, within Belfast itself, labour arguably challenged unionist dominance in ways that Devlinite Hibernianism clearly could not. Thirdly, the expulsions precipitated a boycott of Belfast goods among southern Hibernians, a tactic that would re-emerge on a more considerable scale in 1920.[56] Although the expulsions played no 'part in the political strategy of the unionist leadership', they erupted like a thunder storm into the claustrophobic sectarian atmosphere of Belfast in July, one cultivated by the leadership.[57] Above all, the expulsions, and similar incidents in other eastern towns, demonstrated the near hysterical unionist antipathy for the AOH.[58]

Tyrone unionists exploited the Castledawson outrage at the main County Tyrone Twelfth demonstration in Dungannon. Lord Northland deemed it a 'foretaste of what will occur if Home Rule becomes law.' Ominously he suggested that

> the day may not be far distant when they may be called on to fight openly not upon the weak [and] defenceless in the cowardly and brutal manner of their adversaries but shoulder to shoulder to preserve the liberties for which their fathers fought and died at Derry and the Boyne.[59]

The growth of the AOH under the presidency of Joe Devlin reinforced unionist apprehensions. Prior to the 1910 general elections, the Board of Erin, the majority Hibernian grouping, had eighty divisions in Tyrone and in effect had displaced the UIL, a trend replicated across Ulster.[60] Despite their nominal constitutionalism and antipathy to overt republicanism, many Hibernians held an ultimately separatist outlook. For example, just before the December 1910 general election, the leading Strabane Hibernian, Eugene Conroy, claimed that the AOH 'would never cease their agitation until Ireland got complete separation from England no matter what measure of Home Rule the present government granted'.[61] Separatism aside, the 'Hibs' were charged with sectarianism, violent suppression of political opponents and undue influence on the IPP. Furthermore, under the National Insurance Act of 1911, the AOH qualified as an 'approved society', as did the Orange Order. Participating societies received an administration allowance of 3*s*. 8*d*. per member per year from public funds and by 1913 there were 130,000 registered Hibernians.[62] In November 1911 Horner warned parliament that the Insurance Act 'endowed' the AOH 'with perpetual existence' through an 'enormous grant of public money', which made it 'immeasurably the strongest society in Ireland'.[63] The local unionist leadership feared Hibernianism because it symbolized the loss of the county council and of the patronage, political advantage and social status already suffered by their southern brethren. Indeed, the Hibernians themselves held the near universal opinion that they stood to inherit the earth under home rule.[64]

The Hibernian bogeyman also loomed large in the liberal unionist psyche. The *Dungannon News* claimed that:

> The Home Rule party in Ireland is far from being homogenous. At the one end are the men who appear to want nothing more than a reform in Private Bill legislation then at the other end of the scale, we find the AOH, whose relation to the Home Rule party in Ireland is much the same as that of the Orangemen to the Unionist Party. Both form the driving force, and embrace a large portion of the working population ... In the face of ... the annual resolutions of the Hibernians, what authority has Mr Redmond, or Mr Devlin, or any Irish politician to say that he accepts a subordinate parliament in satisfaction of the national demand? And of what value, in the face of these resolutions, are all the so called safeguards?[65]

Faced with the choice between Orange and Hibernian ascendancy, local Presbyterians appeared to plump for the devil they knew, particularly since future separation jeopardized their economic position. The impressive Protestant cohesion, demonstrated by the numbers who signed the Ulster Covenant, thus becomes more understandable.

On 28 September 1912 just over 470,000 unionists across Ulster signed the Ulster Solemn League and Covenant, or its ancillary women's declaration. In Tyrone, 39,000 out of a possible 43,000 Protestants signed.[66] Thomas Sinclair, the Belfast-born, leading Presbyterian businessman and liberal unionist, penned the Covenant. He also chaired the committee that organized the anti-home rule Presbyterian convention in February 1912. The Covenant, as the title suggests, owed a heavy debt to seventeenth-century history and spoke to a very Scottish and Presbyterian conception of Ulster unionist identity. Nevertheless, Sinclair, at the behest of the UUC, secured the co-operation of all the main Protestant churches and established a clerical sub-committee to help with organization. For a campaign that lamented clerical involvement in nationalist politics, ironically 'Ulster Day illuminated the two-way relationship between the Protestant churches and the Ulster unionist hierarchy'.[67] The sanction of all the Protestant churches helps explain the impressive statistics. In Dungannon, where the different denominations held separate services, a total of 1,278 men and 1,312 women signed, some of whom 'had never previously shown any interest in politics'.[68] Arguably, had 'Ulster Day' not encompassed a religious dimension and gained the full co-operation of the Protestant churches, it is unlikely that a solely political demonstration would have achieved such comprehensive Protestant singularity of purpose, a strategy that Catholics employed in the subsequent anti-conscription campaign of 1918.

The number of Protestants who signed, combined with census data, suggests that proportionally the response to the Covenant was strongest in Armagh, Tyrone and Monaghan.[69] Unionist solidarity appeared greatest in areas with significant Protestant populations and a strong local Catholic presence, although higher church attendance in rural areas may also have contributed. Signatories pledged to defend their 'cherished position of equal citizenship in the United Kingdom', by 'all means which may be found necessary to defeat the present conspiracy'.[70] This indicated that many unionists held a distinct constitutional interpretation. David W. Miller has argued that Ulster Protestants adhered to a contractarian ideology, involving allegiance to a sovereign in return for physical protection, rather than the discourse of nationhood.[71] In the same vein Revd David T. Mackie of Newmills told the Dungannon Apprentice Boys that the Parliament Act was 'a violation of the constitution' and, at Fivemiletown, John Carmichael-Ferrall of Augher Castle, Clogher magistrate and Orange County Grand treasurer, claimed that 'they belonged to the plantation of Ulster planted by the King's ancestor, which gave them a right to appeal to the King to protect them'.[72] Appeals to the empire, constitution and racial identity were neither extreme nor exotic in a contemporaneous British conservative context. However, local unionists also consistently evoked the plantation and Williamite history. In August 1913, at the Apprentice Boy commemoration in Omagh, the duke of Abercorn appealed to the memory of those 'who fell in the historic siege of 1689':

> Gentlemen, the blood of those heroic defenders runs in your veins (Cheers.) They withstood oppression; they withstood that great siege in order to hand down their birth right to their successors. Will you stand firm as they did? (Loud cries of 'Yes' and cheers.) Will you suffer as they did? ('Yes' and cheers.) Will you die if necessary as they did? ('Yes' and cheers) And hand those civil and religious liberties to your successors as they did? ('Yes' and cheers.)[73]

Indeed, unionist rhetoric frequently linked the conquest of Ireland to global British triumphs.[74] It was on the basis of empire that Andrew Horner challenged the home rule bill at Westminster in 1912:

> Do you think the men who are of our blood and race, controlling, as they do, the greatest interests in our Colonies, will stand by and see you coerce

us, your oldest Colony, by force to leave the shelter of the Imperial
Parliament and accept the Government of men whose whole careers have
been abuse and hatred of us and you?[75]

Nonetheless, the cohesion evident in the Covenant did not rely solely on
rhetoric. Some Protestants opposed the general sentiment. When Revd
Alexander MacLurg, Presbyterian minister for Ardstraw near Newtownstewart,
refused 'to hold a religious service and to sign the Covenant, the people brought
down Prof[essor] Leitch who gave a blood and thunder address averring among
other things that a Protestant home ruler was a man who had a thraw [sic] in his
character'.[76] Boycotted by his congregation, MacLurg emigrated to Canada.[77]
Nonetheless, the overwhelming majority of Tyrone Protestants had little
compunction in signing.

There are a number of explanations as to why so many signed the Covenant,
including the supremacist and economic. In his first speech after Ulster Day,
Charles Frederick D'Arcy, the bishop of Down and chairman of the Belfast
Eugenics Society, used comparative levels of insanity and illiteracy within
Ireland to demonstrate Ulster's superiority and validate his support for the
Covenant.[78] At Aughnacloy in May 1912, Horner argued that 'although Tyrone
could only return one Unionist member, still Unionists ... represented the vast
bulk of the industry, enterprise and influence in the county'.[79] He told Fintona
Orangemen in February 1913 that 'the only ascendancy he knew in Ireland was
the ascendancy of industry over sloth, of intelligence over ignorance, and of
thriftiness over thriftlessness [sic], and no act of Parliament could change those
characteristics of the race that inhabited this island'.[80] At a commemoration of
the relief of Derry in Dungannon, William Moore, MP for North Armagh,
maintained that home rule represented the 'government of Ireland by the most
intolerant and least progressive section of the community'.[81] At Carson's rally in
Omagh, John Gordon, an Ulster Unionist MP and future Irish Attorney-
General, claimed that Protestants would suffer under 'a dissolute, law breaking
and unindustrious [sic] people of whom the Irish nationalists are composed ...
[a people whose] ... avowed objects were complete separation, and as a means to
that end the expulsion of all Unionists – the British garrison – from the
country.'[82] Racial supremacism was not the preserve of Ulster unionists. Indeed,
much of the British élite, and some Irish nationalists, accepted eugenics as scien-
tific fact. But what racism really represented was the ideology of power and a
fallacy constructed to legitimize privilege and economic domination. It would
have been unnatural to expect unionists not to employ accepted aspects of the
contemporaneous discourse, no matter how baseless, in their rebuttal of home
rule. This does not, however, preclude commentary on the fact that such opinion
was largely erroneous.

This rhetoric also tends to ignore a liberal unionist perspective that eschewed supremacism. A unionist perspective was possible without total commitment to either popular Orangeism or the extreme invective of some unionist political figures. The *Dungannon News* consistently attacked corrupt IPP machine politics and employed economic arguments in editorials and opinion pieces against home rule.[83] Although typically condescending, the tone differed significantly from platform oratory. The Tory *Tyrone Courier* eventually took control of the faltering *Dungannon News*. The liberal unionist position had limits, however. First, the unionist leadership did not promote this perspective. Furthermore, a near universal colonial identity underpinned the unionist consensus. Walker claims the Irish Presbyterian Convention of February 1912 demonstrated that opposition to home rule was not the sole preserve of Conservatives, landlords and the Orange Order, and that Presbyterians rationally opposed both Anglican and Catholic ascendancy. Indeed, the Presbyterian Convention proclaimed that their opposition was not a matter of 'party politics', but rather a refusal to 'be driven out from the enjoyment of the full rights and privileges of citizenship in the United Kingdom, and to be thrust under an Irish legislature and executive.' Yet, Walker also emphasizes the 'blood and soil' dimension of Ulster Protestant identity to which Presbyterian 'mythologising was central'.[84] Indeed, the conference resolution went on to promote a colonial identity typical of the unionist platform oratory that dominated speeches in Tyrone:

> we Presbyterians are now in Ireland because three centuries ago our forefathers were 'planted' in Ulster by the English government in order that, by their loyalty and industry they might secure the peace and prosperity of our province and promote the mutual welfare of our two countries. Our fathers and ourselves have done our best to fulfil the trust committed to us, we feel that it would be an unworthy requital should we now not withstanding our solemn protest, be deprived of the heritage we now enjoy as fellow citizens in the United Kingdom of equal status with our English and Scotch co-religionists.[85]

Therefore, opposition to home rule was not primarily negative or concerned only with the threat of Rome rule and Hibernian intolerance. Unionist ideology relied on two positive elements, which blended contemporaneous British imperialism and an inherent colonial identity. The complementary appeals to pride in empire and Ulster's place in it permitted the local aristocrat to find common cause with his tenants and the local capitalist with his workers. At Dungannon in February 1914 Uchter Knox, earl of Ranfurly and former governor of New Zealand, warned that 'if Ulster had to go down it would be a prelude to the total disruption of the Empire and the destruction of the monarchy.'[86]

Towards the end of 1912 the Unionist leadership sought to exercise greater control over an increasingly militant rank and file and the UUC decided that

various citizen militia should be united into a single body known as the UVF.[87]
At the County Twelfth in Castlecaulfield in 1913 a gang of Orangemen hauled
Bernard Conway, a local nationalist reporter with the *Dungannon Democrat*, from
the press box. Revd Gordon Scott, Church of Ireland minister near Omagh and
deputy grand chaplain of the Tyrone Orange Lodge, told Lowry that he never
'saw a more cowardly, savage, cruel bit of work in my life and I truly believe that
a few men saved the unfortunate reporter's life.'[88] The previous summer Scott,
'an enthusiastic supporter of the Unionist Clubs', had 'considerably stimulated'
activity by presenting a 'handsome cup for excellence in drill'.[89] Some local
clergymen viewed the UVF as a mechanism for restraint.[90] Horner also sought
to distance the Order from the attack in the Commons.[91] Although the leadership baulked at their brethren's violence, by 1913 Orange intransigence trumped
earlier propagandist concerns and the local leadership had either to tolerate or
attempt to direct the energies of lower-class supporters. The UVF may, as the
RIC inspector-general observed, have sought 'to enlist the hooligans, as the
leaders are anxious to acquire a disciplinary control over that class', but the
necessity to appeal to popular emotion undermined restraint.[92] As Jackson
argues, the UVF resembled 'a kind of Frankenstein monster, called into life by
Carson and Craig, but threatening to defy the authority of its creators'.[93]

The UVF originally operated on the existing structure of the Unionist Clubs
with regiments for each parliamentary constituency. East Tyrone was an exception, with two centred on Cookstown and Dungannon.[94] By May 1913 the RIC
estimated that there were 74 clubs in the county with just under 6,000 members
out of a total of 333 clubs throughout Ulster.[95] A further 1,500 Tyronemen had
joined by September.[96] Unsurprisingly, North Tyrone recorded the largest
membership of 3,000, while the two East Tyrone units comprised a combined
figure of over 2,000 men. The local aristocracy took a prominent early part in the
movement, Abercorn in North Tyrone and Ranfurly in East Tyrone. In
addition, the owners of local linen mills were strongly associated with the UVF.
Even prior to the Larne gun-running, the Belfast police seized separate consign-
ments of weapons disguised as supplies for Adair's Mill in Cookstown and
Herdman's in Sion Mills.[97] Herdman's essentially enlisted its Protestant
workers, while the owners of the four major mills in Cookstown and Dungannon
led battalions.[98] In effect, Lord Northland in Dungannon and Ambroise Ricardo
in Sion Mills sought to enlist every eligible Protestant in the east and west of the
county.[99] During an instruction camp for County Tyrone at Baronscourt, local
employers gave the men a week's paid leave, a move repeated by mill owners in
Dungannon and Cookstown.[100]

The movement's numerical strength was understandably weaker in the
majority nationalist and rural Mid-Tyrone area, centring on Omagh, which had
a roll approaching 1,000 men in September 1913.[101] Rural areas were clearly
more difficult to organize. For example, J Company, Dungannon Battalion in

nationalist Pomeroy had a very high rate of absenteeism, which reflected occupational background and the logistical problems associated with rural companies.[102] Nonetheless, the UVF's county administration was based in Omagh under the direction of Philip Cruickshank, UUC member, editor of the *Tyrone Constitution*, and author of *Home rule and what it means* (1911) and *The Tyrone Regiment, U.V.F.* (1913). The South Tyrone area also registered less than a thousand men by September 1913 and there was no company in Aughnacloy until late 1913.[103] This may have been due to residual liberal Protestant sentiment, but it was more likely a reflection of the area's rural complexion and an inability to enlist large numbers of Protestant factory workers. Indeed, the rural nature of South and Mid-Tyrone lay behind the creation of a mounted infantry unit with fifty in the Mid-Ulster Horse (Omagh) and fifty in the Tyrone Horse (Clogher).

Initially, the Tyrone UVF constituted little more than a formalized version of existing, infrequent drilling. In August 1913, however, the Belfast leadership appointed a permanent salaried military command under General George Richardson. Coincidentally, all four full-time O/Cs represented 'ex-British Army officers drawn to the Ulster Unionist cause by concern at the strategic implications for imperial defence of Home Rule for Ireland'.[104] This led to the force's military re-organization and the instigation of a series of officer training camps, the first in Tyrone at Baronscourt from 4 to 11 October 1913. To this end, Cruickshank received a circular from headquarters which stated that 'ultimate success ... will depend largely on the number of efficient men in the UVF' and a grant of £75. It was anticipated that 200 would attend Baronscourt which was to remain as secret as possible.[105] Nevertheless the RIC monitored proceedings. Constables Stafford and McCabe described how fields were trenched, secured with sand bags and barbed wire, and guarded by sentries, who barred McCabe's entry.[106] The camp appeared to have enthusiastic local officers. 'I must say', Northland wrote to Lowry, 'I really enjoyed our week in camp'.[107] The next step was to motivate the ranks.

The increase in membership noted between September and November can be partly attributed to 'a whirlwind autumn tour by Carson which had developed into a triumphal procession' through thirteen towns in Ulster during which he introduced Richardson to the grass roots.[108] As early as October 1913 the RIC reported that Ulster Volunteers 'now begin to fancy themselves a match for even the British army'; they seem to have disregarded the prime minister's warning that 'force would be met with force'.[109] On 1 October Carson visited Dungannon and Cookstown in the company of F.E. Smith. He heightened local audacity by telling Cookstown Volunteers that he had 'given up on addressing political audiences, and wanted to speak only to those who were prepared to fight'.[110] The composition of the fifteen-strong organizing committee for the Dungannon meeting is revealing. Northland and Ranfurly took the lead. James Dickson, a

Presbyterian, and Robert Stevenson, an Anglican, the owners of Dungannon's two largest linen mills, were members and agreed to give workers the day off. The other Dungannon representatives included Barry Meglaughlin, a solicitor and Tyrone Orange Order delegate to the UUC, and Revd E.F. Campbell; all others were former army officers or local land agents. Four of the five representatives from South Tyrone were leading Anglican landlords, including Moutray, Carmichael-Ferrall and de Fellenberg Montgomery.[111] As a Presbyterian businessman, William Coote, commander of the local UVF, member of the Tyrone Grand Lodge Committee and Horner's successor as MP, was something of an exception in South Tyrone.[112] A similar situation prevailed in Cookstown, where a combination of Presbyterian mill owners, such as John Adair and William Leeper, and landlords, including John B. Gunning-Moore, UUC delegate and member of the Theistic church, Carrickfergus-born and Eton-educated Thomas MacGregor Greer and Viscount Charlemont, directed the local Unionist party and the UVF.[113] Therefore, in both parliamentary constituencies, local landlords and factory owners dominated the leadership.

This is borne out by Timothy Bowman's analysis of the officer corps of the 5th Tyrone Regiment (Cookstown), which came from 'landed gentry and rural Ulster's small professional and middle-class'.[114] Bowman's characterization of the influence of landlords and factory-owners on recruitment as akin to a 'feudal' relationship is particularly pertinent in the case of the 1st Regiment (North) Tyrone.[115] Among the nine identifiable officers and company captains, three were factory owners or managers, three were JPs and two were Church of Ireland ministers.[116] By contrast, the officers of the weaker 2nd (Mid-Tyrone) Regiment had more humble origins than the four other regiments, with eight large farmers and one land agent making up two-thirds of the identifiable officers.[117] Overall a combination of landed gentry and factory owners controlled the Tyrone UVF with an ancillary level of the Protestant professional middle class, the vast majority of whom were also Orangemen. In this respect, it mirrored the deferential structure of the Unionist Party and wider unionist society and placed Tyrone within the pattern identified by Dooley in neighbouring Monaghan and Donegal.[118]

By autumn 1913 Tyrone had over 8,000 Ulster Volunteers. Northland led the Dungannon Regiment, which had eleven companies and had imported serviceable rifles. The Dungannon Volunteers 'pledged themselves to stand by their fellow covenanters in defending themselves and their children' and claimed 'the Government will send Protestant troops to shoot down their brother Protestants in Ireland at the dictates of the Nationalist Party'.[119] That did not transpire and by the end of 1913 the government had adopted exclusion as a solution to the home rule impasse, a policy mooted by Lloyd George and Churchill as early as February 1912 and one also advanced by Carson from January 1913 onwards.[120] When it became apparent that non-constitutional pressure had altered Asquith's policy, local nationalist ridicule of the 'muster of bandoliers, carts and cart horses' of Carson's 'Tyrone warriors' was replaced by genuine anxiety and, in places, an attempt to locate an alternative policy.[121] The formation and spread of the rival Irish Volunteers in Tyrone in 1914 further polarized the situation.

Carson's visit in October 1913 initially led to a flurry of political meetings and speeches but this noticeably declined in 1914. The time for talking appeared to be over. In January 1914 the RIC reported the 'surprise mobilization' of a force of 1,000 Ulster Volunteers at Killymoon Demesne, Cookstown, which subsequently took possession of the town.[122] In March almost 2,000 members of the Dungannon Regiment participated in a mock battle at Ranfurly's Dungannon Park, with Stephenson and Dickson leading two of the units.[123] The same month the county force mobilized 7,000 men at short notice, 'when it was rumoured that the Unionist leaders were to be arrested'.[124] This rapid mobilization partly relied on the formation of groups of motor cyclists to carry dispatches from UVF headquarters and circumvent the post office.[125] From the outset the local UVF wanted officers to live in the district to facilitate the swift transmission and receipt of information. It consciously employed its own messengers lest the post office 'get too inquisitive'.[126] Unsurprisingly, this system faltered in rural areas. The response times and attendance figures for Lowry's Pomeroy Company were far from impressive during a trial mobilization in February.[127] However, following the Larne gun-running, 1,800 Ulster Volunteers mobilized in Dungannon to transport the weapons to various parts of the county. After a second training camp at Baronscourt in May 1914, the Dungannon battalion paraded the town and openly carried their rifles. It was the view of George Fitz Hardinge Berkeley, an Irish Volunteer organizer in Belfast, that Dungannon was 'a place where, sooner or later, blood was likely to flow; an ideal place for a row ... both sides were obviously very bitter'.[128] According to the RIC inspector general, the 'County Inspector of Tyrone who is himself an Ulsterman, says, "the distrust and hatred between Catholic and Protestant was never in my memory half so deep".'[129]

It was not clear if rebellion was, in fact, a serious prospect. Writing in retrospect, Montgomery described the campaign as 'bluff'.[130] But for those involved in 1913 and 1914, the preparation appeared genuine. Moutray's son, who served with the Connaught Rangers in India, sought to return to Ireland in November 1913 to take an active part.[131] William Copeland Trimble of the UVF's Enniskillen Horse informed the younger Moutray that the Curragh 'mutiny' had averted certain bloodshed and hinted at Moutray's plan to use his position in the army to support the UVF.[132] In the event of conflict, Richardson planned to engage the British army on the roads approaching Belfast and then to carry on urban warfare after an inevitable retreat. The western UVF were to concentrate on policing the nationalist population, a prospect that never overly concerned the military leadership. There were also detailed plans for the evacuation of unionist civilians. The Cookstown UVF even secured letters of authority from parents to permit the evacuation of children.[133]

However, the Curragh incident and the increased – though as Charles Townshend rightly points out – exaggerated military capability of the UVF after Larne made actual confrontation with British forces unlikely.[134] The UVF did not envisage making any concerted stand in Tyrone and, if the government opted for coercion, the unionists believed they could only hold a very small area of consolidated Protestant population around Belfast. The outbreak of the First World War halted such plans and the potential area of unionist military dominance did not receive its first test until after 1920 in far more favourable circumstances.

The unionist campaign in Tyrone emerged from the genuine sense of anxiety caused by the Parliament Act (1911), which represented the removal of the last bulwark against home rule. Irish and British unionists seized on Ulster's opposition, primarily as a wrecking tactic against the whole measure, but gradually outright opposition to home rule gave way to exclusion. By March 1914, with the Irish Party's reluctant acquiescence, Lloyd George proposed a scheme entailing temporary exclusion by county option, or that individual counties could vote themselves out of a Dublin parliament for six years. Carson, acting in line with the wishes of Belfast, rejected anything other than the permanent exclusion of six counties and famously dismissed the project as 'a sentence of death with a stay of execution'.[135] The issue of the extent of the area to be excluded proved intractable. As Ireland hovered on the brink of civil war in July 1914, the Buckingham Palace Conference met to reach a desperate compromise, but it ended in stalemate, mired in the muddy by-ways of Fermanagh and Tyrone. Unionist opposition to home rule and support for it from the King, the Tory Party and sizeable elements within the army constituted a reactionary measure in breach of the Parliament Act's democratization of the British constitution.

In Tyrone the question went beyond the religious issue and, while imperial citizenship appeared crucial, within the unionist mindset some citizens were more equal than others. Tyrone unionists did not appeal to democracy or majority rule, but rather to the notion that all government rested on force, that there were things, in Bonar Law's infamous phrase, stronger than parliamentary majorities. In January 1914 Horner told the local UVF that 'the foundations of society in every country, in every age, were based on force. The rights and liberties which were now in peril were won by force by better men than they were'.[136] In June 1914 in Aughnacloy he maintained that 'imaginary boundaries between counties had nothing whatever to do with' the 'British settlers ... the forefathers of the Ulster Covenanters of today.' In Horner's mind then, Ulster was 'more a people than a place' and 'no government, except by conquest, had a right to place any section of its citizens under the government of those whom they had just cause to regard as hostile to their material welfare and their most cherished liberties'.[137]

Arguably, this position implied that two nations inhabited Ireland and that the exclusion of Ulster's 'imaginary boundaries' corresponded to a form of self-determination. This view has certainly entered the mainstream of Irish historiography. It is, however, a problematic proposition. Despite the influence that British commentators such as John St Loe Strachey, the editor of the Tory *Spectator*, had in lobbying for exclusion because 'there are two nations in Ireland ... and therefore two national units', few local unionists shared this perspective.[138] Instead, Tyrone unionists based their position on empire. In Tyrone, the unionist appeal relied on a fusion of high imperial and colonial-settler identity based on socio-economic and political reality on the Ulster frontier, where major aspects of mobilization from control of local government to the very composition of the Ulster Volunteers sought to defend Protestant unionist privilege vis-à-vis Catholic nationalists. Nowadays, it is contentious to attribute a colonial dimension to Ulster unionism, but in the heyday of empire local unionists had little compunction in basing their appeals on this claim, and in this they received the support of the British landed and plutocratic caste, its monarchy and army.

3 'Tyrone for Ulster, Ulster for Ireland
... up with home rule!'

On a snowy Saturday in January 1910 jubilant Hibernians swarmed Dungannon courthouse. The 'Boys of Wexford' and riotous cheers met Tom Kettle, the 30-year-old Dubliner and university lecturer, who had just retained his parliamentary seat. Kettle's campaign slogan encapsulated nationalist expectancy: 'Kettle for East Tyrone, East Tyrone for Ulster, Ulster for Ireland, down with the House of Lords and up with Home Rule!'[1] Before the outbreak of the First World War, nationalists in the county were bitterly divided between republicans, Hibernians and Healyites. But the prospect of seemingly imminent home rule disguised these divisions. The Ulster crisis rocked Hibernian self-confidence. Its quietist response to unionist militancy and crucially its reluctant acceptance of partition undermined the IPP support base. In Tyrone the IRB was eager to follow the unionist example by promoting the Irish Volunteers. The movement developed rapidly in 1914 following the Curragh incident, Larne gun-running and, in particular, increasing fears of partition. The AOH and IPP were forced to give the Volunteers their consent but then quickly manoeuvred to take control of the organization. The outbreak of the war placed Redmond and his party in an awkward position. He did not call unconditionally for recruits until the home rule bill was passed on 18 September. Yet Redmond's appeal for enlistment and earlier acceptance of partition, which was crucial in Tyrone, fuelled the re-emergence of the republican demand and sowed the seeds of the IPP's ultimate demise.

Kettle's victory speech mocked those who claimed that 'the fishermen of Ardboe were not going to support him' because 'Ardboe voted to a man!' This cryptic remark referred to the IRB cells among the area's pollan and eel fishermen.[2] The IRB network stretched from Lough Neagh, through the sizeable towns of Dungannon and Coalisland, westwards into the mountains around Carrickmore and Pomeroy, and northwards to Greencastle.[3] This republican network spilt over county boundaries, running eastwards through the Brantry into north Armagh and northwards along the lough shore to Toome on the Antrim border.[4] A separate cluster around Strabane shared a closer affinity with the small, and fading, network of cells in Donegal.[5]

Typically, around a dozen members attended cell meetings, usually held in public houses, with events such as fairs often acting as cover for county and provincial meetings.[6] Tyrone had over twenty cells. Each elected centre or head was represented on the county-level council. This body sent a representative to the Ulster council, which in turn nominated a provincial president who sat on the supreme council. The meetings generally dealt with housekeeping issues, such as elections, disciplining wayward members and approving new men, as well as collecting subscriptions to buy arms, debating policy and reading 'seditious' literature.[7] W.J. Kelly senior described how cells sounded out young men of 'good character' and 'trustworthiness' before approaching them.[8] In one instance, after receiving anti-recruiting literature linked to the execution of a Indian Nationalist, the Ardboe cell diverted some of its precious gun money to journalists for 'fomenting agitation' and 'harassing the British government' on the sub-continent.[9] One policy of particular note was the infiltration of other organizations as a means of furthering republicanism. In line with national trends, the Tyrone and Armagh county centres were heavily involved in the Gaelic League and GAA.[10] The IRB, therefore, represented a network of polit-ically conscious individuals, pledged to use their influence to further the cause of an Irish Republic, through force of arms if necessary.

Kettle's remarks also alluded to the humble social origin of the artisans, small tenants and labourers of Tyrone, who inhabited a political world below the level of 'respectable' politics. Many commentators held a dismissive, even hostile, attitude to working people. CI W.J. Millar characterized the IRB in Tyrone as 'lacking in character, position, intelligence and leaders', and claimed that they 'may be ignored with absolute safety.'[11] While many lower-class nationalists and unionists acquiesced in these deferential modes, the IRB championed a 'democ-ratic and republican social ideal'.[12] This partly rested on tradition and familial networks, echoes of Fenian and United Irish activism based on non-sectarian and egalitarian concepts.[13] Sizeable seasonal and permanent emigration exposed members to left-wing British politics, with the Scottish IRB unsurprisingly dominated by west Ulster labourers.[14] The socialism of first generation Ulster emigrants, Connolly and Larkin, also received a sympathetic hearing among the working-class IRB, although the leaders were less receptive.[15] Both leadership and base shared an antipathy to the priest in politics, however. In 1910 Patrick McCartan maintained that 'the power of the priest is the greatest obstacle to nationalism in the country' and that the IRB's new journal, *Irish Freedom*, should 'go straight for' this 'reactionary power', which had 'escaped too long'.[16]

The republican position in Tyrone relied on civic virtue combined with antipathy to British rule and opposition to the perceived hypocrisy of constitu-tional nationalism. Yet, the imminent 'home rule' elections apparently placed republicans in a quandary.[17] The previous October IRB member, Hugh Devine, advised Strabane Hibernians 'to keep their powder dry ... for the coming general election' to 'return the present Irish Party' and 'make the House of Commons ring with the demand for Home Rule'.[18] Similarly, Eugene Conroy, a local leader and tailor from Strabane, defected to the Board of Erin.[19] Tyrone republicans appeared torn between an imminent measure of freedom and political principle. The prospect of home rule temporarily plastered over the cracks in nationalism, mirroring the cohesion that the issue generated within unionism.

Before the January 1910 election, the county centres voted to abstain. Yet, 'those who voted against the motion' supported Kettle.[20] Some actually went beyond abstention; the Ardboe cell censured James 'Dundee' Devlin for 'canvassing in the Unionist interest'.[21] This probably emerged from the bitter history between the IRB and AOH. Although Kettle urged a post-election meeting near Coalisland to treat local Sinn Féiners as 'honest Irishmen' and permit them 'freedom to speak their opinions and freedom to argue and reason with them', this contrasted with his previous conduct.[22] In 1907 he had returned early from an American fundraising tour to crush SF.[23] This meant unleashing the local AOH on the Dungannon Clubs which sought to use Griffith's SF policy to organize a non-insurrectionary republican movement among Tyrone Hibernians by utilizing the existing IRB network and the skills of local leader, Patrick McCartan, and young provincial organizer, Seán Mac Diarmada.[24]

By 1910 the Dungannon Club initiative had failed. In September 1911 CI Millar reported that 'The Sinn Féin and IRB are active in a small way but these societies have no influence' and were 'merely "stirring the embers" to keep the societies from total extinction'.[25] This referred to Joseph McGarrity's tour of Ulster, when he supervised the election of county and provincial officers.[26] The tour was part of a wider scheme by McCartan, Tom Clarke and younger Ulster leaders, involved in the abortive SF experiment, to secure control of the national IRB.[27] By April 1912 Clarke, as treasurer, and Mac Diarmada, as secretary, firmly controlled the supreme council. McGarrity wrote to McCartan, trusting that 'no other very objectionable people [stood] in the way of progress now ... let us get down to business'.[28] By October 1912 the RIC reported 'more activity' from the IRB, whose 'numbers are increasing', but derisively commented that 'a considerable number of patriots make a living out of movements of this kind' by taking advantage 'of any unusual excitement to further their own interests'.[29] The 'unusual excitement' of the unionist campaign coincided with the supreme council take-over by younger more radical elements linked to Ulster. By July 1913 the 'biennial election of officers' had again arrived and the Belfast republican socialist, Cathal O'Shannon, told the Strabane cell that provincial membership had doubled, while the figures for Tyrone and Donegal had 'increased considerably'.[30] The available evidence points to considerable recruitment and cell formation in east Tyrone, partly facilitated by a provincial organizer, Peter Burns, an iron-turner from the Falls Road.[31]

Three Tyrone republicans were prominent in the 1916 Rising. Joseph McGarrity from Carrickmore had emigrated to Philadelphia, and, by 1912, was the treasurer of Clan na Gael, the IRB's American sister organization. Patrick McCartan, also from Carrickmore, returned to Ireland, ostensibly to pursue a medical career. McGarrity funded and McCartan led the IRB's attempt to subvert constitutional nationalism in Tyrone through the Dungannon Clubs, formed in 1905 in Belfast by Denis McCullough and Bulmer Hobson.

Pessimistic about the chances of an armed struggle, this younger generation of republicans, which also included Mac Diarmada, sought to use Arthur Griffith's SF policy as a means of achieving a republic through passive resistance, including a programme of Irish MPs abstaining from Westminster in favour of a national council of three hundred. By 1910, however, the IPP could easily rebuke the taunt that parliamentary attendance was ineffective. For the IRB, the SF policy was dead. The young cadre then staged a coup against the ageing leadership dominated by Fred Allen. They received guidance and support from Tom Clarke. Between 1910 and 1912 this group took over the IRB and initiated a decidedly republican and insurrectionary strategy. The combination of Ulster resistance, the formation of the Irish Volunteers and the outbreak of the First World War clearly created the conditions for Mac Diarmada and Clarke's decision, in August 1914, to rise during the war. McCartan led the Irish Volunteers in Tyrone and his actions from the outbreak of the war until Easter Week 1916 are examined in chapter four.

The unionist resistance to home rule undoubtedly fanned the republican 'embers' and, when a rival nationalist force arrived in November 1913 in the shape of the Irish Volunteers, the IRB was crucial to its early development in Tyrone. However, it could not fulfil this role itself because of its acrimonious history with the Hibernians. McCartan described how 'in 1912 and 1913, Tom [Clarke] thought I was inactive and often spoke to me about this'. Progress was 'impossible', however, because 'All the young lads were members of the Hibernians' and 'regarded me as a black sheep', a situation only remedied by McCartan's prominent role in the Irish Volunteer Force (IVF).[32] From the republican perspective, the conversion of sizeable elements of Tyrone Hibernianism was critical to any successful challenge to constitutional nationalism.

Fenians and Hibernians shared a similar social background as well as the desire for complete Irish independence. At a point when home rule was within touching distance, the Board of Erin appeared much better placed to satisfy these social and nationalist objectives. The AOH had eighty divisions in Tyrone and 'overshadowed' the UIL, the official IPP constituency organization, which selected electoral candidates.[33] It also employed boycott, violence and intimidation against perceived Healyism within the UIL. There had been a long history of bitter relations between clerical Healyites and Devlinite Hibernians.[34] Healyites believed that the clergy and middle class constituted their community's natural leaders, while Devlinism championed the claims of the 'rising democracy', namely, the AOH. This represented a difference of tone rather than substance, or, as McCartan remarked, between 'Tweedle-dum and Tweedle-dee'.[35] While both leaderships were largely middle class in origin, the reliance on grass roots support gave Devlinism an aggressively nationalist populist character against Healyite social conservatism and conciliation of unionism. As a result, younger nationalists viewed the AOH as 'more progressive' than the UIL.[36]

Wheatley argues that the IPP's moderate nationalism and tacit imperialism reflected 'Whig' and 'Buttite' tradition among 'many older, landed, and upper middle-class Catholic nationalists ... themselves assimilated into British life and culture'.[37] The Hibernian majority in Tyrone repudiated this perspective, an outlook paradoxically compounded by the IPP. Kevin O'Shiel painted a rather comic picture of IPP meetings, where some 'eloquent "Demosthenes"' began by 'setting our young blood on fire with vivid descriptions of' 1798, before applying the 'bromide' that the Irish Party's brilliant advocacy negated the need for such methods.[38] Therefore, in Tyrone, separatism was 'stronger than is often supposed' and shared a 'common discourse' with constitutional nationalism.[39] Similarly, Devlin's Labourite rhetoric and the Hibernians' role in National Insurance attracted working-class support.[40] John Skeffington, the county president, consistently portrayed the AOH as the engine for 'the freedom of the workers and the poorer classes', although he unequivocally stated that Hibernians would oppose anti-Catholic and anti-national socialism.[41] Arguably, Devlinite criticism of Protestant 'workers' in the Tyrone UVF playing at 'tomfoolery for the cameras in the interests of the greedy, selfish few' who 'despised them', rang hollow after the Board of Erin's vociferous support for William Martin Murphy during the 1913 Dublin Lockout.[42]

The IRB calculated that, with the Irish Party's perceived hypocrisy exposed, Hibernians would naturally adopt republicanism. Unlike the IRB, however, the Hibernians were also avowedly sectarian. Skeffington challenged those who called the Hibernians 'Catholic Orangemen' by claiming that the 'iron rule of the ascendancy party in Ulster' justified an exclusively Catholic body.[43] When unionists regained control of the Clogher Board of Guardians in 1911, George Evans, a Catholic and Hibernian, was suspended as workhouse master with unionists alleging that he had 'immoral relations' with an inmate, Mary Kelly. Claiming that this accusation was religiously motivated, Evans prosecuted the vice-chairman, James Trimble, for perjury, and directed unsuccessful charges of conspiracy against the chairman, Hugh Montgomery.[44] A Dublin judge ruled that Evans would not receive a fair trial in Tyrone due to the influence of those accused.[45] The Local Government Board (LGB) subsequently vindicated Evans, whom it re-appointed against the wishes of the board.[46] In 1914 Clogher RDC returned an equal nationalist and unionist representation, but, as incumbent chairman, Montgomery manipulated procedure to secure a unionist majority; the nationalist members formed a short-lived alternative board in protest.[47] These events poisoned relationships within the local community and vindicated the AOH critique.[48] But when Hibernians held the reins of local officialdom, their conduct tended to mirror that of their unionist adversaries. The police reported how they 'always had things their own [way]' in Strabane.[49] In one humorous incident when a unionist councillor condemned the UDC's refusal to present a loyal address to the new king, George V, Eugene Conroy told him to shut up. A fracas erupted and, amidst 'wild scenes', a flying shoe struck one unfortunate councillor on the head.[50]

In his memoirs, William O'Brien depicted the IPP as the victim of a Hibernian 'Frankenstein of their own raising which in Ireland passes by the name of "Molly Maguire".'[51] He claimed that Devlin's dual appointment as UIL national secretary and Board of Erin president allowed him to 'machine' the party on New York's Tammany Hall model. As UIL secretary, Devlin packed conventions with Hibernian followers and often refused to affiliate branches in areas hostile to the IPP leadership.[52] O'Brienite disgust may also have sprung from Devlin's populist and democratic language. Indeed, the Hibernian *vox populi* antagonized many within the Catholic establishment. At Carrickmore in 1909 Cardinal Michael Logue of Armagh described the Order as 'a pest, a cruel tyranny, and an organized system of blackguardism', which endeavoured 'to compel others to join the order by means of boycotting, threatening … waylaying and beating persons.'[53] Tyrone nationalism lay somewhere between the uprising of democracy that its supporters sought and the Tammany Hall caricature of the Healyite invective.

In Omagh, Kevin O'Shiel described the 'kind of local Parnell split' that emerged between the slighted Healyite hero, George Murnaghan, 'in every sense of the word, an excellent man of affairs' and the Hibernian 'dictatorship' of 'political chancers and adventurers', whose 'tactless partisan outpourings' whipped fresh life into the Orange Order and who were intent on 'weeding out every non-Hibernian Member of Parliament'.[54] The police claimed that the split emerged over a combination of 'business and professional rivalry' and Murnaghan's 'moderate views on local boards'.[55] The Murnaghanites 'comprised the more conservative elements in the Catholic community, solicitors like Mr Alex Donnelly of Omagh, well-to-do businessmen and farmers, a considerable proportion of county and rural Councillors, and at least nine-tenths of the Catholic clergy.'[56] Murnaghan consistently voted with unionists, shared out public appointments and frequently challenged central Irish Party policy, mirroring the position of William O'Brien and Tim Healy's All for Ireland League (AFIL). At the 'Baton' convention on 9 February 1909, called to consider Birrell's land bill, Hibernians effectively drove O'Brien from the UIL, the organization he had founded.[57] By the 1910 elections, Hibernians had marked Murnaghan's card.

In January 1910 the Murnaghanites alleged that Devlin had packed the UIL convention called to select the parliamentary candidate for Mid-Tyrone.[58] Murnaghan claimed that the 'respectable people … were being denied their proper place' by 'a crowd of nobodies' unfit to select a parliamentary candidate.[59] All the priests present left and formed a rival Murnaghanite convention, which claimed 'the priesthood of Mid-Tyrone had been insulted'.[60] In an echo of Tammany Hall, Murnaghan claimed that he was deposed because 'he would not go into dark rooms in John Street [the offices of the Devlinite *Ulster Herald*], Omagh, and take his direction there on what he should do in certain matters'.[61] Murnaghan then stood on an AFIL ticket, confident that unionist voters would support him due to his conciliatory record. The Unionists deliberately delayed naming their candidate. This secured the return of George Brunskill by 300 votes ahead of the official Nationalist candidate, John Valentine, who easily out-polled Murnaghan.[62] In O'Shiel's view 'Conservative Nationalism, then (as now)' represented 'the mass of the nation'.[63] But the majority of Mid-Tyrone nationalists had chosen popular Hibernianism over conservative nationalism. By the December election, the damage wrought precipitated a partial nationalist truce and a successful unity candidate, Richard McGhee, a Lurgan Protestant, prominent Land Leaguer and a former president of the National Union of Dock Labourers.[64]

The following year, however, 'a distinct cleavage' re-emerged between the Board of Erin and Murnaghanites on Omagh RDC.[65] When Murnaghanites supported a unionist as vice chair on the grounds of 'fair play', one Hibernian called the nominator 'a low traitor and a contemptible scrub who would sell his cause for a mess of pottage.' Patrick Muldoon warned that 'they would mark all the nationalist backsliders' for the approaching occasion 'when he got the board purified'.[66] Hibernians subsequently boycotted 'factionist businesses' in Carrickmore.[67] Similarly, Patrick McCartan secured his position as Gortin dispensary doctor through Murnaghanite and unionist votes. He claimed that his income had suffered because the Hibernians supported an independent doctor: 'my opponents have made a mason of me. That explains the support of the Unionists. It also tends to injure me with the Catholics here but it does not matter.'[68] McCartan had established strong friendships with local unionists and his non-sectarianism bordered on the perverse when he lent his car to the UVF during the Larne gun-running.[69]

The Murnaghanite dispute displayed nationalist heterogeneity in stark contrast to unionist homogeneity in Tyrone. Temporary IRB and Murnaghanites support for the Irish Party quickly evaporated after unionist opposition spoiled the home rule honeymoon. The Devlinite consensus itself rested on insecure foundations because many committed supporters clearly viewed home rule as an instalment of Irish freedom, not a final settlement. These constitutional separatists would find common cause with the IRB and Murnaghanites in the post-1916 Sinn Féin. A series of developments during the Ulster Crisis, most notably the threat of partition, further damaged the nation-alist consensus. Significantly, 'Murnaghan's defeat by Valentine, who polled 836 votes more than his rival, [also] exposed the limitations of clerical authority'.[70] The unionist campaign consistently prophesized that 'Home Rule' meant 'Rome Rule', but, although undoubtedly influential, there were definite limits to the Catholic Church's influence over the Irish Party.

The borders of three Catholic dioceses converge within County Tyrone. While Patrick McKenna of Clogher and Tyrone man, Charles McHugh of Derry, could both be described as Irish Party supporters of a 'Faith and Fatherland' disposition, their ecclesiastical superior could not.[71] Cardinal Logue had only recently abandoned Tim Healy in favour of Redmond and Dillon, whom he distrusted for their perceived secularism.[72] Logue carried the generational baton of reaction from Paul Cullen, upholding a tradition of continental style anti-republicanism.[73] Miller argues that under Logue the Catholic Church served its own interests 'with consummate skill and determination' by manipulating the tension between British state power and the popular legitimacy enjoyed by the Irish nation, that is, the Irish Party and then SF.[74] Although convincing, this argument partially obscures churchmen's own origins. The church coveted its institutional authority, but leading clerics also spoke for the dominant class within Catholic Ireland. Logue dismissed unionist opposition as inspired 'not so much by the fear of a religious persecution … as by a fear of losing the ascendancy and monopoly of almost all public positions which the authors of the agitation have long enjoyed'.[75] He was critical of the economic provisions of the home rule bill: 'Ireland can stand no increased taxation. She is already taxed to breaking point'.[76] But the cardinal's greatest concern was education and the Liberal chief secretary, Augustine Birrell's, 'nonconformist mania for secularizing secondary education'.[77] Nonetheless, when Logue and Irish Party loyalist, Bishop Patrick O'Donnell of Raphoe, communicated their uneasiness about possible changes in secondary education, Redmond's 'dismissive response' demonstrated 'clearly the limits of episcopal authority and input'.[78] The IPP's acceptance of partition in early 1914 jeopardized the interests of the church and moderate home rulers.[79] Within this context, the Catholic hierarchy arguably strengthened its role in Ulster politics, but largely in response to the breakdown of IPP authority and the threatened position of moderate northern Catholic opinion of which leading clerics represented a significant constituency.

Before the onset of the partition controversy, moderate middle-class nationalists solidly backed the IPP. Despite Devlin's populism, parliamentary candidacy remained the gift of the UIL standing committee, which he and Dillon effectively controlled. This saw Tom Kettle 'pitch forked' into the Hibernians to guarantee his election at the 1906 East Tyrone by-election.[80] Similarly, under Devlin's orders, the local UIL convention selected John Redmond's son, William Archer, in December 1910. In effect, the UIL represented nationalist opinion because the Board of Erin provided the necessary weight of numbers and electoral enthusiasm. Following Redmond's victory in East Tyrone, rioting erupted in Dungannon, Coalisland, Stewartstown, Cookstown and the Moy in which, according to press reports, rival Orange and Hibernian crowds destroyed property, threw stones, stabbed opponents and fired shots.[81] For all the democratic rhetoric, Hibernians had little or no say over who represented them. The Healyites wanted Hibernians to know their place; under Devlinism; Hibernians were oblivious to the fact that they had been put in it.

The Catholic middle class controlled the UIL. Its remit included the registration of voters as the franchise was restricted to ratepayers. Election victories in notoriously close contests depended on the micro-management of the register and both nationalists and unionists spent the intervals between elections at loggerheads in the revision courts, minutely dissecting the register.[82] This explains the preponderance of Catholic solicitors on constituency executives as they spoke well at public meetings and worked voluntarily in the revision courts.[83] Barry Meglaughlin, Dungannon solicitor, senior Orangeman and Unionist election agent for the East Tyrone constituency, claimed that Kettle's increased majority in 1910 rested on the court of appeal's decision, known as the 'North Tyrone Agreements', which allowed a tenant the vote despite the previous occupier dying intestate and while other adults resided in the house.[84] The IPP apparently extracted the concession from the Liberal administration in Dublin Castle in return for Redmond Barry's seat.

Unionist arguments about a homogenous Ulster only increased the importance of nationalist parliamentary representation. David C. Hogg's election as Liberal MP for Derry City in January 1913 provided an excellent example. Across Tyrone, leading members of the IPP took a fortnight's holiday from their legal offices to campaign for Hogg, whose nomination papers had been signed by Bishop McHugh.[85] Interestingly, like the earlier general election in Tyrone, Derry republicans co-operated with the constitutional nationalists in the city.[86] The result represented a propaganda coup, for, as Armour predicted, 'If Hoggi gets in, the Unionists of the three kingdoms will be in a state of consternation as Ulster will have more Home Rule members than Unionists'.[87] At the 'Great' League convention of 1913 Devlin claimed the nationalist majority in Ulster fatally undermined the unionist case.[88] The IPP's machine appeared impregnable, yet closer investigation revealed chinks in its armour, particularly when unionist intransigence rendered irrelevant the nationalist parliamentary majority in Ulster.

The IPP became preoccupied with responding to the unionist challenge, tailoring its position on empire to British tastes and fatally, as events would prove, accepting partition. Tyrone Hibernians championed loyalty to the 'cause' of 'Ireland a Nation' with references to the empire typically being derogatory.[89] The IPP squared the circle by portraying home rule as limited self-government within the British Empire, while promising socially progressive legislation and appealing to deep-rooted nationalism at home.[90] Tyrone unionists exploited this contradiction. For example, following Redmond's fund-raising tour in America in 1910, which netted $100,000, they portrayed the IPP leader as a 'dollar dictator', who effused separatist rhetoric in America, but espoused loyalty in

Britain.[91] In June 1911 Averill Lloyd JP told Benburb unionists that 'just a few days ago', Redmond claimed he did 'not now want total separation', yet 'if he made that statement before meetings of the servant girls in America, from whom he got his dollars … They would tell him he got their money under false pretences'.[92] In July 1912 W.A. Redmond countered unionist jibes by suggesting that Irish home rule would not 'dismember or disintegrate the Empire' but would be 'a sure means of welding together the many self-governing communities into a common bond.'[93] This argument helped deflect unionist criticism, but was of relatively recent origin to constituents weaned on tales of Fenianism.

John Redmond himself once commented that were he an Englishman, he 'should be the greatest imperialist living'.[94] His son similarly had a liberal and humane interpretation of empire.[95] At the other extreme, *Irish Freedom* preferred 'Ireland never to be free than to win freedom by joining in with the pirate Empire, sharing in the guilt and the spoils of wholesale massacre and theft.'[96] Whereas many constitutionalists genuinely sought incorporation into a 'liberalised and democratised British Empire',[97] British and Irish unionists held a high imperial perspective of colonial expansion and racial predestination. The Redmonds' altruistic vision of an empire of equals did not fully reflect reality. Therefore, the IPP sought to counter the dominant interpretation of the British socio–political élite, while reconciling its own interpretation with a separatist tradition necessary for continued popular support. There was certainly many a nod and wink involved, but the war required real sacrifices for the empire and, on this point, the leadership tumbled from its rhetorical tightrope.

If pro-imperialism sat uncomfortably with nationalist rhetoric, the necessity for political peace in Ulster undermined popular mobilization, particularly Devlin's eighteen-month ban on AOH marches after Castledawson.[98] At Dungannon in July 1913 H.K. McAleer, Board of Erin provincial president, lambasted unionists, who 'were leaving traps for the nationalists to fall into, so as to have some scandal to bring against Home Rule'.[99] Nevertheless, this moratorium and indiscriminate attacks on nationalists in unionist areas, strained Party influence over more militant elements.[100] In September 1912 the RIC IG warned that nationalists were being 'stirred up to a state of intense excitement and bitterness, and in their present temper a large number would probably respond to any call'.[101] Nonetheless during the summer of 1913 the 'rather fictitious' peace held firm because nationalists obeyed 'strict instructions to give no offence' going to 'any length to avoid getting into collision with the opposite party'.[102] Riots erupted in Derry at the Apprentice Boys demonstration on 12 August, with 'the indiscriminate use of revolvers' leading to a nationalist fatality and the serious wounding of a policeman.[103] The Belfast, Portadown and Lurgan contingents maintained an 'almost continuous fusillade of revolver shots' as they travelled through Tyrone, with one woman injured as she stood on the station platform.[104] The Hibernians, nonetheless, still turned the other cheek.[105] The IPP's quietist strategy relied on Devlin's authority, the lack of a viable alternative and the belief that the unionists were bluffing.[106] The formation of the Irish Volunteers in November 1913 transformed this situation. The acceptance of partition, the Curragh 'mutiny' and the Larne gun-running propelled the Irish Volunteers' expansion in Tyrone. After two years of meekly observing Orange intransigence, the IVF provided a means for Hibernians to regain some self-respect and defend home rule.

No issue threatened the IPP's hegemony more than partition. By the end of 1913 this had become the government's solution to the Ulster crisis, shattering nationalists' 'pristine childlike faith in Liberal promises'.[107] In February 1914 Skeffington warned that 'exclusion would simply mean that the nationalists of Ulster would be crushed under the heel of ascendancy, a thing which they had looked forward to Home Rule to relieve them of'.[108] By February 1914 west Ulster nationalist leaders, most notably Bishops McHugh and O'Donnell, organized a rally in Derry against exclusion, lest 'the party might sacrifice them to the Carsonites in the interests of political expediency', and to show Asquith that 'there were two sides to the Ulster question'.[109] Fearing the meeting would inflict the 'gravest injury on the National cause', Redmond vetoed it.[110] In early March the IPP leader agreed to temporary exclusion by county option as the price of peace. Devlin, in reluctant agreement, toured the north to smooth relations with the bishops and several leading Partymen, while Jeremiah MacVeagh, MP for South Down, met Cardinal Logue.[111] The mission succeeded because there was as yet no prospect of a unionist dominated administration in Belfast and because west Ulster nationalists read county option to mean that Fermanagh, Tyrone and Derry city would still come under a Dublin parliament.[112] The acceptance of partition led many nationalists to question the Liberal alliance and even harbour doubts about the IPP's ability to deliver all-Ireland home rule, particularly James Mayne and John Doris from Cookstown who challenged the manner in which Devlin had engineered the acceptance of county option.[113] The Healyites had previously criticized Devlin's secret deals, but here were loyal party members questioning their leaders' integrity, men who would rather abandon the IPP than consent to partition.

When the home rule bill passed its third reading in the House of Commons in May 1914 the leadership officially supported the Irish Volunteers.[114] The Party then cynically pointed to the IVF as a bulwark against further concessions.[115] The bill's final passage proved a pyrrhic victory, however. The amending bill undermined celebrations and Carson's demand for the exclusion of six counties threatened Tyrone itself. On 22 July a nationalist convention in Omagh representing Tyrone, Fermanagh and Derry city, resolved to resist any additional concessions, declaring that 'at the risk of our lives we will never consent to be separated from the Irish Nation'.[116] The IPP supported this meeting, partly because it had lost control, but also because it strengthened its position at the all-party Buckingham Palace Conference (21–4 July), convened to reach a compromise and avert civil war.

The negotiations eventually collapsed on the issue of Tyrone. Although the IPP representatives stood firm, they had lost ground since March.[117] Once conceded in principle, partition had embedded itself in the British political agenda. Physical force, or the threat of it, had put it there. By June Tyrone nationalists, copying unionist militancy, no longer relied solely on the assurances of their leaders. Although the majority remained nominally loyal, the relationship between leadership and base had shifted. At an anti-exclusion rally in Derry in June 1914, Fr William Doherty dismissed

> the weakling members of parliament … [who] are pushing the pawn on the political chess table towards Carson and his friends … nothing can stop that pawn but the low and angry rumbling of your voices swelling over the hills and dales of Derry, the low steady tramp of the march of the Volunteers.[118]

The Irish Volunteers held their first meeting at Dublin's Rotunda on 25 November 1913. Plans by the IRB to establish a force coincided with similar thinking within the wider nationalist caucus.[119] Eoin MacNeill chaired the IVF provisional committee, which included a cohort of IRB men, Gaelic Leaguers and, despite the IPP's disapproval, some party supporters. This diverse grouping agreed on one thing – the impact of the Ulster Volunteers. Tom Kettle claimed that the Irish Volunteers were formed because 'one-fourth of the nation has planned to secede from the other three-fourths, and to make its secession good by duress of arms', and therefore any 'self-respecting man' should 'discipline and practice himself in the art of communal self-defence – in the art of war.'[120]

Although unionist resistance, particularly after the Curragh 'mutiny' and Larne gun-running, spurred nationalists into action, there was less agreement in terms of the ultimate goal. The typical position vehemently opposed partition, but exhibited little hostility to constitutionalism *per se*. In essence, the provisional committee members not specifically aligned to the IRB can be described as constitutional separatists. They viewed a generous measure of home rule as a step towards real independence and backed a unified IPP at Westminster as the best means to achieve this. They were careful though to guard against any slippage on nationalist principle. Hence MacNeill claimed that the Irish Volunteers were designed not to undermine the IPP but to 'under-prop' it.[121] For many the IVF represented a means of reinvigorating Irish nationalism; 'a partial recourse to Fenianism would be the saving of constitutionalism.'[122] F.J. O'Connor, president of the Tyrone Volunteers, shared this view, urging local nationalists to 'band themselves together in a citizen army … not as an army of hirelings to any other country'.[123]

By contrast the IRB sought to use the Volunteers to undermine constitution-alism and generate the conditions for a mass movement pledged to a republican and ultimately insurrectionary programme. McCartan endeavoured to imple-ment this plan in Tyrone, where the IRB controlled the new movement's formative development.

There were three distinct phases in the IVF's expansion. The first lasted until March 1914 and constituted lower-class, autonomous and advanced nationalist mobilization, essentially driven by the IRB, but attracting 14,000 Volunteers, including many Hibernians.[124] The second and largest mobilization, sharing aspects of the first, included moderate nationalists, who joined in reaction to the Curragh and Larne episodes, before the IPP's public support in May. The third phase saw the entry of Devlinites, dated specifically to after 9 May. This date coincided with Board of Erin directives to join and control the movement.[125] The police claimed that membership in the county rose by over 3,500 after Devlin's official endorsement.[126] Redmond captured the movement on 10 June by issuing an ultimatum to the provisional committee. While the IPP sought to neutralize the IVF during the summer, independent companies continued in earnest. This situation persisted until the outbreak of war when Redmond's recruiting call split the movement.

The development of the Volunteers in Tyrone rested on the pre-existing IRB network.[127] Indeed, the IVF and IRB stimulated each other until March 1914 when an influx of independent constitutional nationalists joined the ranks in response to the deteriorating political situation. At an IRB county meeting in Dungannon on 26 December 1913 McCartan and McCullough directed that each cell form a company and then swear in officers.[128] By early 1914 this had been carried out in east Tyrone.[129] Likewise, at Strabane, Cathal O'Shannon instructed members 'to do everything to support the IVF'.[130] Arthur McElvogue, Pomeroy IRB centre and Hibernian, claimed that the IRB were 'the driving force' behind the IVF. By April 1914 republicans had formed companies in Pomeroy, Upper and Lower Kildress, Munderadoe, Aughnagar, Carrickmore, Tremogue, Cookstown, Sixmilecross, Clogher, Donaghmore and two in Galbally, all with an average membership of fifty.[131] The cells in Coalisland and Dungannon appear to have drilled indoors and did not openly establish corps until early summer.[132] Significantly, McElvogue revealed how several IRB men retained AOH membership, thereby getting 'divisions of the Hibernians to help them form Volunteer Companies'. Similarly, McCartan recalled how 'once we had broken into the Hibernians, it was plain sailing after that', with new IRB cells formed in Carrickmore village, Sixmilecross and Greencastle. McCartan also inducted two priests. Fr James O'Daly of Clogher joined the local cell under the command of the local postman, Frank Dooris.[133] Fr Eugene Coyle of Fintona came to McCartan's attention when he personally purchased sixty rifles from the O'Rahilly, IVF director of arms, and organized an independent corps in Fintona.[134] Coyle's association with the IRB apparently dated to the summer of 1914.[135] In May 1915 he wrote to Maurice Moore, inspector general of the National Volunteers, claiming that the Irish Volunteers sought to preserve Ireland 'from disgrace in the eyes of history', and describing Redmond as 'the most discredited politician and leader that Ireland ever produced'.[136]

The initial growth of the IVF did not rely solely on the IRB, however. The early organizers included a cohort of IPP supporters.[137] The formation of companies outside IRB areas was the result of independent, lower-class, Hibernian activism. In January 1914 one hundred nationalists 'without leaders' paraded in Newtownstewart in the north-west.[138] This independent mobilization clearly fed off indignation with the local UVF's frantic activity at nearby Baronscourt.[139] Therefore, the Hibernian grass roots and elements of the clergy, 'restive under the strain of the political crisis', ignored Board of Erin orders prohibiting drill, 'under pain of expulsion'.[140] Consequently, the Irish Volunteers made headway in areas previously untouched by republican activity.

In January 1914 Strabane had 750 Volunteers and Eugene Conroy presided at the meeting of the first 'corps of the Volunteers in Ulster'.[141] Despite O'Shannon's input, constitutional nationalists predominated on the Strabane Corps. Indeed, aggressive Hibernianism was very apparent when the Strabane IVF, assisted by neighbouring units from east Donegal, seized control of the town at midnight on 16 May.[142] Throughout the period the IVF in the hinterland of Strabane was more closely connected to companies in Donegal, a relationship that was later copper fastened by the area's inclusion in the IRA 1st Northern Division [ND]. The Donegal IVF 'sprang' from the AOH, although the CI identified co-operation with local republicans.[143] By February five companies had been formed and by March Donegal had eleven branches with an approximate membership of 2,600.[144] In Tyrone the IRB dominated the earliest stage of development. In both counties a blend of republican and advanced Hibernian mobilization took place; dual AOH and IRB membership clearly facilitated this process in Tyrone.

Outside Donegal, the Hibernian prohibition on drilling enjoyed greater success. In Fermanagh, nationalists reacted unfavourably to the IVF, and less than 400 volunteers had enrolled by April.[145] Despite a positive reception from the UIL, the Monaghan IVF had only four branches in March, centred on the IRB in Carrickmacross and the GAA clubs in Clones and Monaghan town.[146] In Derry city, the IRB formed a company in protest at Bishop McHugh's cancellation of the anti-partition meeting. It also established companies in Magherafelt and Newbridge. Independent Hibernian mobilization was not apparent.[147] In Armagh, the IRB formed companies in the city and Blackwatertown.[148] Open drilling of any sort did not take place in Armagh until May, during the second phase and the IVF's rapid growth in Ulster, which effectively forced the IPP to come to terms with the new movement.[149]

The Curragh incident in March 1914 fell on Ulster nationalists 'with all the staggering force of a bombshell', smashing complacency about UVF bluff and exploding faith in the Liberal alliance.[150] It also strengthened the nationalists' desire to have 'an army of their own'.[151] Indeed, many Hibernian lodges now actively promoted the movement.[152] The Larne gun-running stimulated involvement from moderate nationalists, ordinarily opposed to political violence, and independent companies were formed in every police district.[153] The overarching issue of partition clearly motivated moderate involvement. Just prior to his tour of Tyrone in May, Roger Casement wrote to Moore that 'We shall have to make it clear that the exclusion of Ulster on the lines now suggested in England will be met in Ulster by resistance and instead of peace they will assure strife'.[154] The provisional committee then appointed Captain Jack White, a former member of the Irish Citizen Army, to train the Ulster contingents.[155] Both men visited Dungannon in June. Casement told his audience that 'for twenty years the people of Ireland had played the constitutional game according to the rules ... and if at the eleventh hour they found that the game was not going to be played by those methods ... then they would also have to appeal to force'.[156]

By May the Tyrone Volunteers had over 5,000 members in fifty-nine branches, drawing support from 'all classes of Nationalists, including the AOH and IRB' and 'the Catholic clergy'. The police noted that the 'class of persons joining are labourers, farmers' sons, shop keepers' assistants, factory hands etc.' Significantly, several leading members of the IPP now overtly supported the Irish Volunteers, most notably F.J. O'Connor of Omagh.[157] Independent mobilization reached its pinnacle with Casement and MacNeill's tour of the Sperrins in mid-May. A broad range of opinion, united in opposition to partition, coalesced under the IVF umbrella. Party supporters in Tyrone gravitated towards MacNeill's 'under prop' thesis, 'radicalizing the doctrines of the constitutional agenda while presuming to remain within its bounds'.[158] The genuinely popular nature of the movement, the prevalent hostility to the UVF and the open association of local party supporters forced Devlin to lend his support lest he lose followers. In May the CI reported that the 'majority of the Nationalists in Tyrone are in favour of the movement being placed under the control of the Irish Nationalist Parliamentary party'.[159] The party leadership had reached the same conclusion. Moore, MacNeill, Casement and Bulmer Hobson engaged in unofficial contacts with the Irish Party between April and May, constituting what Tom Clarke labelled a junta, operating 'behind the backs of the provisional committee'.[160] On 9 May Redmond rejected their proposal for an elected representative council, according to Hobson, because 'it might give public expression to' IVF 'disapproval of the partition proposals'.[161] Nevertheless, when the Irish Party finally sanctioned the IVF, the movement exploded throughout Ulster, with the national membership soaring from 25,000 to 69,000 within a month.[162]

On 10 June Redmond issued an ultimatum, threatening to establish a rival organization if the provisional committee did not accept the co-option of twenty-five of his nominees.[163] The provisional committee's acceptance by fifteen votes to nine on 16 June owed a substantial debt to the 'junta', particularly Hobson, whom Clarke never forgave.[164] The latter argued that Redmond intended to 'capture and smash up the Volunteer movement' and that 'had the provisional committee only stood up to Redmond, he would have been smashed within three months'.[165] For those who supported the under-prop thesis, the co-option appeared wholly positive. F.J. O'Connor claimed that the Volunteers represented a 'Citizen Army' organized to prevent 'further concessions'. Their response to any such compromise would be 'away with the government and away with the Home Rule Bill'.[166] James Mayne claimed Liberal bad faith meant that 'they must now rely on themselves to defend their province and their country against the impudent and the arrogant claims of Carsonism'.[167] Constitutional separatists clearly believed that their efforts had guided the IPP back on to the right course. The party's attitude to the IVF demonstrated that this was far from the case.

On 26 July determination mixed with outrage when attempts by the IVF to arm themselves at Howth led to the Bachelor's Walk incident in which British soldiers fired into a Dublin crowd and killed three civilians. DI Conlin of Omagh claimed that the event 'had a very disturbing effect' on Tyrone nationalists, which was apparent in the outraged condemnations issued by the few nationalist-controlled public bodies in the county.[168] It is questionable whether the IVF could have coped had civil war erupted in July 1914. At Clogher, Captain Jack White, who had recently taken command of Tyrone, told those assembled that 'they should not suppress home truths'; they were 'a leaderless' and ill-equipped force, who could rely only 'on their own determination and self-sacrifice'.[169] Lord Clanwilliam of the UUC claimed that 'If war did break out it would probably be a war of extermination. We have the Nationalists sandwiched between our forces and they have only a few old guns to rely on … We have the province in the hollow of our hands'.[170]

Throughout the summer the IRB continued energetically to promote the Volunteers, determined to 'use this organization, if it prospers, to effect the separation of Ireland from England.'[171] They were ably assisted by White, who relished getting 'Tyrone into shape' as 'there are some very good men in the County'.[172] Thus, while the IPP sought to neutralize the IVF, republican companies continued drilling and arming.[173] Hobson attended field operations with the Clogher, Fintona and Trillick companies, while the Greencastle, Cranagh, Kildress and Carrickmore Battalions exhibited 'furious élan' during manoeuvres around Greencastle.[174] White and Darrell Figgis led this camp.[175] White recounted how Figgis, 'the hero of the recent Howth gun-running', apparently saved him from a potential mutiny on the mountain, after he 'gave vent to a passionate tirade of abuse … unbridled in its fury' because the men refused to be quiet in camp. White was 'astounded, as always, by the natural military aptitude of the men'.[176] He lamented the political wrangling at the top of the IVF and the Irish Party's neglect after the Redmondite coup.

On achieving control, the IPP sapped the life from the movement. Publicly, Devlin sought to arm the northern Volunteers with Italian rifles.[177] Fr O'Daly claimed, however, that 'the Redmondites were not sincere in their attitude to the Volunteers', but were obliged to import weapons to placate militant Hibernian followers.[178] In Belfast, Séamus Dobbyn of the IRB recounted how, armed with obsolete rifles, 'training practices developed into mere parades, to open air meetings, where we were addressed by Joe Devlin and some M.P.s'.[179] Devlin imported the 'gas pipes' to keep the Hibernians quiet – literally as they did not work. As Phoenix remarks, having 'neutralized' the IVF 'by placing it under the Party's control', Devlin 'had no desire to see it assuming a leading political role'.[180]

The outbreak of war and Redmond's pledge that the Volunteers would defend Ireland's shores transformed the situation. On 17 September, at Coalisland, Captain White 'characterized as humbug the unloading of a few thousand rusty rifles dating back to 1875, on scattered companies without organization or trained leaders, with the tragicomic contention that this would secure the country from invasion'.[181] Members of the IPP in Tyrone were unwilling to commit to the war until home rule had been granted, however. John Skeffington 'advised them to keep clear of the British army' while another leading party member stated that 'when they got Home Rule they would join the army, but not till then.'[182] White had proposed that, under the auspices of home defence, the IVF seek assistance from the War Office to organize an officer training camp and provide serviceable weapons. He even claimed that 'some Sinn Fein leaders saw the sense' of his proposal, including a local SF priest, most likely Eugene Coyle, who backed the scheme privately.[183] Ultimately, however, Redmond's call for recruits at Woodenbridge, not the war itself, provoked the Volunteer split.[184] In Tyrone the IPP carried the majority mainly due to the passing of the home rule bill on 18 September (two days before Woodenbridge), albeit suspended for the duration of the war. To Redmond's relief, Asquith told Bonar Law that the exclusion of six counties was unacceptable.[185] The likelihood of Tyrone's place within a home rule administration therefore also deflected potential dissent. Nevertheless, only thirty companies in the county even debated the split and only 1,445 Volunteers supported the IPP, whereas 6,699 made no declaration.[186]

The period from 1910 to the outbreak of the war had started brightly for Tyrone nationalists. The tantalizing prospect of home rule temporarily reconciled the various factions. The destruction of the Lords' veto vindicated a political generation of patience and adherence to constitutional methods and the Liberal alliance. Below the surface, however, Tyrone nationalism was a house divided. The unionist determination to challenge home rule by force shattered nationalist harmony. The IRB challenged the perceived hypocrisy of Irish Party rhetoric based on the Fenian legacy and seized on the unionist example to promote the IVF, attracting many of the Hibernian grass roots in the process. The IPP's Murnaghanite adversaries quickly found fault with the details of the home rule bill and, as the fateful issue of partition emerged, many loyal supporters within the UIL began to question the IPP's ability to deliver home rule, or to save Tyrone from exclusion. The Party's failure to deal with the unionist challenge or the disintegrating Liberal alliance pointed towards its subsequent demise. By September 1914 home rule was on the statute book, but doubly fettered by an amending bill and suspension until the end of the war. The twin issues of renascent Irish republicanism and partition would shape political debate in Tyrone for the next decade.

4 Empire or republic?

Britain declared war on 4 August 1914 and, in the words of Churchill, 'the parishes of Fermanagh and Tyrone faded back into the mists and squalls of Ireland, and a strange light began … to fall and grow upon the map of Europe'.[1] The initial wave of nationwide enthusiasm for the war, sparked by Redmond and Carson's common support, was not matched by large-scale recruitment between 1914 and 1916. As will be shown, the Tyrone UVF joined in respectable numbers in the early months of the conflict but this was not sustained. Idealistic hopes of a shared sacrifice on the battlefield were likewise not realized. Fears of conscription in 1915 stimulated a reorientation of nationalism in the county. The seeds of the IPP's final collapse germinated in the 'hothouse conditions of war'.[2] Partition, support for Britain despite the presence of Ulster unionists in the wartime coalition, and the emergence of a republican alternative all undermined the IPP position. The dispute between the Redmondite National Volunteer Force (NVF) and the republican IVF highlighted the reasoning behind growing disenchantment with constitutionalism, even if attempts at insurrection in Tyrone itself during Easter Week 1916 were shambolic. The Rising occasioned a renewed attempt to reach a home rule settlement in the summer of 1916 based on six-county exclusion. The spectre of partition proved decisive. It split constitutionalism in Tyrone and ended the dominance of the IPP.

In his report for August, CI Millar recorded that the war had 'worked a revolution in the state of party feeling in this county'.[3] While the *Tyrone Courier* rallied to the empire, the *Ulster Herald* was more circumspect: 'sacrifices we are told are necessary in the interests of the Empire at this fateful juncture, but if sacrifices are to be made, let them be made in the interests of Ireland'.[4] Nationalist support was conditional on home rule reaching the statute book but the amending bill pointed to the postponement rather than the death of partition. While both Ulster and Irish Volunteers escorted army reservists to train stations in places like Omagh, relatively few nationalists enlisted. This may have been due to Redmond's offer that the Volunteers be deployed for home defence. Millar claimed that the Irish Volunteers were waiting for direction 'from the promoters of the organization'.[5] Yet, even after Redmond's Woodenbridge speech when he committed the Volunteers to serve 'wherever the firing line extends', there was no rush to the colours. Despite a general 'desire' for British success, there was a 'lamentable failure' in nationalist recruitment until the end of 1914.[6]

By contrast, under Ambroise Ricardo, Tyrone unionists enlisted in larger numbers in 1914. While in neighbouring counties the UVF 'held aloof' or were 'slow in making a move', in Tyrone 200 Ulster Volunteers rushed to join in

August 1914.[7] Ricardo had started recruiting for the 36th (Ulster) Division even before War Office sanction and had 'therefore almost literally kidnapped into the 36th Division [Catholic] recruits who should have gone to the 10th [Irish] Division.' By October the 9th Battalion Royal Inniskilling Fusiliers (Tyrone) had 650 men. The same month Ricardo distributed a handbill to Ulster Volunteers, urging them to join for the 'Empire and Ulster'. Outwardly satisfied, he privately conceded that 'We have done fairly well, but require 300 men to complete; if we do not get these at an early date there is a great risk of our being filled up from outside which would be a great slur on our country'.[8]

During 1915 just under 1,000 men enlisted in Tyrone. The figure comprised 340 National Volunteers, 523 Ulster Volunteers and 175 non-aligned recruits, who were probably agricultural labourers.[9] These modest numbers matched rural recruitment across Ulster which, 'like those in south-western Ireland, did not peak until 1915', coinciding with IPP support for a large-scale recruiting campaign.[10] Tom Kettle represented the Nationalists at these cross-party meetings.[11] At Strabane, he warned that 'if the war was … prolonged until another winter, then they must have conscription'.[12] Nonetheless, F.J. O'Connor attacked the initiative, claiming that 'Jingoism and Imperialism do not find a response among the Nationalists of Ireland'.[13] By the end of 1915, despite large attendances, recruiting meetings had little effect. The RIC reported that this was 'in a great measure due to the influence exercised by the Sinn Féiners [an umbrella term for anyone opposed to war effort], which handicaps the speakers in their efforts to overcome local prejudice to military service.'[14] Economic motives proved even more important. In November 1914 CI Millar claimed that 'even the most enthusiastic [about the war] like to turn a penny out of the public distress.'[15] There was an inclination to exploit high war-time prices, or work in the much safer surroundings of a local linen mill, which had received significant 'khaki orders'.[16] By 1916 Montgomery had 'given all attempts at recruiting up as hopeless', claiming that 'the anti-recruiter here … simply wants to stay at home and keep his sons at home to make money while others are fighting'.[17] He identified 'a whole strip of the country from near Clabby to Ballygawley which has sent hardly any recruits, Protestant or Catholic, but who all turned out at the sports.'[18] For the Tyrone tenantry, unionist and nationalist, the allure of the by-ways of Tyrone trumped the muddy trenches of Flanders.

Tyrone formed part of the 27th regimental recruiting area.[19] Between the outbreak of the war and mid-January 1916 Tyrone had contributed 2,123 men or 1.5 per cent of the total population. In proportional terms this was ahead of Donegal (1,032/0.6 per cent) but behind Fermanagh (1,082/1.75 per cent) and Derry city and county (3,778/2.68 per cent).[20] The latter had a larger unionist population and a concentration of unemployed and lower-class urban males in the city, which had a tradition of military recruitment. Overwhelmingly agricultural, Donegal had a much smaller unionist population (21.1 per cent) and by

1916 military recruitment shrank to a handful from 'the unemployed classes'.[21] Within Tyrone CI Millar identified a trend in September 1914 that persisted until 1916, noting that the UVF had 'responded fairly well' with the majority 'from about the principal towns'.[22] During the same period, the Belfast recruiting area, which contained over 100,000 less people, produced 28,001 recruits.[23] Interestingly, 'Belfast Catholics ... were four times as likely to enlist as Catholics from other parts of Ulster' and proportionately contributed as many recruits as the city's Protestant population, an indication of both their relative poverty and the strong response elicited by Joe Devlin's recruiting call.[24]

After a surge of recruitment by the UVF in the autumn and winter of 1914, it plateaued in west Ulster before declining in 1916 with only 336 enlisting in Tyrone and 122 in Fermanagh; Derry city alone registered 'fair' recruitment during the year.[25] Reflecting on enlistment in Herdman's Linen Mill in Sion Mills in 1918, Ricardo was surprised to 'find that 130 employees have served & the two sides are just equally represented!! At first our men went – but latterly I hear the others have gone in dribbles & ours have not. All honour to every R.C. who has gone, he has had & will have to incur considerable odium from his own.'[26] Unlike Ricardo, most Tyrone unionists were worried that nationalist labourers, who trickled into the army out of economic necessity, might tarnish the lustre of early, patriotic, unionist enlistment and consequently rob them of useful post-war propaganda. In October 1916, in an obvious allusion to plummeting unionist enlistment and the questionable religious and social background of those currently taking the shilling, the duchess of Abercorn wrote to Carson: 'I have heard they would have to replace Ulster Division losses outside; *unless* there is conscription there cannot be much voluntary material to put in of the right sort'.[27]

Paradoxically, overtures to nationalists undermined unionist enlistment. Writing in 1918 Montgomery identified 'an idea afloat that the stoppage of [unionist] recruiting here, and the opposition to compulsory service was due to recruiting being in the hands of anti-national persons'. This referred to George Evans, the recruiting agent in Clogher from November 1915 until July 1916. In addition to his acrimonious history with unionists, local nationalists apparently viewed Evans 'as a renegade and threatened his life at the time of the rebellion soon after which he was sent away to join a training corps somewhere'.[28] In October 1916 William Coote, South Tyrone MP, raised the case in Parliament and asked why Evans was not at the front.[29]

Shared Irish sacrifice in the First World War has received a lot of recent attention. However, Tyrone unionists derided nationalist recruitment figures. They regarded the loyalty of Redmond and his followers as cynical, not backed by real sacrifice, and merely designed for propaganda effect. Indeed, there are legitimate doubts about the truly Irish composition of the 10th (Irish) Division.[30] At the very outset in August 1914, William Moore, MP for North

Armagh, told Apprentice Boys in the Moy that 'they had to show that Protestant Ulster was heart and soul with the empire' in this 'life and death struggle'. He believed that Redmond's call for defence represented neither loyalty nor patriotism but merely 'another move' in the 'often declared' policy 'of driving British rule bag and baggage out of Ireland'.[31] By 1916 Montgomery claimed that while his speeches provided 'sufficient eyewash for the British elector', Redmond 'winked the other eye at his followers here' who remained aloof. 'If we spoke publicly about this we should be held up as incorrigible bigots.'[32] Rather than shared sacrifice, the war generated further acrimony. Unionists consistently challenged nationalist commitment even though unionist recruitment figures were far from exemplary. By 1916 this was exacerbated by war weariness and horrific reports from the trenches, which affected both nationalist and unionist recruitment. Horner captured the mood in the Commons in December 1915: 'Can we expect men to come cheerfully forward to join the Colours if the feeling gets out, as it undoubtedly is getting out, that we are asking these men to go abroad without a hope, or only a small hope, of their ever returning to this country?'[33]

By spring 1915 insufficient recruits had enlisted. The government passed the National Registration Act on 15 July 1915 to ascertain the number between the ages of fifteen and sixty-five engaged in each trade. Many interpreted this as a preliminary to conscription, a view strengthened by the formation of a coalition cabinet in May 1915. The registration measure was not applied in Tyrone. Unionists believed that the government spared the blushes of Redmond and Tyrone nationalists.[34] Andrew Horner, who raised the issue in a series of newspaper articles, informed Carson that there had been 'a good deal of intrigue' as nationalists feared a poll because of the low level of Catholic recruitment.[35] At Tyrone County Council, Montgomery claimed that the act had been 'opposed in the most backward and barbarous' parts of the country and asserted that Tyrone's inclusion with the agricultural south and west represented a slur on the county. This led to protests from nationalists and a heated debate.[36] Any measure of conscription, however, would threaten nationalist sympathy for Britain. The *Ulster Herald* claimed that 'compulsory military service … would be attended with bloodshed and imprisonment unprecedented.'[37] Many unionists were also opposed, fearing conscription would 'be worked unfairly against Protestants and Unionists'.[38] Montgomery told Dawson Bates, the future NI minister of home affairs, that, in 1916, when he sought to pass resolutions at the local and county councils, Carson advised him to 'drop it'.[39]

Fears of conscription played into the hands of the Irish Volunteers, which after September 1914 were synonymous with the IRB.[40] They remained primed to exploit any weakness in the Redmondite position. McCartan claimed that after the split 'practically the only people who remained with us … were the IRB men and of these we had about 500 in the Co. Tyrone'.[41] An insurrection represented the medium-term objective. At a meeting of county delegates in a Dungannon pub in December 1914, Denis McCullough 'advised those present not to give up their rifles if any attempt to seize them was made', and later informed the Dungannon cell that 'they might soon have an opportunity to strike a blow for the freedom of Ireland'.[42] In January 1915 Father O'Daly told the Clogher company that 'the Irish Volunteers had come to settle the Irish Question in the old way, the only way ... it could ever be settled'.[43] This attitude was prevalent across the IRB in mid-Ulster. At Toome in October 1914 Ernest Blythe thought it better 'to resist death at home and die on your own threshold, than to be shot down doing England's dirty work on the Continent'.[44]

Until the spring of 1915 the IVF engaged in anti-recruiting as a core activity while it attempted to consolidate its position. In the towns, such as Dungannon, republicans proposed neutrality on the split and reverted to the core numbers prior to the Devlinite influx after May 1914.[45] By contrast, in rural villages and townlands such as Donaghmore, Pomeroy, Kildress, Galbally, Cappagh and Derrytresk, the IRB monopolized control by engineering showdowns within local companies.[46] The RIC estimated that there were 517 Irish Volunteers in Tyrone at the end of 1914.[47] Frank Burke, the IRB military organizer for Ulster and leader of the isolated IVF in Carrickmacross, County Monaghan, claimed that in Ulster, except for 'Belfast and Tyrone, the organization [IRB] elsewhere was scrappy'.[48] The IVF companies in the north Armagh and Derry Brigades represented extensions of the Tyrone IRB network, while the cells in Strabane and Sion Mills communicated with about 250 'Sinn Féiners' in Donegal.[49] By February 1916 the county board of the Tyrone Irish Volunteers represented twenty-four companies with over 500 members.[50] Father Coyle, who dismissed the 'de-nationalized' upper class and 'West Briton' press, placed his hope 'upon the farmers and labourers of the country ... artisans and labourers in the towns. Only among these classes in Ireland, as a rule, is preserved the true tradition of Irish nationality'.[51] In January 1915 the police provided a less sanguine analysis, noting that the Dungannon IRB 'belong to the working classes and have no influence in the locality'.[52] With the exception of McCartan, his family members and a few priests, the Irish Volunteers came from a working-class community with a tradition of republican activism.

From the outset, republicans opposed constitutionalist support for the war. Anti-recruiting posters appeared across the county and in Dungannon the Union Jack was burnt.[53] According to Ben Novick, republican propaganda consistently linked 'support for the war-time policies of the IPP with support for the historic evils of British rule'.[54] In November 1914 Devlin appealed to Dungannon Hibernians: 'If England is our enemy, then England must be fought, but if England is our friend, then we must act in a spirit of friendliness.' He ridiculed local men 'prepared to go out on the hillsides' to 'combat the British army', as 'they could never hope to win for Ireland what had been won for her in the bloodless revolution of the past thirty years'.[55] He believed that the nationalist war record would bring the Orangemen round and that the British government was no longer Ireland's adversary; republicans disagreed on both counts.

Opposition to the war benefitted the Irish Volunteers when the creation of the coalition cabinet in May 1915, which included Carson, precipitated a conscription panic.[56] By August 1915 their determination 'to resist conscription and fight for national independence' had provided the force with 'an influence which its comparatively small membership would scarcely warrant.'[57] This coincided with moves to reorganize the Tyrone IVF. Headquarters sent the former American soldier, J. J. 'Ginger' O'Connell, north in the summer of 1915 'as a compliment to Mr Joseph McGarrity of Philadelphia, a Tyrone man by birth'.[58] Seven training camps were held between June and August 1915. The RIC admitted that the July camp was a 'bold step forward'.[59] Although the police underplayed his influence, the rival NVF organizer, Captain John Eckersley, claimed that O'Connell's activity embodied a 'sort of secret society', which found particular local favour.[60] After O'Connell's departure in late July, Captain Hugh McCrory, another American army veteran, assumed control of the newly constituted Tyrone Battalion.[61] O'Connell himself admitted that 'had the appointment of Sir Edward Carson not taken place, my efforts towards the reorganization of the Volunteers in Mid-Ulster would have been met with no success.'[62]

The efforts to promote the IVF did not go unchecked. The RIC took 'exhaustive interest' in O'Connell's doings. The local constabulary also 'discreetly approached' H.K. McAleer and other leading Hibernians and priests to counteract the IVF and encourage recruitment.[63] The older priests, particularly Monsignor O'Doherty of Omagh, opposed the IVF. However, O'Connell noted that younger curates were less hostile and recognized 'the Party to be the sham it was increasingly proving itself to be'.[64] The NVF also sent Captain Eckersley north to counteract the initiative. O'Connell recounted, however, that Eckersley's 'employers did not care whether he effected anything or not – provided he rendered my efforts useless.' By June 1915 Eckersley complained that most local nationalists dismissed the NVF as a 'humbug'.[65] A fortnight later he directly attributed his failure to O'Connell's training camps.[66] After Eskerley's departure, F.J. O'Connor claimed that young men had turned their backs on the NVF. He blamed the 'jingo speeches' of the local recruiting campaign and criticized Redmond's attitude towards the force, claiming there was 'no serious desire or intention of making it a military force in any sense'.[67] By October 1915 the NVF 'had virtually collapsed'.[68] By contrast, before his departure, O'Connell noted 'the beginnings of real progress' and widened his analysis of 'the great contributing causes', namely, 'the conscription scare; MacNeill's meeting at Cappagh, the Deportations, and the first training camp'.[69]

Eoin MacNeill's visit to Cappagh on 29 June invigorated the local expansion of the IVF. As part of an unceasing propaganda drive, the *Irish Volunteer* described Cappagh as the 'largest gathering in County Tyrone since [Daniel] O'Connell's monster meetings'. MacNeill claimed that 'a demented ... English-driven Orange Army' would be let loose 'upon the helpless Catholic people of Ulster, who would be driven out of the province or massacred where they stood'.[70] The *Democrat* derided this 'gathering of 90 Irish Volunteers, and the presence of two of the school of fame seekers, which as a rule, crises always produce'.[71] O'Connor privately admitted, however, that 'the MacNeillite Volunteers are gathering strength' at constitutionalism's expense.[72] A meeting of the IVF in Carrickmore on 22 August eclipsed the NVF parade in Omagh organized for the same day.[73] While the IPP held nominal nationalist ascendancy, the momentum rested with the IRB.[74]

The training camps and the anger provoked by the deportations of Ernest Blythe, Denis McCullough and Herbert Moore Pim emboldened Tyrone Volunteers and increased recruitment.[75] When the RIC attempted to arrest Pim in July 1915 at Carrickmore, the Volunteers formed a guard and Mick McCartan shouted 'another step and down you go.'[76] The *Tyrone Courier*, however, reported that 'firearms were discharged by the Sinn Féiners, but the authorities are very reticent about the affair'.[77] On Sunday 18 July 1915 Dunmoyle, Carrickmore, Clogher, Coalisland, Donaghmore and Dungannon companies, including over one hundred cyclists, carried out manoeuvres from Donaghmore to Dungannon, ending in a parade, which the *Irish Volunteer* claimed was so large that 'no street in Dungannon held it'.[78] The nationalist community's genuine fear of conscription benefitted the IRB and the Irish Volunteers. The NVF, tarnished by jingoism, appeared unwilling and unable to present any sort of challenge to the rumours of conscription. By the time of the 1916 Rising, the police reported that

> The efforts of Mr Redmond and his party, however, to encourage recruiting, and the fear of conscription, brought considerable support privately to the Sinn Féiners, who boasted loudly that they were opposed to recruiting and conscription. In this way, it may be said that at the outbreak of the rebellion the Sinn Féin movement had several hundreds of supporters or sympathisers in the district.[79]

The 1916 Rising in Tyrone was a fiasco. The responsibility lay with McCartan and McCullough. Orders were received from Pearse and Connolly that after assembling in Coalisland, the Belfast and Tyrone Volunteers would march to Belcoo, in Fermanagh, to join with Liam Mellows's Connacht contingent and 'hold the line of the Shannon'.[80] Interestingly, Connolly was adamant that 'not a shot' was to be fired in Ulster.[81] Both McCartan and McCullough believed that the Germans intended to send soldiers as well as arms. Essentially, Mac Diarmada and Clarke did not have enough faith in either, probably because McCartan's opposition to an unprovoked rising echoed the thinking of Hobson and MacNeill, that any action should be in self-defence.[82] Hobson had already burnt his bridges in June 1914; he was placed under armed guard during the Rising. On Spy Wednesday, MacNeill temporarily agreed to the insurrection after the revelation of the 'Castle Document', a fabrication penned by Joseph Plunkett.[83]

McCullough learned of the Rising when he met Mac Diarmada on Palm Sunday in Dublin.[84] On his return, he prepared for the mobilization in Coalisland.[85] McCullough claimed that when he arrived in Tyrone on Good Friday McCartan and Fathers Coyle and O'Daly told him that the Tyronemen were reluctant to carry out orders. The priests had demanded the meeting after learning of the Castle Document on Holy Thursday.[86] The crux of the matter was the German landing. McCartan and Frank Burke, the IRB organizer, were sent to Dublin to seek clarification. They met Mac Diarmada, who apparently under 'severe mental strain',[87] disingenuously assured them of the landing.[88] Later that night, Tom Clarke candidly informed McCartan that 'there was nothing definite about the German landing but … he believed they would come'.[89] McCartan then spent the night in Clarke's home, 'bubbling over with enthusiasm'.[90] He returned to Omagh at nine o'clock on Saturday morning by which time he had learned of the capture of Roger Casement and the *Aud*.[91] However, when he met McCullough and the priests at Hugh Rodger's house in Beragh that afternoon, he confirmed countywide orders for mobilization the next day.[92] The priests recommended a localized campaign, to which McCullough replied that he intended to carry out the military council instructions or none at all.[93] McCartan claimed that the clerics would not go out without a German expedition and that, amidst the rancour, word arrived from Coyle's company in Fintona that MacNeill 'was coerced into agreeing and Hobson was kidnapped. This did not tend to inspire much confidence it was from bad to worse'![94] They then decided to send Josie Owens of Cumann na mBan to Dublin for further information. She arrived back before midnight but had little to report whereupon it was decided 'to wait for a day or two for developments.' The Belfast men were ordered home and the Tyrone men placed on stand by. McCartan later claimed that Josie brought a brutally simple message from Clarke: 'It is hopeless but we must go on.'[95] Either way, he always maintained that he was merely awaiting fresh orders, a decision vindicated by the countermand that MacNeill drafted late Saturday night and which Eimar O'Duffy, the Dublin novelist, delivered to the Volunteers in Coalisland on Easter Sunday evening.[96]

On Holy Saturday night, therefore, McCullough had decided to abandon all plans: 'That is the great story of the turn-out of the Belfast men in Easter Week … I acted on my own responsibility in doing so and in ordering my men back.'[97]

McCartan claimed that the Dublin leadership's decision not to take him into their confidence meant that uncertainty reigned in Tyrone and that the Rising failed because of poor communication. 'We have failed in Tyrone – miserably failed', he wrote to McGarrity on Easter Friday, 'but it is not the fault of Tyrone but of Dublin.' In subsequent letters to his mentor he described his personal 'hell'.[98] Had he Clarke's confidence, McCartan claimed the Tyrone Volunteers could have

> captured Omagh and burned the barracks ... we could have had all the men in Tyrone and Derry ... in five districts on Sunday, cleared the police barracks on Sunday night ... destroyed wires and railways and got into position on Monday night ... We would have marched out of Tyrone probably 1,000 strong, but at worst 500, and all well-armed. Is it any wonder I feel like cursing the Dublin men?[99]

The Tyrone leaders apparently formulated this plan during the myriad of inconclusive meetings between Good Friday and Easter Tuesday, a view supported by evidence in a very well-informed RIC report.[100]

A detailed examination of the available evidence suggests that McCartan and McCullough decided not to act because they disagreed with the Rising. Frank Burke recalled that when he took Pearse's orders to McCullough, he 'cried'.[101] They were also clearly resentful at their own marginalization and jealous of Mac Diarmada's prominence within the IRB and James Connolly's co-option to the military council, of which they were not members despite McCullough's nominal presidency and McCartan's membership of the IRB supreme council! Above all, however, they were not prepared to risk conflict without some prospect of success and apparently seized on the news of Casement's capture to cancel the mobilization. McCullough returned to Belfast and went into hiding. Despite the desire of the Belfast IVF to do something, he made no contact with his comrades during the week of the rebellion.[102]

During the mobilization, such as it was, the Belfast women stayed in Derrytresk, while the men occupied an old building in Coalisland, now renamed Liberty Hall. On Easter Sunday morning the Belfast and Coalisland contingents paraded from Liberty Hall to ten o'clock mass.[103] The Dungannon, Donaghmore, Galbally and Cappagh Companies gathered beneath the ancient High Cross in Donaghmore village, attended mass and then took possession of their arms.[104] Sixty men mobilized in Carrickmore at 7 p.m. on Sunday in anticipation of the arrival of Volunteers from Coalisland.[105] Clogher and Fintona, under the influence of the two priests, did not mobilize.[106] McCartan, McCullough and Herbert Moore Pim drove to Coalisland on Easter Sunday morning, stood down the Dungannon company en route, and then ordered the Belfast men to deposit their weapons in Coalisland and march 'to Cookstown to catch the 7.30 p.m. train.'[107] On their way to Cookstown, the Belfast contingent met the South Derry Volunteers, who promptly turned back. Around four o'clock, Eimar O'Duffy arrived in Coalisland with MacNeill's countermand.[108] At ten o'clock that night, McCartan gave the Tremogue, Carrickmore, Sixmilecross, Pomeroy and Greencastle companies the 'order to demobilize and to remobilize on Monday night.'[109] He went to work the next morning.

The leadership's decision did not meet with approval among the rank and file. In heated discussions outside Liberty Hall Coalisland, at around half past two, McCullough called rank on several Belfast men, while Nora Connolly, who was adamant that Dublin would rise, verbally attacked McCullough.[110] She also 'had angry words' with McCartan in Carrickmore.[111] Connolly then sought clarification in Dublin where she received orders for the northern units from her father and Pearse, 'to mobilize all men in the county, seize all police barracks and hold up all trains with military supplies going south'.[112] On Easter Monday she disembarked at Dungannon, the first railway terminal in Tyrone, and reached Carrickmore late in the evening to inform McCartan.[113] The re-mobilization in Tyrone took place on Easter Tuesday.[114] But McCartan, under the influence of the priests, once more refused to act, again pointing the finger at Dublin: 'they and they alone are to blame for the fiasco here'.[115] Once more, the rank and file appeared willing to fight, but the leadership refused to obey Pearse's order.[116]

The only meaningful action in Tyrone during Easter Week was the seizure by the Dungannon Volunteers of a number of old Italian rifles from the NVF headquarters at St Patrick's Hall, Dungannon.[117] The following week the British military swooped across Tyrone and arrested thirty men.[118] They were sent to Richmond Barracks in Dublin and then to Frongoch detention camp in Wales. Joseph McCarthy of New Ross, County Wexford recalled meeting W.J. Kelly senior, 'who was always talking of Tom Clarke and had a fiery disposition' as did his son who was also interned.[119] When Rory Haskins, a Protestant IRB member from Belfast, informed the Tyrone internees of McCartan's assertion 'that they were unwilling to take the field in Easter Week', they 'forcibly expressed their indignation of Dr McCartan's version'.[120] On this point, the ordinary Volunteers had strong grounds for complaint.

This begs the question – what could have been achieved by the Tyrone Volunteers? Fifty Volunteers from the Fingal (Dublin) Brigade under Thomas Ashe achieved notable success in north Dublin, overcame a superior force of RIC at Ashbourne on Easter Friday and held out until the end of hostilities in Dublin.[121] By March 1916 the Tyrone Irish Volunteers numbered fifteen companies with roughly 600 men.[122] They were well-drilled and had taken part in the mock mobilization organized throughout the country on St Patrick's Day 1916.[123] The available evidence suggests that the IVF had approximately 300 weapons of various calibre, a ratio of one firearm to two Volunteers; this was well above the national average of a rifle for every ten.[124] They were reasonably well-trained and armed and had the Belfast men remained in Tyrone, a further 150 men could have been added to their number. As late as Easter Tuesday night, before the military arrived, McCartan could have called on several hundred Volunteers gathered in Carrickmore.

This raises a further question regarding 'well-disposed citizens' and local unionists. Townshend argues that UVF assistance and 'voluntary unofficial scouting work around Omagh', meant that the 'rebels would, in effect, have had to operate in enemy territory'.[125] In fact, nationalist mid-Tyrone had the weakest UVF battalion in the county. According to Bowman, across Ulster, the UVF only mustered 2,000 men, mostly around Belfast.[126] While DI Conlin claimed that the police had effectively scuppered the efforts in Tyrone, CI Millar expressed uncertainty as to whether the RIC and local loyalists could have stopped a serious outbreak. In his view 'the arrest of Casement and the sinking of the German vessel' 'brought about the immediate return of the 150 Belfast Sinn Feiners, and with their departure the danger of a rising in Tyrone was over.'[127] Arguably, the Irish Volunteers could have seized control of large parts of Tyrone. Both McCullough and McCartan had ample opportunity and resources at least to attempt this. After spending most of their adult lives planning for a rebellion, when the moment arrived, they faltered.

The British response to the Rising led to a change in the public's view of the outbreak. In addition to widespread arrests and martial law throughout the country, sixteen rebels were executed. Dungannon's Tom Clarke was shot on 3 May. The executions in particular transformed the generally bemused, and in places hostile, reaction of Tyrone nationalists to one of admiration: 'from being objects of contempt and rejection', the rebels rapidly 'became heroes'.[128] Nationalist condemnation of martial law was immediate. Fr John McKenna of Knockmoyle denounced military rule and warned that Tyrone nationalists could not 'promise not to be Sinn Feiners in the future'.[129] It was against this backdrop that the IPP sought to secure nationalist consent for six-county partition.

The Rising occasioned a renewed British attempt, under pressure from potential American war allies, to implement a home rule settlement. After a cabinet meeting on 21 May, Lloyd George was charged with mediating between the IPP and Unionists. Not for the last time, he employed deliberate ambiguity in relation to partition. While the 'Welsh Wizard' offered Carson permanent six-county exclusion, with the hint of a Belfast administration, he let Nationalists believe that the scheme was temporary, with continued representation at Westminster. In retrospect, the scheme held little chance of success. Significantly, it forced Tyrone unionists to accept the abandonment of their brethren in Donegal, Cavan and Monaghan. As the cabinet demanded 'Home Rule at once', Carson argued that the party that rejected 'Lloyd George's arrangement ... will stink in the nostrils of the patriotic British public'.[130] At a UUC meeting on 12 June Tyrone delegates unenthusiastically backed the six-county scheme. Montgomery subsequently claimed that the UUC's public reluctance disguised the satisfaction felt by Belfast's Old Town Hall.[131] Ricardo recalled that 'James Craig ... talked to me for an hour about his 6 County scheme. I told him I believed he had gone mad!'[132] As Montgomery correctly argued, the very acceptance of exclusion in 1914 left the covenant redundant.[133] By 1916 Tyrone unionist leaders had reconciled themselves to six-county partition. There was no such acceptance by their nationalist counterparts, however.

The Lloyd George exclusion scheme marked the beginning of the end for the IPP. The exclusion of majority nationalist Tyrone, Fermanagh and Derry city without a plebiscite alienated the Catholic middle class and clergy in Tyrone. The UUC vote on 12 June in favour of the scheme as a 'definite' solution heightened nationalist concerns about the permanence of partition.[134] The IPP's difficulties were compounded by the opposition of the northern Catholic hierarchy. The bishops viewed the provisions for administering the excluded area as an embryonic Orange parliament, which would 're-establish in the north the rule of bigoted Irish Protestants'.[135] At the beginning of June Bishop McHugh showed Devlin a resolution from F.J. O'Connor and George Murnaghan 'against the exclusion of any part of Ulster'.[136] The UIL county convention on 7 June expressed its 'unmistakable determination to resist by every constitutional means any attempt to perpetrate such an outrage on the country ... temporary or permanent'. The unionist allegations regarding permanent exclusion only reinforced nationalist opposition and fear. The *Herald* argued that the unionist version amounted to the establishment of 'another Pale', a view shared by local unionists.[137] Despite mounting hostility, the IPP called a provincial conference in Belfast's St Mary's hall on 23 June in a high stakes bid to win approval for the scheme.

The IPP's acceptance of partition split Tyrone constitutionalism. Sympathy for the executed rebels and opposition to martial law galvanized local opposition.[138] Even T.J. Harbison, a party loyalist who voted against exclusion, claimed that he had 'never known our people to be more unanimous ... that there should be no exclusion' but clung to the belief that the party would 'never entertain the idea'.[139] This mirrored Redmond's disingenuous public position on 3 June that 'no agreement' had been 'entered into by anyone'.[140] Devlin pessimistically questioned the advisability of an Ulster convention given that 'the only support for the proposals will come from this city [Belfast]'.[141] Just two days later, Devlin confidently predicted that delegates would 'yield to his persuasion'.[142] Clearly, the constitutional leadership sought to grasp the lifebuoy from the coalition cabinet and frantically set about securing a positive vote at St Mary's hall. The final result – 475 votes in favour and 265 against – relied on Devlin's effective control of over a third of the votes.[143] As Kevin O'Shiel put it, Devlin had 'machined' the vote through the mobilization of his Hibernian foot soldiers.[144]

The Tyrone delegates divided, 102 against to 52 in favour.[145] Of those opposed, a number of perspectives can be discerned, the Murnaghanites being the most obvious. Another was a coterie of Omagh solicitors, who orbited F.J. O'Connor and Michael Lynch, the proprietor of the *Ulster Herald*. Disenchanted with the party, they formed a new organization called the Irish Nation League (INL), a deliberate echo of Parnell's Irish National League, and in the summer of 1916 openly challenged the IPP. By the end of July Redmond had repudiated the Lloyd George proposals on learning that exclusion was to be permanent. But the damage to the standing of the IPP proved irreversible. The depth of opposition to partition was captured in John Doris's resignation speech to the East Tyrone UIL executive in August. He was against partition whether temporary or permanent and claimed 'the wrong was first committed when the exclusion of the four counties was agreed to'. He 'would see Mr Redmond, Mr Dillon and Mr Devlin disappear from public life before he would see the rights of Tyrone given away'.[146]

By the time Pearse proclaimed the Irish Republic on Easter Monday 1916, constitutional nationalism and republicanism appeared to have chosen diametric paths – the former for Ireland and the British Empire, the latter for Ireland alone.[147] The concept of shared sacrifice on the battlefields of Europe was alien to Tyrone. Local unionists resented nationalist rhetorical support without any practical sympathy. The UVF enlisted well in the early stages, but by 1916 even the unionist community held aloof, preferring to reap the economic rewards of high agricultural prices. By 1916 Tom Kettle's dream of a united, home rule parliament lay in virtual ruins. The Easter Rising fatally undermined his and his party's support for England's war. The veteran Dungannon republican and 'embodiment of Fenianism', Tom Clarke, conceived and instigated the insurrection.[148] Referring to Clarke's execution, Kettle prophesized that 'these men will go down to history as heroes and martyrs and I will go down if I go down at all as a bloody British officer'.[149] He was killed on 9 September 1916 during the Irish assault on German positions at Ginchy. In Tyrone rumours of conscription from 1915 onwards gave a fillip to republicans who had opposed nationalist support for the empire from the outset. The Tyrone Volunteers were poised to rise during Easter week, but a combination of poor communication and incompetent leadership produced an embarrassing anti-climax. Nonetheless, republican support in Tyrone was growing prior to the Rising. The ascendancy of the re-constituted SF over the IPP in Tyrone owed a great deal to the fallout from the St Mary's hall conference, when the IPP's forced acceptance of partition alienated large sections of its middle-class and clerical support. One thing which remained constant, however, was local unionist opposition to rule from Dublin, whether within the empire or outside.

5 From St Mary's hall to the Dáil: Sinn Féin, 1916–18

Between the summer of 1916 and the December 1918 general election, a significant reorientation of nationalism occurred in Tyrone, which encompassed an
initial period of flux before Sinn Féin emerged as the dominant force. Nationally
the party secured 73 of Ireland's 105 parliamentary seats, a clear mandate for
self-determination. The IPP fought hard to arrest its own slow decline, bolstered
by the still significant AOH and SF's acquiescence to the Cardinal Logue-
brokered general election pact. But for this, CI Millar believed, SF would have
captured both North-East and North-West Tyrone in 1918. The post-Rising SF
bore the moniker of Arthur Griffith's party, largely because the British misiden-
tified the IRB's insurrection – never had guilt by association been so politically
profitable. The second coming of SF represented a broad coalition, a mass-
participatory separatist movement, which drew support across the nationalist
spectrum from idealists to political pragmatists. Key to its remarkable success
was the fear of partition and the conscription crisis of 1918 which had 'an
immense hold on the peasantry'.[1] Grass roots unionists shared the nationalist
antipathy to conscription. In Tyrone the 1918 general election represented a
referendum on self-determination and, perhaps more pointedly, whether Tyrone
should be ruled from Dublin or Belfast.

The INL was a clerically backed, middle-class organization, which promoted
advanced constitutionalism and cultural nationalism. In Omagh, the
Murnaghanite-John Street gang alliance successfully challenged Devlinism.
Significantly, the Catholic business and professional class in Cookstown, among
them John Doris, Dr James Gillespie, James Mayne and Daniel Chambers, also
joined the INL. But Cookstown nationalists generally sided with the Harbison
family and the AOH. Neither Omagh nor Cookstown had witnessed any Irish
Volunteer activity. Therefore, the INL represented 'an anti-partition protest ...
heavily influenced by the clergy', which infiltrated areas untouched by republican activism, demonstrating the IPP's unpopularity after St Mary's hall.[2] By
October 1916 there were twenty branches with just over 1,000 members, most of
whom were deemed SF supporters in the sense of exhibiting sympathy for the
executed rebels.[3] Nevertheless, F.J. O'Connor blamed the INL's failure on the
general 'panic which they [the people] have as the result of our policy to destroy
the present Parliamentary Party'.[4]

The League's moderation, middle-class profile and clerical leadership
actually restricted its growth. By autumn 1916, in the words of the CI, it could
not 'steal popular enthusiasm', as 'constitutional agitation is quite out of fashion
now'.[5] The INL constituted a sort of separatist purgatory, 'a place or state of

punishment where some parliamentarians suffered for a time before they joined Sinn Féin'.[6] By September 1916 O'Connor argued that genuine nationalism represented a symbiosis of physical force and constitutionalism, while the *Herald* floated the idea that Ireland should be represented at any post-war peace conference.[7] By December O'Connor accepted in principle abstention from Westminster in favour of a native assembly. In March 1917 Patrick McCartan described the League's programme of conditional attendance as 'the one for the country'.[8] This demonstrated an abrupt evolution from the INL's initial position, which O'Shiel characterized as giving 'constitutionalism a last chance'.[9]

When a SF party emerged from the Mansion House conference of April 1917 the bourgeois INL acted as local intermediaries before amalgamating in September 1917. The chronology is interesting. As late as May 1917 O'Connor still maintained that the INL spoke 'for a very large body of moderate opinion'.[10] In addition, Nation Leaguers had acquired a very useful set of electioneering skills, honed in the cauldron of Tyrone. These were put to good use in the watershed North Roscommon by-election in February that saw Count Plunkett returned for SF. Before the 1918 general election such expertise proved invaluable, particularly in rural constituencies, like North Roscommon or Cavan, where there had not been a meaningful election in decades.[11] McCartan was clearly keen to keep the INL on side. In March 1917 a fellow republican inmate in Fairford Prison in Gloucestershire, J.J. O'Kelly ('Sceilg'), promised George Gavan Duffy, INL national organizer, that if the League 'throws itself earnestly into the preparations', it 'will be entitled to and awarded much credit' and 'corresponding influence.'[12] This policy almost backfired, obliging McCartan to write to Gavan Duffy only two days later, urging him to 'make the position of Sceilg and myself clear' to the 'ultra-suspicious' Griffith that 'we would [not] support the Nation League *against* Sinn Féin'.[13]

In March O'Connor wrote to Gavan Duffy that 'there is no such thing ... as a Sinn Féin party', only 'numerous little groups each a trifle uncertain of the other, each groping for a policy'. He asserted that Plunkett's abstentionist position and perceived personal obstinacy antagonized moderate constitutionalist opinion, such as the INL, which was sympathetic to a new nationalist organization opposed to the IPP.[14] But by early July when SF's steady progress was evident, Murnaghan revealed to Gavan Duffy that he favoured 'friendly cooperation with the advanced section' but was unsure if it was 'politic to ask for the establishment of an Irish Republic'. He believed that the INL should be 'on a controlling body as a steadying factor.'[15] Though not in full agreement with the SF programme, Murnaghan became a member of the SF standing committee at the end of July. He proved very influential following O'Connor's untimely death on 1 June. The national leadership followed Murnaghan's direction on northern policy, from the contentious question of the 1918 Logue pact right through to the Anglo-Irish Treaty of 1921. In August 1917 Murnaghan and O'Shiel, his law partner, established the Omagh SF cumann.[16] In an ironic twist, the conservative, Catholic, Healyite element in Tyrone politics, which had opposed popular participation and the Irish Volunteers prior to the Rising, assumed the leading position in SF thereafter.

The INL stalled because it relied on the Catholic middle class and clergy. Nevertheless, the Leaguers represented a variant of a wider popular impulse towards a radical departure. The SF movement that emerged between 1917 and 1918 constituted an umbrella organization. The IPP's acceptance of exclusion also provoked popular discontent. The RIC reported the initiation of a boycott in Fintona against a party member who had 'voted for exclusion at the Belfast conference'.[17] Fintona had also witnessed popular discontent at the post-Rising arrests. The boycott continued well into 1918.[18] The most prominent victim was Owen Rogers, the local Board of Erin chairman, who complained to John Dillon that 'not 10% of the people speak to me'.[19] Therefore, the respectable, Catholic, Irish-Ireland mentality was not the only revolutionary impulse.

The initial priority for the IRB was the revitalization of the Volunteers rather than the promotion of SF. Its post-Rising efforts were confined to clandestine drilling and support of the National Aid campaign. Proper re-organization only commenced after Christmas 1916 with the release of internees and Michael Collins's reorganization of the IRB.[20] Jack Shields, the first O/C Tyrone Brigade, recounted how a meeting in Carrickmore in June 1917 resolved that the IRB should reorganize the IVF.[21] Unlike much of the north, a structure already existed in Tyrone to facilitate and control the Volunteers. However, the IRB's dominant influence actually retarded activism. The residual leadership, embodying an older generation, awaited central instruction, which did not exist until early 1917, rather than promote local initiative.[22] Hence Séamus Dobbyn, IRB provincial organizer, thought little of the IRB in rural Ulster: 'they were doing nothing … thought themselves superior', and 'were not even supporting the IRA'.[23]

In early 1918, with the exception of W.J. Kelly, all Volunteer officers in Tyrone were members of the IRB.[24] Kelly claimed that in 1917 younger IRB men, including Shields, Frank Dooris, Mick McCartan and Albert Tally, reorganized the Irish Volunteers, because 'the old officers of the pre-1916 vintage … wanted to retain their influence to cancel or change things'.[25] This younger generation did not, in fact, fully emerge until 1919, with their appointment as the officer corps of the Tyrone Brigade.[26] This generational take-over in Tyrone was not necessarily replicated in other counties. For example, in Tipperary Augusteijn identified a divergence between elder constraint and youthful activism but the younger generation there abandoned the IRB. Significantly, while this sparked local initiative in Tipperary, Tyrone Volunteers continued to look to the IRB and GHQ. As such, 'the official non-violent policy of GHQ therefore facilitated the development of ever-growing differences in activity between the various counties' – with Tyrone's fight retarded by a dependency on central direction, while the Tipperary brigade were masters of their own revolutionary destiny.[27]

A guerrilla movement was more likely to find recruits among those who habitually transgressed the common law. Below the level of small town respectability, poteen distillation, cockfighting, faction fighting at local fairs, poaching and attacks on landlord property and gamekeepers kept local magistrates occupied.[28] Ardboe Volunteer and teetotaller, Thomas Martin, opposed poteen-making and recounted how he threatened to execute an illegal distiller to gain information on his confederates.[29] Similarly, many lower-class nationalists employed republicanism as camouflage for punitive attacks on local authority figures.[30] Interestingly, the first arms raid in Tyrone at Plumbridge was against Colonel Lowry's gamekeeper, and was 'perpetrated by local Sinn Féiners, who have a very strong hold in the district'.[31] As early as August 1917 when the RIC arrested James McElroy, a local Volunteer and champion set dancer, at Lamas Fair for 'sneering' at them, shots were fired by the Volunteers when the police refused to release their prisoner.[32] That month a similar manifestation took place in Mountcharles, Donegal.[33] Large social events, such as hiring fairs, where lower-class men gathered to seek employment, also served as occasions for tentative public defiance, where growing popular discontent, often encouraged by republicans, further exacerbated relations between the nationalist community and the police.

The prominence of Irish-Irelanders during Easter Week led many observers to attribute a retrospective republican instinct to the Gaelic League. The secular canonization of Pearse and other intellectuals suited the prejudices of the middle-class Leaguers and in particular their clerical backers. It also played down the revolutionary Fenianism of Clarke and Mac Diarmada, providing the Rising with posthumous moderate appeal. This is not to argue that republicanism did not extend beyond 'ethno-linguistic specificity'; it clearly did.[34] However, Irish-Ireland represented a milieu that attracted separatists of all social hues. In this context, the popular nationalist community filled a political vacuum through grass roots mobilization in the GAA and Gaelic League, particularly under martial law. By June 1916 both were the main outlets of republican activism.[35] Indeed, government suppression radicalized the GAA and the IG noted 'Gaelic Athletic sports and football matches afforded evidence of the disloyal revolutionary spirit abroad'.[36] Tyrone Hibernians unsuccessfully attempted to contest separatist dominance of cultural organizations. John Skeffington complained bitterly to Lissan Hibernians in November that 'no movement had the right to claim it [national sport] as individual property'.[37] John T. Donovan, Board of Erin secretary and MP for West Wicklow, conceded however that SF had 'a virtual monopoly' over their 'national language, music, games and drilling exercises'.[38]

By the end of 1916 the GAA in Tyrone had sixteen clubs.[39] There were eleven in the east Tyrone league, several named after executed republicans: Plunketts Pomeroy, Dungannon Clarkes, Clonoe O'Rahillys, Fintona Pearses, Kilskerry MacDonaghs, Donaghmore O'Donovan Rossa. These 'Easter' clubs all originated in areas with Irish Volunteer companies. For instance, Dungannon members abandoned the Craobh Rua and formed the Thomas Clarkes.[40] On the anniversary of the Rising, punitive acts of defiance such as flying tricolours took place across Tyrone and in neighbouring counties. By the summer of 1917 the National Aid Tournament, in support of republican internees and their families, was the county's most prestigious competition.[41] The following year the military disrupted the annual Cappagh sports when the organizing committee did not seek a government permit.[42] Across nationalist Ulster, Eoin O'Duffy and his associate, Seamus Dobbyn, exploited the GAA to increase popular support for republicanism.[43]

Unlike the GAA, disparate social strands coalesced in the Gaelic League. There, clerical and middle-class leaders mingled with a large-scale influx of grass roots republicans.[44] Arguably, the Gaelic League helped make republicanism respectable. By 1918 the *Herald* claimed that through the sacrifice of 'Pádraig Pearse and Thomas Ashe, the path of the Gaelic League is covered with names and memories that are glorious and undying'.[45] At Kilskerry aeridheacht (open-air concert), speaking from a platform 'extensively decorated, with the tricolour remarkably conspicuous', Fr Matthew Maguire 'was thoroughly convinced that if only Irish-Irelanders continued on the lines they had hitherto pursued only a few short years would elapse until the final victory was gained, namely – the restoration of the language, national games, and an all round Irish-Ireland civilisation'.[46] Republicans also made use of the torch-lit processions that had characterized traditional Hibernian mobilization. In June 1917 the government decided to release republican internees as a sign of good faith before the ill-fated Irish Convention. Their return was greeted in Strabane, where 'tar barrels blazed in the streets' and 'loud cheers were given for the prisoners and the executed Republican leaders', before the obligatory tricolour 'was hoisted on the telegraph wires in Butcher Street'.[47] After de Valera's Clare by-election victory the following month, 'several hundred people with Sinn Féin flags' paraded through Carrickmore, lit 'bonfires, and cheered for the victor and the republican leaders.' There were similar scenes in the Rock, Termon and Pomeroy.[48] Each successive SF by-election victory in 1917 heralded similar celebrations. In September de Valera and Griffith visited Carrickmore and Omagh, the former a republican stronghold, the latter virgin SF territory.[49]

Nationalist female activism in Tyrone pre-dated the Ulster crisis. Quite apart from Alice Milligan, the Omagh poet and Protestant republican, Tyrone women were active in the Dungannon Clubs and Gaelic League in the early twentieth century and later in Cumann na mBan. The latter organization supported SF but was more closely aligned to the IRA. O'Shiel noted how both the Cumann na mBan and IVF 'were very touchy and resentful of any suggestion of control by the despised "politicians"... particularly so the ladies'.[50] An interest in Irish-Ireland appeared to be a defining characteristic and was put to good use in organizing céilithe and Irish classes.[51] This very much fitted with the reasonable level of education and lower middle-class background of the identifiable leaders, who worked as secretaries, teachers or in other non-manual employment. Familial association was another trend; the Owens sisters of Beragh had an established record of participation, while Nellie McGrath of Omagh joined with her two sisters.[52] The involvement of male siblings in the Volunteers was also prevalent. Alice Mallon and Alice Donnelly, the leading members of the Cookstown branch, had brothers who were Volunteers, all of whom suffered internment at some point, as did Alice Mallon herself.[53]

The IPP maintained its residual strength in Tyrone and neighbouring Armagh. This was demonstrated in successive by-election victories in early 1918. The IPP's support reflected continued AOH allegiance but loyalty to Joe Devlin, its northern leader, in particular. SF success in the Longford by-election was due to large-scale Hibernian defection to Joe McGuinness.[54] In Tyrone, conversely, the well-organized local Devlinite Hibernians represented SF's most aggressive opponents. Across nationalist controlled local bodies, recent SF converts battled with Hibernian die-hards. In April 1917 Omagh Board of Guardians appointed Pat McCartan as locum doctor, a move that created heated exchanges before his eventual selection.[55] Writing from Fairford Prison, McCartan claimed that his appointment demonstrated 'the degree to which his [Griffith's abstentionist] principles are gaining adherence' even among those who once opposed him. A similar stand off occurred when James Grugan returned from Frongoch and was re-elected manager of Carrickmore co-operative creamery.[56]

Unionists appeared content to let the nationalist population fight it out. As the East Tyrone by-election in April 1918 approached, unionist sympathy clearly lay with the IPP, even if leading unionists drew some pleasure from its discomfort.[57] Elements within the loyalist grass roots expressed concern, however, at republican audacity. An anonymous Orangeman from Fivemiletown, for example, wrote to Montgomery in July 1917 complaining that 'our Contry is swarming with Sinn Figners and ... the[y] are going to invaid our home and I fear very much youre own is in danger.'[58] Unionist leaders did not take the republican threat as seriously. Montgomery dismissed the local SF leader, John McCarney, a 32-year-old agricultural labourer, as not a very 'formidable person'.[59]

While moderate nationalists stood to lead SF, the IRB, through the Irish Volunteers, effectively backboned the movement in Tyrone. SF's early expansion typically relied on a visit from a leading separatist organizer, proselytizing initiatives by the IVF, or both.[60] There were five cumainn in the county in July. One had been established by the Clogher IVF while the secretary of the Fintona cumann was local Volunteer adjutant, Patrick J. Maguire.[61] In September 1917 the Volunteers established the first SF club in Coalisland with the assistance of outside organizers. By the end of that month Tyrone had twenty-five cumainn.[62] The organizing committee and platform party at Coalisland reflected a wider social mix than de Valera and Griffith's in Carrickmore, because the local middle class remained largely Devlinite. Of those named at Coalisland, Dónal Ó Donnaile (Daniel Donnelly) was a Dungannon Gaelic Leaguer and chemist, while Pat Campbell from the Rock and John O'Neill of Cookstown were IRB men. The speakers, Eoin MacNeill, Herbert Moore Pim, Denis McCullough and Louis Smyth were very familiar with local republican politics. Pim asserted that SF was 'not a party in the common conception of the word. It was the uncompromising spirit of Ireland. Sinn Féin would unite Ireland. Ulster Unionists would have no compromise, and Sinn Féin would have no compromise.'[63] The *Dungannon Democrat* criticized the audience's plebeian character.[64] The RIC noted that 'the movement is confined principally to the lower classes, very few men of influence or position being members.'[65] A pattern emerged of lower-class political mobilization around the new movement, largely orchestrated by the Irish Volunteers. The three Derry cumainn that existed in September 1917 were closely linked to IVF companies, while the nineteen branches in Donegal appeared to rely on a combination of scattered IRB contacts and the enthusiasm of the 'younger and more irresponsible class' without 'any special stake' in the country.[66] But an existing IVF network was not a precondition; both Monaghan and Fermanagh had seventeen clubs by September.[67] There were only two small IVF groupings in Enniskillen and Derrylin, while in Monaghan the IVF was confined to Carrickmacross. Although the INL was organized, particularly in Fermanagh, activists tended to be young and attached to the Gaelic League, or the GAA in Monaghan. In its earliest manifestation in west Ulster, SF represented the radical voice of youth.

In Tyrone the IVF harnessed this youthful enthusiasm for the benefit of the new party. The overlap between Irish Volunteer involvement and SF activity led to the creation of a combined South and East Tyrone Executive, which corresponded to the area of pre-Rising Irish Volunteer activism.[68] Once local SF cumainn were formed, however, Volunteers tended to distance themselves from the political side of the movement. Albert Tally, O/C Tyrone Brigade IRA by 1920, claimed that after the 1918 general election 'the Volunteers did not associate very much with the Sinn Féin clubs', they merely 'helped them when necessary' and kept them 'travelling in the right direction'.[69] Irish Volunteers tended to have an innate suspicion of politicians, a legacy perhaps of their aversion to IPP machine politics. This would have important implications later when the fate of SF in Tyrone, and indeed the county itself, became as much a political as a military matter and the traditional republican community's aversion to politics left it voiceless and rudderless.

By the end of 1917 SF had forty cumainn in Tyrone, bucking the provincial trend, where 'it had achieved only 48% of its peak membership in Ulster'.[70] Half of these clubs were in the North and Mid-Tyrone constituencies, where the INL and IVF both contributed to the movement's development.[71] In East and South Tyrone, none stretched beyond previously republican areas, with the exception of a small club in Cookstown. The police reported that Armagh had only fourteen clubs, 'an ignorant lot' with no 'leaders of standing'. The relatively low number of cumainn can be attributed to the small IRB network, the impact of Cardinal Logue's denunciation and the fact that the AOH was 'combating' the new party.[72] The AOH was also particularly strong in Derry city and its rural hinterland and consequently only nine SF cumainn were founded.[73] The SF movement did not face the same degree of Hibernian opposition in Donegal, where the 'young people' and the 'less responsible classes' had established thirty-four cumainn.[74] Likewise, in Monaghan, young former constitutionalists linked to the GAA had helped found thirty-five.[75]

Once again, Tyrone encapsulated all the trends of the neighbouring counties. It remained remarkable for the existing republican network and the early defection of respectable middle-class nationalists such as Dr James Gillespie of Cookstown and John Donnelly from Galbally, a member of the East Tyrone UIL Executive. Greater numbers of respectable nationalists joined SF across Ulster in 1918. In the Mid-Tyrone constituency, where the INL was strong, the IPP lost more support. The Omagh Board of Guardians had a two-thirds defection rate. However, only three members of the SF Mid-Tyrone comhairle ceanntair had been UIL delegates, including two former Murnaghanites.[76] Apart from the Omagh solicitors, former IPP members played no significant role in SF. After the 25 October 1917 Ard Fheis, Murnaghan and Lynch were among six INL delegates on the SF executive. Phoenix rightly views the St Mary's hall conference as a watershed because, by degree, the 'impromptu counter-leadership which it produced' became the 'local leadership of the reconstituted Sinn Fein movement in the north'.[77] Given the trends in neighbouring counties and the nature of SF's early development in Tyrone itself, it is debatable whether this grouping's allegiance in 1917 materially affected the new movement's early strength, which relied primarily on an upsurge in grass roots' sentiment and the organizing input of the IVF. When the Irish Volunteers and subsequently SF established themselves in a rural area, the local community converted en masse. In February 1918 the UIL failed to muster a meeting in Galbally, while Irish Volunteers and Gaelic Leaguers from Galbally, 'Commandant [Albert] Tally, Andrew Quinn and Patrick McGeoghan', established the neighbouring Cappagh SF club.[78]

By the beginning of 1918 SF looked set to displace the IPP. It had won a succession of by-elections and emerged as a consolidated political movement with de Valera unanimously elected as president of both the political and military wings. Nevertheless, the movement in Tyrone would face adversity before it subdued its constitutional rival. The limits of SF's growth became apparent with defeat in three consecutive by-elections in three months, the last in Tyrone itself on 4 April. The ill-fated Irish Convention which sat between July 1917 and March 1918 still convinced some IPP supporters to maintain their allegiance. This was an effort by Lloyd George to resolve the Irish question and mollify American opinion. It represented constitutionalism's 'last throw'.[79] Although invited, SF refused to attend. Due to its strategic importance, Tyrone was strongly represented at the Convention. T.J. Harbison represented the nationalist side. A reluctant Montgomery, who viewed the entire project 'as waste of time', attended for Tyrone unionists.[80] As Jackson has noted, ultimately the IPP failed 'to use the convention to force a settlement, and instead came to be suffocated by its proceedings'.[81] The report of the Convention, unsurprisingly, revealed that the Ulster unionists, committed to six-county exclusion, had rejected any form of All-Ireland home rule. This further undermined the Irish Party.

During the Convention the IPP engineered successful by-elections in South Armagh and East Tyrone in an attempt to halt the 'invincible force' SF appeared to have become following its by-election victories in 1917.[82] The Tyrone contest arose when William Archer Redmond successfully contested his late father's seat in Waterford in March 1918. The stakes were high as SF squared up to the AOH, which felt strong enough to deliver another significant electoral blow to its opponent. Harbison, the Devlinite candidate, criticized SF radicalism and thereby attracted some unionist support. John Dillon, the IPP leader, agreed with Harbison's candidacy because 'he opposed us [the IPP leadership] at the Belfast Convention [St Mary's hall]'.[83] During the campaign Harbison felt 'precluded from disclosing anything relating to the [Convention] proceedings'.[84] He was supported not alone by local Hibernians but by the Catholic hierarchy and senior clergy. East Tyrone lay in the Armagh diocese of Cardinal Logue, who viewed SF's programme as utopian.[85] When O'Shiel and Daniel Donnelly attempted to address a SF meeting in Clonoe, just outside Coalisland, Canon Thomas McWilliams, who had signed Harbison's nomination papers, 'ordered the people to go home and not be wasting their time listening to such blackguards'.[86]

Recognizing that victory was unlikely, the SF national executive nonetheless bowed to local pressure and nominated Seán Milroy. In April 1918, however, many SF sympathizers were not even on the dated electoral register.[87] At a rally in Dungannon addressed by de Valera, Milroy decried conscription and stated that 'he stood for the sovereign independence of Ireland and Mr Harbison stood for Mr Lloyd George's Convention farce. They had never refused to go to Parliament, but they had refused to go to a British Parliament'.[88] The IPP received a hostile reception throughout rural East Tyrone, largely because the local Volunteers acted as election workers and stewards. The IPP's failure to hold a meeting at Pomeroy contrasted with the village's large SF meeting, under the stewardship of Malachy McGuone, a local Volunteer.[89] There were several violent clashes between IPP and SF supporters. In Galbally and Cappagh, John Muldoon and Mr H. McMillan, Belfast, who 'mounted a chair and tried to address the crowd', were met with an incessant chorus of 'Amhrán na bhFiann' and a hail of rotten eggs. At Kildress, 'stone throwing and other forms of rowdyism' made it difficult for Patrick Crumley, MP for Fermanagh South, and P.J. Whitty, MP for North Louth, to address a meeting.[90] In Coalisland O'Shiel lamented a 'disgraceful and senseless attack' by young Sinn Féiners on a party of IPP MPs, including Devlin. He recalled how two young boys entered the SF hall, 'their faces flushed and shining with excitement and delight, [and shouted] "O, Muster Shiel, Muster Shiel, hurry down quick till Harbison's meetin' and watch the Hibs g'ttin' pelted wi' eggs"!'[91]

Harbison won the election with 1,802 votes (compared to 1,222 for Milroy). The poll was close to the 3,108 votes William Archer Redmond received in 1910 and suggests widespread unionist abstention. These figures relied on an eight-year-old register and local loyalists had clearly mobilized against SF. The *Irish Independent*, admittedly no fan of the IPP, claimed that up to 500 unionists had voted.[92] This was far short of the estimated one-third of unionists who voted against SF in the South Armagh by-election.[93] Alice McSloy recalled that the Orange Order lent their drums to the Ardboe Hibernians to celebrate.[94] Nonetheless, the result 'seemed to bode ill for the [Irish] party's future cohesiveness in the area, particularly if an election were held on an up dated register'.[95] In his victory speech, Harbison praised the 'sterling Nationalists of East Tyrone'. He believed the result was a blow again 'mob law' and SF intimidation and claimed that only through 'constitutional agitation … could any democratic nation hope to achieve its objects.'[96] Joe Devlin claimed that East Tyrone had rejected the SF 'gospel of hatred of England, hatred of their fellow-countrymen in Ireland, hatred of everything, hatred preached in the school, hatred preached from the platform'.[97]

The election campaign was nevertheless beneficial for SF, which had spread into AOH strongholds. The police reported that it had 'strengthened the Sinn Feiners, who were never more aggressive, disloyal and pro-German.'[98] After the election in Ardboe, Milroy told a crowd of Volunteers that 'they did not expect to win the election. These last three elections were simply outpost skirmishes, they were only preparing for the grand battle at the General Election'.[99] W.J. Kelly believed that the result 'brought home to the minds of all northern republicans the necessity of organizing local companies of the Volunteers and local branches of Sinn Féin' and the Cumann na mBan.[100] Seán Corr recalled that the contest won many 'converts to the Sinn Féin cause', with new companies established in Stewartstown, Coalisland, Cookstown, Ardboe and Ballinderry.[101]

Branches of Cumann na mBan had been established in all the major towns and villages; many came into being after the East Tyrone by-election and through the work of provincial organizer, Alice Cashel of Galway.[102] SF also capitalized on the failure of the Irish Convention. At Clara on the Tyrone–Monaghan border in April, Count Plunkett suggested that the AOH should now be called 'the Allied Orange Hibernians'.[103]

The threat of conscription in Ireland reached a new pitch in March–April 1918. It transformed SF's fortunes and its relations with the Catholic Church, relegated the IPP's short-lived electoral renaissance to an historical footnote, and undermined the Hibernian counter-offensive in Tyrone. Nicholas Smyth recalled how the conscription crisis 'roused the Irish people of all shades of political opinion'.[104] The CI remarked on the 'general fusion of all the nationalist organizations of this county'.[105] SF took the leading role in opposing conscription and the popular discontent facilitated the reorganization of the Irish Volunteers 'in most of the local parish areas in Tyrone'.[106] Even former moderates such as Murnaghan and John O'Hanrahan 'advised the people to get their guns ready and … when the police and soldiers came to conscript them, they … would be carried away on stretchers'.[107] In Strabane, which had witnessed higher nationalist recruitment during the war than any other district, another former moderate, Edward Gallagher, the 'prime rascal' in the local 'divilment', told a meeting to 'resist conscription by every means'. This resulted in a 'boycott of all Protestants by people working for them' and the disappearance of Catholics from the local soldiers' relief committee.[108] On the county council, unionists were fearful that nationalists might take advantage of a temporary majority 'to force a resolution against Conscription'.[109]

The conscription crisis emboldened the Volunteers. The arrest of Christy Meenagh, a local Volunteer, at a SF céilí in Aldrummound led to a mêlée, with members of the crowd suggesting that they should 'take the prisoner from the police and take the barracks'.[110] A similar situation arose in Trillick in May when the RIC had to disperse a crowd with a baton charge.[111] Such incidents 'polarized relations between police, populace and Volunteers', and correspondingly led to 'diminishing acceptance of the Crown forces as the legitimate authority'.[112] By the summer of 1918 leading Volunteers such as Pat McKenna, president of Errigal Truagh SF and local Volunteer commander, flaunted the law; their resultant arrest further radicalized local opinion.[113] The CI concluded that 'a general result of this anti-conscription agitation has been the strengthening of the influence of the Sinn Féin party'.[114] O'Shiel recalled that the 'military wing was, naturally, in the ascendant' and that 'below the open political surface the I.R.B. men – Dan McAuley, Peter Haughey and others – were working silently and efficiently in perfecting, plans for local resistance should the attempt be made to enforce the measure'.[115]

Although the Volunteers prepared for hostilities to resist conscription, or in the event of SF's exclusion from the Paris Peace Conference, nationalist support for SF did not equate with support for an armed struggle. Even Volunteers appeared reluctant to raid unionist homes for arms – principally because the occupants had a superior arsenal. One notable case did take place in 1918 when the home of William Coote MP was raided by Volunteers from Sixmilecross.[116] Interestingly, after the restoration of unionist dominance in 1923, one of the raiders appears to have personally apologized to Coote.[117] A planned attack on Broughderg Barracks did not materialize due, W.J. Kelly claimed, to 'a want of organization amongst us'.[118] The Volunteers were noticeably quiet in 1918, although the Strabane men, with assistance from Donegal contingents, raided Baronscourt Castle, seat of the duke of Abercorn, in May.[119] This provoked serious discussions within the local UVF. While on leave from the front, Ambroise Ricardo advised that loyalists voluntarily surrender their arms to Omagh Barracks, where they would be 'safe and in the country in event of unforeseen emergencies.' He described the 'folly' of storing the arms under UVF guard at Baronscourt, as 'constant bait to Sinn Feiners'. This measure was adopted with 'most of the centres in N. Tyrone' handing in their weapons.[120]

Some loyalists, however, shared their nationalist neighbours' antipathy to conscription. Nicholas Smyth claimed that in Dromore 'a number of young Ulster Volunteers came along to us and offered to join the Irish Volunteers in their determination to fight conscription'.[121] A similar thing happened in Clanabogan near Omagh. In Omagh itself, O'Shiel established a short-lived news-sheet, *The Conscription News*, in the belief that conscription exercised 'the minds of all – Protestant and Unionist no less than Catholic and Nationalist' and recalled that the readership was 'surprisingly numerous and still more surprisingly heterogeneous.'[122] This also happened elsewhere in Ulster. Montgomery decried 'the lie that Protestants and Unionists are as much opposed to Conscription as Nationalists', which 'is repeated hundreds of times in papers and speeches'.[123] In a letter to Montgomery, Dawson Bates wrote: 'It is essential that we should retain control over the rank and file ... they do not believe Conscription ... will be administered impartially, and that they in the North will have to go, while the men in the South remain behind'.[124] Montgomery replied by reminding Bates that Carson had checked his attempts to 'get resolutions in favour of Conscription passed at the Tyrone County Council', and that, if nationalists proposed anti-conscription resolutions, unionist councillors were intent on submitting counter-resolutions.[125] But the unionist population did not share their leadership's enthusiasm for compulsory military service. This may explain why Belfast's Old Town Hall fell quiet, leading one of Montgomery's correspondents to lament that 'we are being badly let down by our Leaders'.[126]

On 18 May the British government used a spurious 'German Plot' to arrest seventy-three national SF figures. Aware of the government's plans, the leadership engineered the situation to great propaganda effect.[127] This facilitated

Arthur Griffith's victory in the East Cavan by-election in June to the familiar cry of 'put him in to get him out'. Tyrone Sinn Féiners believed that victory in East Cavan would atone for the defeat in East Tyrone: 'the triumph was celebrated in Clogher by a procession headed by the local members of the Cumann na mBan branch, the Volunteers and members of the Roger Casement Sinn Féin club'.[128] In his report for June 1918, the CI claimed that SF represented 'the only active political org. in the county' with fifty cumainn and a series of well-attended outdoor meetings. He also noted that relations between republicans and Hibernians had become even more bitter following the East Cavan election.[129] In September the ill-feeling led to a murder.[130] Although a Hibernian presence still existed, the available evidence suggests that like large swathes of west Ulster, SF could now claim to represent the vast majority of nationalists.

Before the 1918 general election Tyrone's electoral constituencies were redrawn and the number of seats reduced from four to three. This along with Cardinal Logue's electoral pact complicates an analysis of SF's growing dominance. To prevent the nationalist vote being split, the cardinal proposed the equal allocation of eight marginal seats in Ulster between the IPP and SF. SF agreed on 28 November and a reluctant John Dillon acquiesced the following day.[131] SF received North-West Tyrone; Harbison got a free run in North-East Tyrone, while a free contest took place in William Coote's safe Unionist seat in South Tyrone. The pact was criticized by some. John McCoy, a leading Armagh Volunteer, lambasted this 'stupid blunder', which saved the IPP from electoral oblivion outside Belfast and suggested that this 'sectarian policy' knocked 'the bottom out of all the castles in the air' that advanced 'Protestant/Presbyterian republicans were building up'.[132]

Government hostility to SF candidates generated widespread sympathy, a resource the IPP could no longer tap.[133] Griffith won North-West Tyrone, while still incarcerated, despite a concerted, unified unionist campaign by William Miller, a local solicitor, UVF organizer and county councillor.[134] In the North-East constituency Harbison confidently predicted beating 'both Tory and Sinn Féin'.[135] However, the votes received by Denis McCullough (5,437) and John Skeffington (2,602) in South Tyrone undermined Harbison's assertion.[136] In total, SF won more than two-thirds of the nationalist vote. The constituency's unionist majority relieved the pressure to secure nationalist representation. Indeed, both constitutional and republican camps portrayed the vote as a mini-referendum on local nationalist sympathies.[137] By December 1918 the IPP had fatally undermined two key political pledges. The first was attendance at Westminster. In 1917 the *Dungannon Democrat* claimed that SF's abstentionist policy would create 'an Orange platform in the House of Commons'.[138] But during the conscription crisis John Dillon accepted conditional abstention and led the IPP out of the House of Commons. Second, Harbison derided the appeal to any post-war peace conference and mocked that if SF knocked at the conference door, 'Edward Carson would knock three times'.[139] By December 1918 he had performed a volte-face and signed a pledge in 'support [of] the claims of Ireland, as an independent nation, to unrestricted self-determination and to support Ireland's appeal for such to the Peace Conference'.[140]

For two years unionists, Hibernians and SF vied for mastery of Tyrone. Harbison's victory masked SF's dominant position within Tyrone nationalism. Nationalists switched their political allegiance because of SF's links to the Rising, its forceful opposition to conscription and the general impression that the new party was in the ascendant. Like any nationalist popular front, SF constituted a broad church. The general election confirmed that SF had a democratic mandate for their Irish Republic, securing 73 out of the 105 Irish seats. The twenty-seven TDs, who were not in military custody, duly convened the first Dáil Éireann on 21 January 1919. But unionists drew a different lesson from the election, which returned Lloyd George and his Tory-dominated cabinet. J.R. Fisher, the unionist journalist and future representative on the Boundary Commission, confidently predicted 'that the Election will result in an absolute Unionist majority of the whole House'.[141] The Conservatives achieved this result despite the enormously widened franchise provided by the Representation of the People Act, which Coote had described as 'a most dangerous franchise bill ... dangerous for us'.[142] The coalition pledged to implement home rule legislation with partition central to any provision. But Ulster unionists did not share Lloyd George's enthusiasm for the two nations theory as a means of countering Irish self-determination. Fisher described it 'as a *reductio ad absurdum*; recently it has come into the field of practical politics', but 'We have never asked for it or accepted it for its own sake.'[143] The Government of Ireland Act (GOIA) of 1920 represented the culmination of the process by which a truncated 'Ulster' separated itself from the rest of Ireland. Tyrone, where two of the three successful MPs had stood on a platform of self-determination, would be included in its territory.

6 Ulster Pale or Irish Republic, 1919–20

Between the formation of Dáil Éireann in January 1919 and the GOIA of December 1920, SF strove to create a counter-state. Tyrone nationalists, both politicians and militants, rejected British rule, while unionists sought to counteract the republican threat. The period from 1918 until the local government elections of 1920 also represented the zenith of Irish trade unionism. Commenting on labour's strong performance in the January 1920 UDC elections, the *Irish Times* remarked how 'in Unionist Ulster the ancient order of things has felt something like an earthquake'.[1] Politically, Tyrone unionists also attempted to frustrate a nationalist seizure of the County Council and to avoid a damaging internal split over the abandonment of covenanters in Cavan, Donegal and Monaghan. Serious IRA operations in Tyrone began in 1920. The military campaign and resulting outbreaks of loyalist violence in Belfast, Lisburn and Banbridge during the summer of 1920 led to the creation of the Ulster Special Constabulary (USC), whose task was to preserve the 'Ulster Pale'.[2] Yet rival manoeuvring in Tyrone operated beneath the shadow cast by the GOIA, which gave legislative expression to Tyrone's place under a northern parliament.

In May 1919 Louis J. Walsh, the Draperstown solicitor and SF Antrim county councillor, wrote to Joseph MacRory, Catholic bishop of Down and Connor, that if SF failed at the Paris Peace Conference, 'there is a terrible danger that the "hotheads" may play into England's hands by adopting extreme measures'. He favoured passive resistance over violence and believed there was a 'limit to the amount of coercion' the British could apply 'in the face of the World'.[3] In the first half of 1919, SF mobilization in Tyrone concentrated on the peace conference and agitation against British repression, which Michael Mulvey, editor of the *Ulster Herald,* described as the conduct of 'an inmate of a criminal lunatic asylum ... one moment in a stupor, at another ... its blood boils with apoplectic rage'.[4] The party organized large public meetings on 5 January in Omagh, Dungannon and Strabane to demand the release of SF leaders such as Daniel Doherty of Strabane.[5] In March 'Sinn Féin meetings were held at nearly all the Catholic churches in the county in protest against the government treatment of political prisoners'.[6] Under the DORA and the subsequent Restoration of Order in Ireland Act (ROIA) in August 1920, a growing number of Tyrone men were jailed. Such action further incensed nationalist opinion, not only cementing the existing SF base but in places generating support for a more belligerent course.

Before 1916, 'British rule in Ireland had been characterized by moderation and forbearance, the republicans' policy of radicalizing Irish nationalists by goading the Crown forces into repressive measures had succeeded beyond all possible expectations'.[7] When John O'Hanrahan was released from prison in May 1919, after a three-month sentence, Murnaghan stated that 'the idea of making lengthy speeches had passed away', independence 'could only be secured by the determination and will of the people to accomplish it by every means at their disposal'.[8] In August 1919 the military proclaimed SF meetings in Benburb, Fintona and Stewartstown, leading to a serious confrontation in Coalisland. The CI believed that SF was 'much exasperated' by the proclamation and 'meditating reprisals'.[9] In September the *Ulster Herald*'s offices were raided by the Crown forces.[10]

In response, SF organized a conference of Ulster MPs in the Omagh SF hall. Seán Milroy presided. The MPs included Arthur Griffith (East Cavan/North-West Tyrone), Eoin MacNeill (Derry City), Joseph Sweeney (West Donegal), Joseph O'Doherty (North Donegal), P.J. Ward (South Donegal), Seán MacEntee (South Monaghan) and Paul Galligan (West Cavan); Ernest Blythe, MP for North Monaghan was in jail.[11] Griffith stated that 'English politicians and their agents in Ireland conspire to create amongst us sectarian animosity. We exhort the people of Ulster of all creeds to beware of those who prostitute the name of religion … to set Irishmen against Irishmen.' In the same vein, MacNeill urged 'the most conciliatory attitude towards those who differ from us'.[12] The editor of the *Herald* quipped that Carson and Devlin represented 'a dead creed and dead passions. They are both playing England's game'.[13] These resolutions provided a further indication, if any was needed, of the change in nationalist demands.

By the autumn of 1919 there was universal recognition that the Peace Conference would not deliver, a fact privately acknowledged by the national leadership in mid-January.[14] As early as May, the British cabinet believed that in such an event, 'de Valera proposes in co-operation with labour; and supported by the Irish Volunteers, to organize the utmost passive resistance.'[15] With the assistance of the ITGWU and the Labour Party, the emerging Dáil ministry countered British authority over local government, established an alternative justice system with a republican police force, and raised the Dáil loan. By July 1920, £317,849 had been collected from 150,000 contributors or fifteen per cent of the households of Ireland. Tyrone raised £5,334, with the north-east area, where the IRA was stronger contributing £2,307. The national average by constituency was £3,629. In Ulster, the heavily nationalist South Monaghan and South Donegal constituencies contributed the most, the latter raising £13,000.[16] Lord French, the lord lieutenant, believed that 'Sinn Fein itself was breaking into two parties', moderates and extremists, a phenomenon that had characterized SF in Tyrone from its inception.[17] The autonomous and largely organic development of an IRA military campaign in the south-west did not materialize in Tyrone, however. Dáil Éireann was declared illegal on 11 September 1919 and on 26 November 1919 SF, the Irish Volunteers, Cumann na mBan and the Gaelic

League were banned. In November 1919 the RIC reported that the local nationalist press was strongly SF, contained not 'one word of condemnation of the murders ... throughout the country' and wrote 'as if the people of Ireland were being ground down by tyrannical laws'.[18] The 'slowly increasing severity' of government repression convinced a substantial section of nationalists to support violent opposition.[19]

The release of republican prisoners provided an opportunity to demonstrate SF strength and organization, while elevating the status of local Volunteers. The homecoming of Robert Slane in November 1919, for example, led to 'great scenes in Sixmilecross', with the released man carried 'shoulder high' at the head of a torchlight procession. The military had arrested Slane, an ex-Frongoch internee and Sixmilecross IRB man, in June 1918 for possession of 3,000 rifle cartridges.[20] Daniel Doherty, president of the Roger Casement SF cumann in Strabane, had been arrested in November 1919.[21] On his release from Wormwood Scrubs in June 1920, 'a dense throng lined the streets', to welcome 'the man who suffered so much for Ireland at the hands of an evil, tyrannical oppressor'.[22] SF efforts were reinforced by the labour movement, which staged a successful general strike for the release of republican hunger strikers in the spring of 1920. The *Herald* reported that 'the Mountjoy prisoners – though some of them were on the point of death – have been released unconditionally ... All Ireland owes a debt of gratitude to organized labour for its prompt and effective action'.[23] Similar scenes took place in May 1920 with the release of Frank Dooris, O/C Tyrone Brigade IRA, who had been on hunger strike in Belfast gaol.[24] In October 1920 the RIC noted how the death of Terence MacSwiney 'and other hunger strikers ... has intensified the already bad feeling against the police and military'.[25] Government oppression proved counterproductive and merely reinforced existing opinion. While the northern IRA contemplated following the lead of its southern comrades in the spring of 1920, the politicians sought to secure a majority on Tyrone County Council.

In 1919 the government endeavoured to counter SF's progress and safeguard southern unionist representation by introducing proportional representation (PR) for local government elections. William Coote opposed this in parliament and tried to have Ulster excluded. Harbison then alleged that Tyrone unionists only held their majority through gerrymandering and that PR would end systematic discrimination.[26] Coote retorted that Tyrone County Council had 'given more positions to Nationalists and Roman Catholics' than nationalist councils across Ireland had given to unionists. Jeremiah MacVeagh, Nationalist MP for South Down, then dismissed Coote's claims of tolerance with a raft of statistics. In Dungannon there 'were only two Catholic employees under the Unionist council. Out of a total salary and wages list of £575, only £36 goes to Catholics, and that goes to two street scavengers.'[27] James Stronge, Grand Master of the Orange Order, feared that PR would 'hand the Tyrone County and District

ULSTER AT BAY

AS IN 1690 AND NOW.

MACAULAY, writing of the Siege of Derry, 1690, says—" There, at length on the verge of the ocean, hunted to the last asylum, and baited into a mood in which men may be destroyed, but will not easily be subjugated, the imperial race turned desperately to bay."

1 Ulster unionist propaganda against home rule, referring to the strong colonial–settler identity that underpinned unionist ideology.

2 An Ancient Order of Hibernians parade near Dunamanagh *c.*1911.

3 An Orange Order parade in Leckpatrick, 12 July 1911.

4 The Irish Unionist MPs after the 1910 elections. The soon-to-be 3rd duke of Abercorn is seated in the front row fourth from the left on Edward Carson's right. Andrew Horner is standing in the back row, second from the left.

5 The 2nd duke of Abercorn signs the Ulster Covenant at Baronscourt, Sept. 1912.

6 Ambroise Ricardo, George Richardson and the 3rd duke of Abercorn at Baronscourt, autumn 1913.

7 Uchter Knox, 5th Earl Ranfurly (1856–1933).

8 Viscount Northland (1882–1915).

9 The UVF at Baronscourt, autumn 1913.

10 The Dungannon UVF outside their drill hall in 1914.

11 Joseph Devlin MP (1871–1934).

12 Tom Kettle MP (1880–1916).

13 The Redmonds: William ('Willie') Redmond MP (*left*), John Redmond IPP leader (*centre*) and his son, William Archer Redmond, MP for East Tyrone, 1910–18.

14 The Belfast Dungannon Club. Bulmer Hobson (*back row, second left*), Denis McCullough (*back row, second right*) and Seán Mac Diarmada (*front row, second right*) all had links with republican politics in Tyrone.

15 Joe McGarrity and Bulmer Hobson meet on the latter's American tour prior to his falling out with Mac Diarmada and Clarke in June 1914.

16 Members of Shanless (Coalisland) Irish Volunteer Force on parade in early 1916.

17 Eoin MacNeill addresses the IVF *as Gaeilge* at Greencastle, May 1914.

18 Patrick McCartan and Liam Mellows before their departure for America in 1917.

19 Sinn Féin 1918 general election poster from Arthur
Griffith's campaign in North-West Tyrone.

The three Tyrone MPs after the 1918 general election.

20 (*right*) Arthur Griffith SF North-West Tyrone.

21 (*bottom*, *left*) T.J. Harbison IPP North-East Tyrone.

22 (*bottom*, *right*) William Coote UPP South Tyrone.

23 Platform party at the SF meeting in Armagh, addressed by Michael Collins on 4 Sept. 1921. *Front row*: third left, Eamon Donnelly (SF organizer in Ulster); Michael Collins; Harry Boland. *Second row*: first from left, Kevin O'Shiel (Omagh Sinn Féiner); sixth from left: Eóin O'Duffy (Monaghan TD and Ulster IRA leader). *Back row*: fifth from left, George Murnaghan (Tyrone SF leader) and ninth from left, Joe McKelvey (O/C 3rd ND).

24 The government proposes to enrol "well-disposed persons" in Ireland. A cartoon by the British satirist, David Low, caricaturing the nature of Lloyd George's Irish policy and the new Ulster Special Constabulary.

25 Eoin O'Duffy in 1922.

26 Charlie Daly in 1921.

27 The command of the ATIRA 1st ND, Mar. 1922. Seán Lehane, Charlie Daly and Jack Fitzgerald standing left to right.

28 Members of the ATIRA on the Tyrone/Donegal border, 1922.

29 Paddy Mullan and Frank O'Neill (3rd Brigade 2nd ND) in Free State uniform.

30 James Craig inspects the USC ranks at Sion Mills in 1922.

31 USC in an armoured vehicle with mounted Lewis gun in Strabane, 1922.

32 Internees from Castlederg awaiting transfer to the Argenta, May 1922.

33 Members of the abortive Boundary Commission: Chairman Richard Feetham is in the centre. The unionist representative, J.R. Fisher, stands to his right, while the Free State commissioner, Eoin MacNeil, stands to his left.

Councils over to the … Sinn Feiners', but Ulster members had received southern representation seeking their support.[28] Montgomery warned the leading Cavan landlord, Lord Farnham, that the loss of Tyrone County Council to SF would 'do the Unionist cause more harm than the opening of Southern Councils to Unionist minorities will do it good.' It also threatened Tyrone's future exclusion, as control of the councils had been a 'strong argument in favour of including Tyrone in the Ulster Pale' at the Buckingham Palace in 1914.[29]

Nationally the local government elections of June 1920, held using PR, returned SF majorities in all but four county councils. The victory in Tyrone signalled the effective reconciliation of nationalism under a SF banner. However, the new councillors' subsequent record indicated that pragmatism underpinned their newfound republicanism. SF and the constitutional nationalists agreed an electoral pact. Of the dozen agreed candidates, only Barney McCartan was a republican prior to 1916, while four, including T.J. Harbison, were constitutionalists. This mirrored local SF editorials, which ridiculed Devlin, but spared Harbison.[30] Prior to the poll unionists withdrew candidates from the rural divisions in Dungannon and Cookstown, where 'for the first time in centuries … this citadel of Toryism and landlordism has fallen into the hands of the Catholic people'. Notably, the police arrested George Murnaghan, 'one of the ablest election agents and best exponents of proportional representation in the county'.[31] The nationalists gained the predicted majority, nonetheless. Alex E. Donnelly, the new council chairman, declared that 'the English Parliament was trying to rush through … a Bill to partition Ireland, and to cut off Tyrone along with the other North-East counties from the rest of Ireland. That Bill was tottering to its grave, and this election gave it a blow from which it would never recover.'[32] Tyrone unionists alleged that the SF majority relied on intimidation and personation, but an election petition to this effect was defeated in October 1920.[33] When the nationalist RDC met to co-opt its members at Dungannon courthouse, the local UVF occupied the town, while the deposed former chairman attempted to use procedure to elect a unionist majority.[34] The nationalists eventually won out after an appeal.[35] The RIC reported that the result confirmed 'that Constitutional Nationalists are losing ground and that all Nationalist persons are throwing in their lot with Sinn Féin.'[36]

With a supposedly SF county council, logic dictated that the Dáil's policy of arbitration courts, established in August 1919, would follow. In November 1919 John O'Hanrahan had represented cases at an arbitration court in Dromore.[37] However, there was no concerted effort in this regard until the summer of 1920. The system of Dáil courts emerged from land agitation in the west in May 1920. O'Shiel related how Griffith appointed him a land commissioner, when 'east bound trains brought to Dublin large numbers of terrified [unionist] land owners, who came beseeching the Dáil Government for protection'. In line with his own social conservatism, many of O'Shiel's judgments favoured the original proprietors.[38] The development typified the reactive nature of the Dáil ministry, in reality little more than a paper administration. The court system, like initial IRA activity, relied on local initiative. With courts already in existence in twenty-eight counties by June 1920, 'the Dáil government, viewing developments with something like injured dignity covering neglect of duty, was forced to act'.[39] This coincided with a more comprehensive court system based on parochial and local government units.[40]

By August 1920 the Tyrone SF executive initiated 'arbitration courts', while IRA 'police' patrolled rural Tyrone, from Strabane in the west to Coalisland in the east.[41] In line with the national pattern, 'the courts dealt with civil matters, the IRA with criminal cases'.[42] At a SF court in Gortin four young men were charged with breaking into a local pub and stealing 'a quantity of liquor'. With a little persuasion by the IRA they gave an undertaking to pay and were released.[43] The destruction of poteen was a favourite activity. The Dáil's publicity department reported that the IRA emptied eighty gallons into a Tyrone river.[44] On 23 December 1920 the IRA killed Joe Mullan in an exchange of shots with distillers in Dunamore.[45] Land disputes, so central to court work in other counties, were not significant in Tyrone. The British counter-offensive in autumn 1920 undermined the courts and the republican police.[46] Michael 'Mack' McCartan, the Carrickmore Volunteer commander and president of Gortin court, was charged by the RIC in December 1920 with holding a republican court on 24 November 1920.[47] Although nationalist solicitors did take cases, many recently converted Sinn Féiners continued to ply their trade in more lucrative Crown courts as arbitration was less expensive for litigants. Within the six counties, the system of Dáil courts was largely confined to south Armagh, south Fermanagh, mid-Tyrone and the adjacent mountainous areas of south Derry, all without sizeable unionist populations.[48]

The court system only really flourished and spread to the towns after the truce in July 1921 mainly due to the absence of the British military. At parish level, judges were typically leading Sinn Féiners with no legal training. In Clogher sixteen cases were settled before a hearing, while the remaining five cases concerned debts.[49] The Coalisland parish court dealt with the sale of black-berries and a dispute between a husband and wife over the sale of ducks.[50] District courts took place in the major towns and the cases tended to be of a more serious nature. Those at one sitting in Omagh ranged from slander to damages claimed by Henry O'Neill against John Gallagher, both of Dromore, for injury caused to a cow chased by the plaintiff's dog.[51] While moderate republicans, typically with some legal training, usually chaired the district court, Volunteers acted as stewards, although no uniforms, weapons or flags appeared at St Patrick's Hall in Dungannon. Interestingly, constitutional nationalist lawyers and some unionists also used the courts during the truce period.[52]

The republican police dealt with cases of a serious criminal nature and the training camp at Cranagh Hall near Plumbridge operated as the county gaol.[53] In September 1921 the IRA in Strabane, assisted by 'Sinn Féiners from County Donegal', arrested John McCutcheon and Charles Hagan, two local labourers, for robbing a 90-year-old pensioner.[54] In one particularly notable incident the functionaries of the police and courts clashed when the IRA arrested James Grugan, the parish clerk and manager of the Carrickmore creamery. The IRA had requested permission to execute Grugan for threatening the life of their commander, Charlie Daly.[55] The Dáil courts functioned until the transfer of security powers to a unionist administration in Belfast in November 1921. The resulting onslaught from the USC, however, demonstrated how the 'political realities of the Northern situation prevented the Dáil courts from winning the kind of acceptance by the community which they had in the South'.[56]

Labour was 'rampant' across much of Ireland after the 1918 general election.[57] Both the IPP and SF courted working-class support. For unionists, labour arguably represented a greater threat than nationalism. There was considerable trade union activity across Tyrone in 1918. The most determined industrial action took place in Dungannon, Cookstown and Coalisland, with ten significant strikes in the first nine months of 1918.[58] Workers also took strike action in the shirt factories in Strabane. In the summer of 1918 protest spread to rural areas, and among textile and UDC workers in Omagh.[59] By January 1919, with the engineers' strike bringing Belfast to a standstill, the Tyrone CI observed that workers believed that they could 'get any terms they demand by going on strike and naturally they do so'.[60] The strikes initially focused on obtaining improved wages but as the year progressed there was a growing demand for union recognition and a closed shop policy in places.[61] Significantly, until the conscription crisis of April 1918, trade unionism crossed denominational boundaries. The area's mixed workforce also explains the strength of the Belfast-based Workers' Union, as opposed to the pro-republican ITGWU.[62]

Unionist employers developed a strategy to fracture working-class solidarity. In March 1918, at Brown's soap works in Donaghmore when workers attacked 'blacklegs', drove a hijacked company lorry through the front gates and 'paraded the village with a red flag,' unionist workers taunted them with Union Jacks 'supplied by the factory owner'.[63] This anticipated the creation of the Carsonite Unionist/Ulster Workers' Union (UWU) in December 1918, which sought to divert potential unionist recruits from the ITGWU.[64] These tactics reached their peak in Tyrone in 1919 when 220 workers struck at Fulton's woollen mill, Caledon.[65] Peadar O'Donnell actually led the strike for higher wages and trade union recognition. This followed the ITGWU's successful campaign during the Monaghan asylum 'soviet' and prompted the majority unionist workforce to seek O'Donnell's assistance.[66] Fulton was a prominent local businessman, spokesman for the 'leading residents in the Clogher Valley' and an associate of Fred Crawford and Dawson Bates.[67]

Writing in September 1920 Crawford recounted the strike from Fulton's perspective and claimed that nationalists, who struck to remove the mill's unionist foremen, filled servicemen's jobs during the war. He alleged that the local Catholic priest, 'the leader of the Sinn Feiners in the district', organized the strike to persecute Protestants.[68] In fact, Fulton's intransigence and poor pay provided the motivation. The local union secretary was an Orangeman, but O'Donnell later recollected how 'gradually the Union Jacks gave way and the red flags took their place'.[69] After four weeks, with 130 workers still on strike, Fulton introduced UWU 'blacklegs', and readmitted strikers on a sectarian basis. When the strike eventually collapsed in July 1919, Fulton celebrated by holding a social under a banner which read: 'Caledon's double celebration: overthrow of the Hun and the Irish Bolshevists'.[70] The village remained a hotbed of sectarian tension, partly because Fulton manipulated religion to preserve his own interests.

By 1919 early working-class solidarity had dissipated due, in part, to a general post-war slump, especially in linen, which fuelled competition for scarce employment. Furthermore, activity relied on the ITGWU, whose 'leaders hold strong communistic and revolutionary principles' and whose 'members are Sinn Féiners'.[71] For instance, the RIC attributed the strike at Spamount woollen mill in Castlederg directly to 'Sinn Feiners'.[72] Protest also shifted westward with the then unionist county council, the largest local employer, increasingly becoming the target.[73] In May 1919 CI Millar noted continued serious 'unrest … amongst the labouring class' and 'rumours of a strike of agricultural labourers'.[74] By May there were strikes at the council quarry and among Omagh's bricklayers.[75]

The SF leadership supported strikes involving council workers.[76] Murnaghan defended James McGinn of the Omagh Bricklayers and Masons' Union against a charge of intimidating a 'blackleg'.[77] The previous August the ITGWU had organized a strike over wages in Carrickmore quarry that succeeded after two months.[78] In May 1919 the county surveyor dismissed the five union leaders and this forced the remaining twenty men out. The area was strongly republican and one of the strike organizers was a local Volunteer.[79] The SF-controlled Omagh RDC sent a deputation to the county council in support of the strikers. Although John Donnelly admitted that 'as a farmer, he was just as much afraid of the Labour Union as anybody else', he felt the council had acted unfairly. William Coote retorted that they 'really came there to support this sort of Bolshevism which was going on all over the country'.[80]

This was not the case for 'while Sinn Féin would not tolerate injustice or oppression, neither would it associate itself with class war'.[81] Notably, in June 1919 SF commissioned a report from Ulster Protestant, W. Forbes Patterson, to investigate new avenues for republicanism in Ulster. He suggested that SF emphasize the Dáil's 'progressive' and 'radical' Democratic Programme in order 'to weld labour interests and Irish nationalism together'.[82] In Tyrone the SF leadership reflected the same bourgeois antipathy to socialism as the national leadership, epitomized in the figure of Arthur Griffith, its vice-president who had sided with big business during the Dublin Lockout. When nationalists gained control of Tyrone County Council in June 1920, support for strikes quickly stopped. For example, in July Omagh bin men, or 'scavengers', failed to secure better conditions.[83] The nationalist council also defeated the strike at Omagh asylum in December.[84]

There has been significant debate regarding the nature of the Irish revolution. Peter Hart has argued that 'there was no socially revolutionary situation in Ireland even in prospect'.[85] Campbell counters that 'the revolution in Ireland resulted in the creation of a conservative state, but not all Irish revolutionaries were conservative' and that 'there were radical impulses', which 'demonstrate that the revolution was neither innately or inevitably conservative'.[86] SF's social conservatism was not universal. While its separatist demand captured the nationalist, working-class imagination, throughout the revolutionary period, the central executive, and then the Dáil Ministry, dealt almost exclusively with its middle-class counterparts in Omagh. Many within the working class, which had a long-term republican commitment, held a very different conception of the revolution. There was clearly a left-wing republican constituency. In Coalisland local republicans had supported trade unionism since the 1890s, particularly at the Roan Linen Spinning Mill and Congo colliery.[87] The town experienced militant strikes in 1918. When northern workers generally ignored the Trade Union Congress's anti-conscription 'workless day' in 1918, Coalisland 'shut down'.[88] As late as February 1920 a strike at Stevenson's yard demonstrated that workers still demanded fairer wages.[89] The IRB cell in neighbouring Old Engine was comprised mostly of former miners and workers at the local brickyard, all of whom were members of the ITGWU. After partition, local workers clashed with Sir Samuel Kelly, the deputy lieutenant of Tyrone and Belfast coal magnate. He bought the local colliery, two spinning mills and the brickyard in 1921 and began production in 1924, with 200 Scottish miners. However, the miners contained a hard core of militants who attempted to create a soviet, precipitating eventual closure. The miners mobilized support from republican internees who had been released from the *Argenta*, and newly demobilized A Specials.[90] Kelly also expelled the Transport Union from the brickworks and brought in 'scabs' from Dungannon. One local republican described the struggle: 'The strike at the brickworks still continues and looks very blue. We are down and out all through the signing of the f**king Treaty'!'[91]

Labour exercised the minds of Belfast unionists perhaps even more than the SF revolution taking place in the south and west. In early 1919 a massive engineers strike had crippled Belfast industry for a month. This class consciousness was also apparent in the local elections of 1920, when twelve labour councillors won seats on Belfast Corporation. SF's virtual monopoly of local government and the disquieting progress of labour in the unionist citadel itself led Carson to link the two issues in a particularly incendiary speech at Finaghy on 12 July 1920.[92] One week later the funeral in Banbridge of Colonel Gerald Smyth, divisional police commissioner for Munster who had been assassinated by the IRA, sparked widespread loyalist violence. In Belfast some 10,000 Catholics and several hundred 'rotten' Protestant trade unionists were expelled from the city's shipyards, mills and foundries.[93] Over the next two years 23,000 people were driven from their homes in Belfast, while approximately 50,000 people fled the north because of intimidation.[94] The death toll in Belfast alone in the same period numbered 500. Of these almost sixty per cent were Catholics in a city where they made up only a quarter of the population.[95] The government's apparent ambivalence and provocative unionist rhetoric before the outbreak led to calls for SF to respond. On 6 August 1920 Seán MacEntee, TD for South Monaghan, petitioned the Dáil on behalf of his fellow Belfast citizens to boycott goods and withdraw savings from Belfast-owned banks. The Dáil cabinet voted for a limited boycott on 11 August 1920.[96]

Tyrone County Council immediately supported the boycott and ordered all local bodies to 'cease trading with Belfast'.[97] Several SF cumainn then publicly advocated measures that led to the burning of Inglis bread carts, a favourite target of local republicans, at Dungannon, Omagh and Beragh.[98] It was proposed to use the network of SF branches for the campaign.[99] The national leadership appeared to be reacting to, rather than instigating, policy. In January 1921 the Dáil set up a separate body under the control of Joseph McDonagh to administer the boycott and by July 1921 there were 600 committees. Those in Tyrone ordered the confiscation of Belfast cheques and notes.[100] In August 1921 Dungannon traders received a circular marked Dáil Éireann. It urged the withdrawal of the financial support 'which makes it possible to carry out these periodical massacres of Catholics, and send hireling orators like Coote into every quarter of the province to inflame the passions of the Orange Mobs'.[101] The Omagh committee published a blacklist of 38 unionist and 17 nationalist traders who still dealt with Belfast.[102] The boycott typically involved posting a blacklist, picketing of businesses carrying Belfast goods, their destruction, and intimidation against those prepared to give evidence against Volunteers arrested in relation to the campaign.

The campaign, which officially ran until the Treaty, covered the whole county, outside Cookstown.[103] It is debatable how much economic damage was actually inflicted on Belfast but in Tyrone unionist businesses suffered.[104] As for the Dáil courts and the IRA campaign, the counter-state was predicated on passive and then active resistance to British rule by a critical mass within the local population. Where republicans were strong, as in Coalisland, the threat of intimidation usually sufficed to get unionist traders to conform. In early 1922 J.J. Fleming, a unionist JP in Gortin, complained to Bates of the 'tyrannical boycott', that local nationalists had refused to work for him and that he had been threatened by the IRA.[105] In strongly republican areas the IRA was able to enforce the boycott as was the case in neighbouring Monaghan, where Eoin O'Duffy, the IRA leader, reported to GHQ in April 1921 that 'several merchants, including Unionists, have fallen in with our wishes and paid stiff fines to have their names removed from the black list'.[106] Monaghan, located outside the proposed six-county area and with a seventy-five per cent Catholic population, had advantages in maintaining the monopoly of legitimate force that Tyrone did not enjoy.

The boycott generated support because it coincided with northern nationalist outrage at the treatment of their co-religionists in Belfast. One aspect of Dáil policy appeared to be less well received. Across Ireland, SF and labour dominated local government after 1920. But only a handful of bodies immediately gave up financial aid from the LGB, despite a Dáil decree in September 1920 to that effect.[107] In December 1920 W.T. Cosgrave, Dáil minister for local government, enquired why the Omagh Board of Guardians continued to recognize 'the enemy institution' of the LGB. Michael Lynch, the SF chairman, marked the correspondence as 'read' and duly ignored it.[108] The CI detected 'some symptoms that the better class and more level-headed businessmen are beginning to see the futility of their continuing allegiance to Dáil Éireann', noting that nationalist bodies still recognized the LGB.[109] In August 1921 Murnaghan claimed that Dáil policy was impossible because 'all the local government officials in that area were opposed to them', since they had been previously appointed by unionists.[110] Clearly, however, many councillors, of very recent republican vintage, favoured continued power over adherence to the Dáil. Faced with the loss of LGB grants, without which asylums and other council-controlled bodies would suffer, the more prudent though perhaps less patriotic option was to take the money.

Rather than killing home rule, Ulster unionists accepted their own version of it. In May 1917 Lord Curzon, the former Indian viceroy and future foreign secretary, drafted a scheme for the British cabinet that counties could vote themselves out of a northern parliament on a fifty-five per cent majority 'for the transparent purpose of enabling a minority in Tyrone and Fermanagh to decide the issue'.[111] The British coalition government's 1918 election manifesto contained home rule with six-county exclusion. This led Carson to inform Craig that 'We are in smooth waters at the moment'.[112] He subsequently told Montgomery that 'our policy should be that, in the event of it being found that devolution was a necessity, we demand a subordinate parliament for Ulster'.[113]

The IPP challenged the Government of Ireland bill in parliament. Devlin claimed that abstention permitted a 'British Government, inspired by an Orange Ascendancy Party, to govern and control Ireland on whatever lines they chose'.[114] Nonetheless, after the 1918 election, he felt that attendance would only prove 'the futility of Parliamentary representation', embarrassing SF 'in their efforts to secure representation at the Peace Conference' and allowing them to

blame the party, when their 'promises do not materialize'. Devlin eventually
yielded to his five colleagues, including Harbison, who wished 'to act according
to our mandate' and 'take an active part in opposing' the upcoming Government
of Ireland bill.[115] In February 1920, in a letter to Bishop O'Donnell of Raphoe,
the IPP's one true remaining ecclesiastical ally, Devlin predicted that 'a
Parliament … for Six Counties' which would establish 'permanent partition …
with all the sufferings and tyranny of the present day continued, only in worse
form'.[116] He claimed that the government had 'a clear and definite arrangement
with Sir Edward Carson, and any attempt to extend the area would meet with his
strongest hostility'.[117]

The Belfast unionists had thrown their fellow unionists in Cavan, Donegal
and Monaghan 'to the wolves with very little compunction'.[118] The UUC had
countenanced this as early as 1916. Both Bates and James Craig discouraged
Montgomery from maintaining links between the UUC and the southern Irish
Unionist Alliance.[119] Stronge claimed that Bates, 'like some others … is too
exclusively Belfast in his views', yet he was 'reconciled … to the idea of partition. One felt that if we have no friends south of the Newry Mountains, it might
be better to draw the boundary line there and be frankly "West Britons" and not
Irishmen'.[120] In September 1919 a parliamentary committee chaired by Walter
Long recommended six-county partition with dual Belfast and Dublin parliaments elected by PR. The GOIA, which was passed in December 1920, closely
reflected these proposals but also contained provisions for a Council of Ireland
to co-ordinate matters of common concern to the two parliaments. Hopes that
this would evolve into a single Irish parliament were illusionary as unionists had
a veto on the transfer of powers to it.[121]

The acceptance of the act by the UUC on 10 March 1920 threatened to split
Tyrone unionism. Unionists in Cavan, Monaghan and Donegal naturally felt
betrayed.[122] Initially Montgomery and Stronge voted against acceptance.
Ricardo resigned from the UUC in 'anger & disgust', and claimed that 'Carson
on 10th fell from the pedestal that many had placed him on'.[123] Elsewhere, he
criticized 'the narrow Belfast clique' who ruled from Old Town Hall and claimed
that he represented 'a strong minority of loyalists', who wished to give 'the
simple covenanter an opportunity…to prevent the Covenant being torn up'.[124]
This led to rather empty soul-searching about the actual meaning of the 1912
Covenant and intra-unionist squabbling in the press. As the Government of
Ireland bill made its way through parliament the logic of a six-county partition
became increasingly clear. This was captured by John Gunning-Moore, a
Cookstown unionist: 'the whole question of "breach of Covenant" turns upon
numbers … the whole 9 will be such a rickety parliament that it must [almost]
at once be absorbed into the Dublin one.'[125]

Unionist leaders recognized Carson's 'considerable triumph' in getting
Tyrone and Fermanagh 'included in the Northern Pale' and that, 'if the whole

thing is thrown back into the melting pot again, we may be the sufferers'.[126] On 5 May, in anticipation of an emergency UUC meeting attended by Carson, the North West and North East Tyrone Unionist Associations backed the six-county scheme as did unionists in South Tyrone. Clearly, in terms of the acceptance of six-county over nine-county exclusion, Ulster unionist policy was 'not a question of ethics and honour, but a question of arithmetic.'[127] At the UUC meeting on 27 May only eighty out of 390 delegates supported the nine-county manifesto.[128] Stronge admitted, however, that he did not look 'forward to governing Carrickmore, Crossmaglen ... with sedition organized over the border & little or no support from England'.[129] In fact, the British government were preparing to provide unionists with their own force – the USC. By May 1920 local unionists were committed to six-county partition. Any lingering doubts dissolved in the face of a developing IRA campaign which had reached Tyrone itself.

The IRA campaign went through several specific phases. Tyrone followed the national pattern where getting weapons represented 'the be-all and end-all of revolutionary activity.' The failure of the Tyrone IRA to achieve this partially explains why the county did not register activity during 'the transition from arms raids to attacks on RIC barracks ... in the winter of 1919–20'.[130] The campaign in Tyrone did not begin in earnest until the late spring of 1920 when there were a limited number of raids on barracks and ambushes. This continued until the formation of the 2nd ND in March 1921, which is discussed in the next chapter. The establishment of IRA GHQ in March 1918 formalized IRB influence over the IRA, with Michael Collins as director of organization and Richard Mulcahy becoming chief of staff. GHQ's lack of direct control, however, facilitated varying degrees of local initiative across the country. Tyrone was particularly dependent on outside direction and resources from GHQ.[131] In return, GHQ encouraged northern operations in order to relieve the pressure on Munster and to challenge partition. After April 1920 the strategy in Tyrone focused on the consolidation of the core No. 1 Brigade area, followed by expansion into quiet or unionist districts. GHQ's divisional reorganization in March 1921 confirmed this thinking. In April 1921 Mulcahy claimed that 'a proper military grip of the Second Divisional Area would result in breaking Carsonia up internally, because it would cut off the western unionist centres ... from Belfast. The centre of this area is a continuous mountainous mass, [which] affords an ideal base for operation.'[132] The 2nd ND in Tyrone comprised two brigade areas. No. 1 Brigade centred on the republican heartland stretching from Coalisland and Dungannon to the mountainous region between Carrickmore and Greencastle. The majority of IRA volunteers and military operations originated there. No. 2 Brigade stretched from Omagh south and west through Drumquin to the small areas of consolidated nationalist population around Trillick, Dromore and Fintona.

Activism in Tyrone was held back by a combination of the very real fear of loyalist reprisals, poor leadership and inadequate arms. In December 1919 the CI noted that 'Sinn Fein outrages such as raids on barracks and attacks on police would spread here were it not for the fear that there would be reprisals on leading Sinn Feiners by the loyalist portion of the population'.[133] In Tyrone, GHQ appointed leaders due more to their IRB membership than their military ability. Jack Shields of the Benburb Company, Dungannon Battalion, was O/C until his arrest on 12 September 1919.[134] He clearly felt that the IRB influence, particularly from Belfast, retarded activism.[135] His company area was 'five miles from Dungannon and the direct road through to Dungannon contained a most hostile Unionist population', which 'meant a practical isolation of our area from Battalion Headquarters'.[136] Likewise, his successor, Frank Dooris, commanded the Clogher Company[137], which was also in a unionist area.[138] Only after Dooris's arrest in June 1920 did GHQ appoint a commander from the mountainous mass, Albert Tally.[139]

The IRA in neighbouring counties began offensive actions much earlier than in Tyrone and displayed decisive local leadership. In December 1919 the Donegal IRA, under the command of Joe Sweeney, ambushed a body of RIC escorting republican prisoners near Dungloe.[140] In February 1920 the Monaghan IRA, under the command of O'Duffy and Ernie O'Malley, attacked Shantonagh barracks. On 9 May the South Armagh IRA, under the command of Frank Aiken, attacked and burned an armed RIC barracks in the loyalist stronghold of Newtownhamilton.[141] It is necessary to note that these areas did not contain the same proportion of unionists and would later not exhibit the same concentration of USC as Tyrone. If other counties were not content to wait for central direction, why was this not the case in Tyrone? Shields suggested that each battalion acted to some extent independently and, in line with GHQ policy, 'no attacks were to be made on Crown forces and the Volunteers were to act in a purely defensive manner'.[142] Nicholas Smyth highlighted a distinct lack of activity in South Tyrone until late 1919. Before the arrival of Charlie Daly during the autumn of 1920, Smyth thought that 'each company was more or less acting independently on its own'.[143]

In January 1920 GHQ sanctioned operations against Crown forces as an 'active defence strategy' and a campaign to smash government communications.[144] But the lack of initiative persisted and this partially explains why operations did not begin until the GHQ directive to destroy vacated police barracks at Easter 1920. In Tyrone just four were burned in April, while Gortin barracks was attacked on 1 May. A fortnight later, the IRA burnt tax offices in Broughderg, Pomeroy and, most notably, in Dungannon.[145] The Dungannon Battalion then destroyed barracks at Donaghmore and Castlecaulfield, and on 7 June raided Cookstown RIC barracks during which Volunteer Patrick Loughran was fatally wounded. This attack represented the first attempt to extend operations into hostile unionist territory.[146] Constable Leonard of Cookstown approached IRA acquaintances from Keady with the plan. The IRA received a map and Leonard left the back door open, the purpose was to seize all the arms and ammunition and, if possible, disable the barracks.[147] This campaign of 'wanton criminal incendiarism, directed principally against ... police barracks', in the No. 1 Brigade area continued throughout July and August.[148] The IRA burnt the barracks in the Moy on 15 July and nearby Charlemont fort a fortnight later.[149] On 26 August the Letterkenny Company, 4th Battalion, Donegal No. 2 Brigade IRA, with the assistance of a local, Volunteer James Curran, raided Drumquin barracks in the No. 2 Brigade area.[150] Constable James Munnelly received a fatal gunshot to the head when he opened the barracks door. Although wounded in the hip, Sergeant Bradley managed to throw a grenade, which brought the attack to an end.[151] Between April and August 1920 the IRA destroyed a total of twelve barracks, razing most of the rural police barracks in No. 1 Brigade area and attacking two well-defended barracks in Cookstown and Drumquin, which saw fatalities on both sides. Operations began in areas of consolidated strength, followed by attempts to take the campaign into hostile or quiet districts. There was also an increase in arms raids, seizure of mails and destruction of property, particularly in connection with the Belfast boycott. Cumann na mBan assisted with first aid, provisions, communications and intelligence. Tyrone women drilled, learned about weapons and transported them, but never appear to have fired any.[152]

Significantly, sympathetic RIC helped plan the raids on Cookstown and Drumquin, as well as an abortive raid on Clogher barracks.[153] Friendly policemen usually formed the premise for direct attacks on barracks, which were beyond the capability of the poorly armed Tyrone IRA.[154] Policemen with republican sympathies tended to make loyalists wary, particularly in the majority unionist Cookstown area, where there were no active IRA men. The Cookstown attack led to follow-up raids by the RIC with the active assistance of the Cookstown UVF.[155] Tally recalled that joint patrols of 'police and military became most active and tough towards the IRA' with common 'raids and arrests'.[156] This included his own arrest in September 1920 along with 'the nest of rebels' in the No. 3 Brigade around Tom Morris, GHQ organizer for South Derry.[157] This proved beneficial as it led to the appointment of an outsider in the person of Charlie Daly, a 24-year-old Kerryman, who quickly endeavoured to instil his 'imperturbable offensive spirit' into the Tyrone IRA.[158]

After the Cookstown raid, the CI claimed that 'the great danger at present in this county is [loyalist] reprisals'.[159] Since March Fred Crawford had been reorganizing the UVF, mindful of Carson's injunction that this should not disturb the Government of Ireland bill.[160] The onset of the IRA guerrilla campaign and the nationalist seizure of Tyrone County Council galvanized Tyrone unionists and Ricardo led the reorganization in Tyrone from late May 1920 onwards. That month Montgomery identified the establishment of a force of Cookstown 'Special Constables', who assisted the local police.[161] On 13 June DI George Hall left the Cookstown UVF in charge while he went to investigate an attack on the Rock barracks.[162] The activity of the Tyrone UVF chimed with Crawford's appeal to Carson and Craig in May for official government recognition. He argued that 'We in Ulster will not be able to hold our men in hand much longer', and that 'we will have the Protestants … killing a lot of the well-known Sinn Fein leaders and hanging half a dozen priests'.[163] By 20 May Crawford, Craig and Carson had co-ordinated a joint submission to Bonar Law requesting the formation of a state-backed security force based on the UVF.[164] Pre-occupied by the south-west, the government sanctioned this, although Hamar Greenwood, the chief secretary, thought it 'politically unwise to announce this publicly'.[165] The county commanders of the UVF then met and agreed to accept the policy formulated earlier in Tyrone. Ricardo regarded the appointment in June of Wilfrid Spender to reorganize the provincial UVF as 'A1'.[166] On 23 July 1920 Craig told the British cabinet that the Specials would prevent 'mob law' and 'prevent the Protestants from running amok'. General Tudor warned that the government should not differentiate between the violence of 'rebels and loyalists'. Lloyd George, however, 'was not thinking of such differentiation, but of releasing troops and police'.[167]

Until the creation of the USC, local unionists tended to avoid confrontation.[168] In June the RIC admitted that 'the police and military force in the county is quite insufficient to cope with a possible outbreak'.[169] By autumn 1920, despite its pitiful arsenal, the Tyrone IRA had consolidated republican areas and spread operations. When the IRA burnt Moy barracks and Charlemont fort, William Murray, the local unionist JP, formed a conciliation committee with 'respectable' nationalists on 11 August 'at a most critical time when there was serious danger of a conflict between rival factions'.[170] The introduction of the USC transformed the situation. In the summer of 1920 loyalist violence predominated where the balance of forces favoured the UVF, such as Belfast, Lisburn and Banbridge, or Cookstown in Tyrone. The creation of the USC facilitated the westward spread of unionist violence. This may explain Murray's very different approach at the end of 1921 when he wrote to Dawson Bates demanding 'energetic and immediate action to suppress the boycott of Belfast goods … this intolerable interference with the rights of law abiding and well-disposed people will be dealt with in direct fashion if those in authority fail in their duty'.[171] Cabinet members consistently used the loyalist population's propensity for retribution to justify arming the same community. In May 1922, referring to the violence in Belfast, Churchill informed the cabinet that 'Whether it was a case of six of one and half a dozen of the other he did not know. He would be sorry to try and arrive at any other ratio.' Churchill then outlined that the government had nineteen battalions, 48,000 Specials and 'orders had been given to accede to Sir James Craig's request for arms and munitions to equip these', because 'at any moment, patience may be ruptured and we shall find ourselves in an atmosphere where people see red'.[172]

After a meeting in September 1920 the three Tyrone UVF leaders, Ricardo, Stevenson and McClintock, issued a secret memo, assuring supporters that no nationalist would join the USC and that the government's 'appeal to "all well-disposed citizens"' 'may be looked upon as camouflage'.[173] The commanders admitted that 'at present we are working with the Military but they may be moved at any time'. Second, in Tyrone the A Specials would 'enable all the vacant police barracks to be re-opened'. They encouraged acceptance of the force because 'we are rapidly approaching an absolute crisis and ... the powers that be may say "very well you will not help us to help yourselves and you have got to accept the rule of the Sinn Feiner"'.[174] The new USC members had no doubt what they were fighting for. Basil Brooke, the future northern prime minister, issued the following declaration to the new force in Fermanagh in November: 'By answering the call of the Empire you are helping your country and defending yourself'.[175] That month Crawford gave an indication of future tactics: 'There is only one way to deal with the campaign of murder that the rebels are pursuing ... where the murder of a policeman or other official takes place, the leading rebel in the district ought to be shot or done away with'.[176] Henceforth, the local IRA faced a more determined, better-equipped and locally knowledgeable adversary.

While the creation of the USC continued apace, the IRA campaign itself changed. GHQ's active defence strategy had shifted to one of open confrontation. This was personified by Charlie Daly, who sought to use active IRA units to bring quieter areas out. Nicholas Smyth recalled that Daly, who 'impressed us very much with his example and bearing,' had 'left us under no illusion ... [that] a number of people would have to be prepared to make the supreme sacrifice ... [that] volunteering was not going to be an easy job'.[177] Daly had a GHQ order to raid for arms, which indicates just how poorly armed the Tyrone IRA was. The *Ulster Herald* claimed that 200 men and 50 vehicles were involved in raids around Gortin.[178] The *Tyrone Courier* reported how, with 'great daring and success', the IRA carried out 'the largest and most extensive raid for arms which has yet taken place in Ireland', remarking that over 100 local Protestants received 'receipts for the weapons ... in the name of the Irish Republic'.[179] The situation was, in fact, far more modest. The IRA had commandeered the car of John Devlin of Omagh 'at the point of the revolver' and raided about seventeen unionist homes in the rural area to the north of Omagh town.[180] Smyth related how the IRA concentrated 'on Unionist and Hibernian houses ... at McConnell's one of our men was wounded in the face by the discharge of a shotgun'.[181] The UVF in Trillick responded by trying to shoot the local curate, Fr John Ward.[182] Such reaction was a precursor of the approach soon to be adopted by the USC.

In October 1920, as a reprisal for the death of Terence MacSwiney, the

Tyrone IRA received an order to attack Crown forces. The objective was to seize police weapons and bolster their limited arsenal.[183] No. 1 Brigade carried out three ambushes. Two in the Dunamore area resulted in casualties to Crown forces. On 8 October Constable Dennison survived seven shotgun pellets to the back of the head when he resisted attempts to deprive him of his revolver.[184] Constable Martin Hoban was wounded in an ambush in Dungannon on Sunday 31 October, the day of MacSwiney's funeral.[185] In reprisal, police and loyalists ransacked and looted the nationalist half of the town, bombing the family home of W.J. Kelly, a matter raised in the House of Commons by Joe Devlin on 2 November.[186] The *Tyrone Courier* recorded the aftermath, when 'explosions and incessant discharging of rifles took place in [nationalist] Anne Street and Irish Street'. The following Sunday, 7 November, Dean P.J. Byrne denounced the IRA men from the pulpit as 'murderers in their heart', a strong condemnation considering they were probably among the congregation.[187]

On 23 November Daly personally led an attack by the Carrickmore Battalion on the RIC at Ballygawley, which resulted in the wounding of three police and two civilian drivers.[188] James McElduff recalled that Daly offered 'them a chance to surrender', which was ignored and that Daly administered an act of contrition to one injured policeman, who pretended to be a Catholic.[189] Seán Corr believed that DI John Patrick Ferris was the intended target due to his previous aggression against the IRA in Cork.[190] Ominously, a 'large number of [Ulster] Volunteers turned out for the purpose of assisting the police'.[191] Daly's influence also extended to the quieter No. 2 Brigade area where reprisals by Crown forces were more intense. One such incident occurred in Dromore in April 1921 and is discussed in the next chapter. Tyrone Volunteers were reluctant to carry out operations in 'orange' districts as they could not protect local nationalists from the inevitable backlash.[192]

In November 1920 Hamar Greenwood earmarked Tyrone as the first rural area to receive A and B Specials.[193] That month, 300 Specials, mostly ex-servicemen, went for training at Newtownards.[194] In December the police reported that despite the continued 'disturbed and unsatisfactory' conditions, the numerous searches and arrests, aided by the UVF, had a 'deterrent effect on the evilly disposed section of Sinn Féin'.[195] Daly's arrest in Dublin two weeks before Christmas 1920 further upset IRA operations until his release the following month.[196] By January 1921 the Crown forces now included platoons of A Specials, equipped with rifles, side arms and military transport. As a result, the RIC reopened nine barracks without any IRA opposition.[197] In effect this largely undid the IRA efforts during the spring and summer to destroy abandoned barracks.

By the end of 1920 the IRA had destroyed vacated barracks and raided two occupied ones, as well as carrying out several ambushes. A SF-nationalist combination had captured Tyrone County Council, Dáil courts appeared in the county and a contribution had been made to the Dáil loan. The strength of the counter-state in Tyrone should not be overestimated, however. The courts displaced the British system nationally because of the breakdown of British authority and the marginalization of the RIC. They succeeded because they originated among the people, enjoyed communal sanction and, crucially, the IRA could enforce decrees. Max Weber argued that the state represented 'a human community that (successfully) claims the monopoly of the legitimate use of physical force within a given territory'.[198] The bureaucratic renderings of the tiny Dáil ministry were irrelevant without the 'vital ingredients' of 'decentralization and local initiative'. Indeed, the Dáil's total expenditure in the first six months of 1921 amounted to less than £40,000; 'by any standard, this revolution was on the cheap'.[199] In Tyrone the counter-state operated in a hermetically sealed bubble in areas of concentrated nationalist population. This ceased when the RIC, aided by the newly-formed USC, challenged the republican monopoly on the legitimate use of physical force at the end of 1920.

By then Tyrone unionism had weathered a potential split over the issue of six-county partition. The republican threat quickly restored unionist solidarity. The unionists' own security force and the knowledge that Tyrone would comprise part of a new northern government cushioned the blow of losing the County Council. The USC was established during the framing and parliamentary passage of the GOIA which represented 'not so much a sincere attempt to settle the Irish question as a sincere attempt to settle the Ulster question.'[200] By November 1920 the British government had sanctioned 2,000 full-time paramilitary police (A Specials) and 19,500 part-time reservists (B Specials), entirely comprised of the UVF.[201] Ernest Clark's appointment as assistant under-secretary for the six counties in September and that of Charles Wickham as divisional commissioner of the RIC in November signalled de facto partition. In Tyrone the Weberian question had evolved from which grouping wielded legitimate force to which one wielded the greatest.

7 Parliament, peace and partition, 1921

On 11 November 1920, the night the Government of Ireland bill passed the Commons, T.J. Harbison claimed that, due to gerrymandering, half a million nationalists 'will not have more than eight or nine seats out of fifty-two in the new parliament'. Therefore, Tyrone nationalists were 'legally justified in using every form of resistance ... to prevent this Act... from coming into operation', a measure introduced at 'the dictates of a narrow-minded set of reactionaries in the North-East corner of Ulster', who 'will have us under their heel for all time'.[1] The act received the royal assent on 23 December 1920 and was due to come into operation in May 1921 with elections, under PR, to parliaments in Belfast and Dublin. SF's unopposed election nullified the southern parliament. As Harbison spoke, border nationalists assembled en masse at a SF protest meeting in Omagh.[2] The IRA was reorganized in March 1921. In opposing the northern regime its principal adversary was the USC rather than a reinforced RIC as in the south. The truce of July 1921 ended violent IRA activity but the Specials, although nominally stood down, continued under the remobilised UVF, a move secretly sanctioned by James Craig. The truce period also exposed divisions between political and militant republicans. From the beginning of 1921 until the signing of the Anglo-Irish Treaty on 6 December, the nationalist community had to acknowledge the traumatic reality of partition, while unionists sought to cement their control of Tyrone.

Robert Lynch argues that 'the creation of IRA Divisions in Ulster' in March 1921, 'signalled the birth of the Northern IRA itself' but that GHQ organizers in the North 'met only disinterest and incredulity'.[3] Tyrone Nos 1 and 2 Brigades had already killed one policeman, wounded eight others, and attacked or destroyed twelve barracks; one Volunteer was killed and four wounded. Although not comparable to Munster or Dublin, violence in Tyrone matched quiet areas of Leinster and Connacht in 1919–20.[4] Arguably, from March onwards the USC and 'the mixture of Orange and Green in most districts' made conditions far more hostile than quieter areas in the rest of Ireland.[5] GHQ directed that five divisional areas be created in Ulster. Eoin O'Duffy, the Monaghan commander, was ordered to organize the 2nd Northern Division (ND) with assistance from 'a useful officer [Daly]', who 'already had some experience of Tyrone'.[6] The Tyrone section of the 2nd ND covered the entire county with the exception of small peripheral areas around Strabane in the west which came under Joseph Sweeny's 1st ND; Brantry in the east was part of Frank Aiken's 4th ND; and Clogher in the south was in the 5th ND nominally under Dan Hogan but still under O'Duffy's effective control. Mulcahy advised that 'the Northern Divisional Staffs, by reason of their familiarity with

Northern conditions, are the best judges ... of [the] application of the general Offensive principle'.[7] His description of the six counties as 'a bridgehead that the English cannot afford to lose and must spend lavishly to defend' succinctly described British policy.[8]

O'Duffy reluctantly left Monaghan, where he had earned his reputation, and only on the condition that he retained control there.[9] In Tyrone he had to initiate an immediate offensive, create a new officer corps and impose a levy to pay the officers a £5 salary.[10] He informed Mulcahy that he 'had to scrap every Coy. Battalion and Brigade Officer' and reorganize the entire Division.[11] O'Duffy, who remained in position until May 1921, proved unpopular among ordinary Volunteers because of the levy, his high-handed attitude, self-promotion, frequent complaints of local incompetence and general lack of camaraderie.[12] W.J. Kelly later claimed that O'Duffy's appointment 'was a mistake as Charlie Daly was a better man for the job', a view shared by Volunteers, for whom Daly was a favourite.[13] O'Duffy was critical in reports to GHQ of the Tyrone officers' lack of initiative and 'easy going' approach to work. The Tyrone IRA apparently regarded 'reasonable orders' as 'Prussianism'. He also suggested that unlike Monaghan, Tyrone Volunteers got 'their arms too easily' from the likes of McCartan but had 'they to risk their lives ... like other counties they would think more about them'. The character of the men under his command represented his chief gripe. The Gortin commandant was 'the principal poteen-maker in the County – his only occupation ... "running stills"... the priests and people are disgusted ... the only decent self-respecting young fellows are those outside the IRA'.[14] O'Duffy's petit bourgeois origins explain both his position in the republican élite and his vitriol for the Gortin IRA.[15] His conception of Irish-Ireland echoed the puritanical 'disgust' felt by the local priests and respectable youth, all fellow recent converts to separatism. Ironically, the very poteen-makers O'Duffy chastised came from an Irish-speaking area that had a company of Irish Volunteers before 1916.[16]

O'Duffy lost little time in ordering an offensive across the division. On the night of 5 April 1921 all armed enemy patrols were to be attacked. The results were mixed. In Carrickmore Constables O'Brien and Curly were wounded. Frank Curran's Aldrummound Company launched two separate assaults on Mountfield barracks, lasting over six hours. During an ambush in Pomeroy, a sympathetic policeman named Staunton 'created a panic among the police' by shouting that they were 'completely surrounded. The police then rushed across gardens to the barracks.'[17] In Coalisland the RIC returned fire when attacked. Verey light signals brought USC reinforcements from Dungannon, which put the IRA to flight. In the No. 2 area, the IRA seriously wounded Special Constables Fyffe and Torrent in Drumquin and Special Constable Hill in Dromore.[18] The latter incident led to reprisals in Dromore, which demonstrated the different nature of the violence perpetrated by the IRA and the USC.

It has been suggested in some accounts that tit-for-tat sectarian reprisals were carried out in Dromore.[19] However, there is little basis for this claim. It rests largely on the misinterpretation of an event that occurred on 21 November 1920. Sergeant McGowan, who was in charge of the RIC barracks, appeared to have lost his nerve and indiscriminately shot a girl named Eileen O'Doherty in the legs and her brother Dan, an IRA Volunteer, in the face.[20] The RIC reported a rather sketchy ambush in Dromore that night, which may have been exaggerated to cover the wounding of civilians.[21] No reprisals were carried out in Dromore by the IRA in November 1920 and in general very few occurred before the truce. The two civilians killed by the IRA in the period were local poteen-makers.[22] The only incident that can be deemed a reprisal occurred on 17 April 1921 when, during a series of local arms' raids, twenty men fired into the house of Albert Hopper, a local B Special, wounding Hopper and his sister.[23] Following the wounding of Constable Hill in Dromore on 6 April 1921, the USC 'took over the town, fired a large number of shots in the village, broke windows in the R.C. houses, and terrorised the inhabitants generally'. They then shot three Dromore Volunteers on the road outside the village: John Devine, Charles Slevin and Daniel Doherty, who had been wounded by McGowan in November.[24] O'Duffy was determined to 'wipe out the Dromore stain' by emulating the tactics of the USC.[25] But Volunteers from the No. 1 Brigade simply refused to obey his orders to carry out reprisals against USC members in Dromore.[26] A number of possible reasons for this can be advanced. First, O'Duffy's authoritarian style rankled with his officers, perhaps proving that the powers of divisional commanders 'remained limited: persuasion and goodwill worked better than the direct exercise of authority'. Second, in the field the new IRA divisions were 'just too big' and 'too ambitious for their actual resources'.[27] Finally, Seán Corr and W.J. Kelly had a long involvement in republican politics, which made direct reprisals against unionists anathema. It would take a further year of USC reprisals to overcome this restraint. In 1921 rather than encouraging or ignoring counter-reprisals, the IRA restrained the tendency for revenge. They focused on ambushing patrols. For example, at Esker, near Dromore, on 15 May an ambush led to the deaths of Special Constable Magill and Volunteer Edward McCusker.[28] There were also some chance encounters. Following an ambush at Altmore in mid-May, W.J. Kelly was approached in Dungannon by DI Henry Jordan Walshe as he went to mass. Revolvers were drawn and the policeman was wounded in the hip. Kelly, who later recalled that Walshe was not considered 'a very dangerous enemy,' attended devotions, where altar boys hid his revolver in the sacristy.[29]

Between April and May 1921 three raids on barracks and thirteen reported ambushes had taken place. The IRA and Crown forces each suffered four fatalities and five and eleven wounded respectively. There was one civilian casualty. By this stage the Dungannon and Coalisland IRA had taken refuge in the mountains around Galbally, Cappagh and Pomeroy. Knowledge of the local countryside helped members of the rural companies to avoid arrest. ASUs or flying columns were formed in Tyrone in spring 1921, almost a year later than more active counties. However, the genesis was the same: increasing pressure from the Crown forces.[30] Charlie Daly succeeded O'Duffy as commandant in May. Reflecting on the IRA campaign in Tyrone under his watch, he suggested that 'taking into consideration the ... hostile civilian population with superior equipment backed up by Regular Forces, and the apathy of our own civilian population, this area did far more than several Southern Counties situated under far more favourable circumstances'.[31] Until the divisional reorganization of 1921 this was a relatively accurate summary but thereafter activity in the South far outstripped Tyrone.[32]

This is not surprising considering that by early spring 1921 there were 3,515 A and 11,000 B Specials in the six-county area.[33] At the time of the truce there were about fifteen reasonably active IRA companies in Tyrone, each with around fifty men, but only half-a-dozen in each company were armed.[34] Therefore, just over 100 poorly armed Volunteers faced a combined force of almost 3,000 heavily armed, paramilitary police comprising RIC, A and B Specials. By April 1922 there were some 4,300 B Specials in the county.[35] In addition, there were 650 men of the Rifle Brigade in Strabane, a military depot in Omagh and, after the Anglo-Irish Treaty, a battalion of the North Staffordshire Regiment at Clogher.[36] The Tyrone IRA therefore operated under military conditions less favourable than anywhere outside the proclaimed districts in the south-west.[37] An additional factor was that 'half of the Catholic families were not sympathetically disposed to physical force methods'.[38] This is reflected in police reports, which distinguish between moderate and 'evilly disposed' Sinn Féiners.[39] In August 1921 Daly lamented the 'slave-mind and lack of enthusiasm and military spirit in the population'.[40] This was to be expected given the acute fear of reprisals. From June 1920 until the truce in July 1921, fifty people were killed or wounded in the No. 1 and No. 2 Brigade areas. These figures are small in comparison to the national average taken from the beginning of 1920 until the truce.[41] Of the twenty-seven people killed or injured by the IRA, twenty belonged to the Crown forces. The IRA killed one and wounded two civilians. Although the Crown forces killed and injured a similar number, the figures hide the different nature of loyalist violence and intimidation.

The USC campaign in Tyrone was characterized by a lack of discipline and reprisals. Between April and July 1921 the USC carried out forty-eight recorded cases of violent intimidation, compared to eleven by republicans. The vast majority took place in unionist areas or were conducted by groups operating from unionist strongholds. On 19 May B Specials from loyalist Tullyhogue, under Sergeant Hutchinson, raided the Hayden farmhouse in Rock. The Haydens had 'no sympathy with the IRA'.[42] Nevertheless, Joseph Hayden was shot in the head by Hutchinson as he lay in bed and his brother, James, was stabbed with a bayonet and left for dead.[43] When Charles Wickham, divisional commissioner of the RIC, wrote to John McClintock, Tyrone County Commandant USC, that he was 'not satisfied that the B men of this district are sufficiently under control … Anything in the shape of partisan action will bring discredit on the Force', McClintock did nothing.[44] John McKenna, RIC head constable in Cookstown, claimed that McClintock and DI George Hall attempted to pin the murder on three local loyalist guides, one of whom, William McMinn, threatened to tell 'the whole truth' if he was not released from Derry jail.[45] Although the USC administered the law, it did not appear accountable to it. After the transfer of security powers to the Ministry of Home Affairs (MHA) in November 1921, Dawson Bates virtually gave the USC immunity from prosecution. The Hayden case was dropped.[46] Likewise, there were no prosecutions for the Dromore murders of April 1921. Special Constable Andrew Griffin took part in a violent raid in October 1921, just a week after his acquittal for the Dromore reprisal.[47]

The structure of the USC partially explains the nature of the counter-insurgency campaign. The full-time A Specials operated alongside an existing RIC barracks or formed independent platoons. Many ex-servicemen gained employment as an A Special during the post-war economic downturn.[48] The Dungannon RIC district contained seven mixed RIC/A Specials barracks (prior to January 1921 only Dungannon, Coalisland and Pomeroy operated), with a combined strength of 150 men. In addition, the independent A Special No. 7 platoon of fifty men commandeered the Ranfurly Arms Hotel in Dungannon. By early 1922 there were nine A platoons and twenty-eight mixed barracks in Tyrone (see Map 5).[49] The B Specials were part-timers, armed with a rifle and Webley revolver, who mobilized once a week and during emergencies, supposedly accompanied by regular police. Officially, they stored their arms in the 'A' or RIC barracks but in reality kept them at home. There were approximately 1,200 B Specials, concentrated in unionist villages such as Castlecaulfield, Laghey, Newmills and Killyman and in towns such as Dungannon and the Moy, where strengths ranged from 30 to 300 men. Strikingly, the mountainous region from Galbally to Carrickmore contained only twenty-five USC in Colonel Lowry's platoon in Pomeroy.[50] Until his resignation in June 1922, Major Robert Stevenson, a former Irish rugby international who served with the British army in India, was district commandant in Dungannon. He revealed that the regulation requiring the RIC to accompany all patrols was ignored as was 'the original arrangement that no raids could be undertaken by S.C. without consultation and consent.' In his view, the B Special represented 'the ordinary Protestant countryman and in many cases corner boys', being 'supplied with arms and clothing by his Government and "authorised" to get "on top", as it were, of his R.C. neighbours [who] they have always been taught to hate'.[51]

Between April and June both IRA and USC employed terrorist tactics. In this cycle of violence, the unionist *Tyrone Courier* reported how both the IRA and USC raided a local constitutional nationalist, John Monaghan of Clogher. The IRA caused no harm; the USC put a rifle in his mouth before relenting, they then 'beat him and burned his house'.[52] To some extent, this incident typified the general trend. Republican actions predominantly consisted of arms raids and military operations, and were usually followed by very violent and often indiscriminate counter-reprisals. The USC around Cookstown epitomized this tendency. When the Kildress IRA fired on Cookstown Specials at Drumshanbo on 23 April, the USC shot a Catholic civilian, Michael Lagan, through the lungs and wounded his sister, Kate.[53] On 30 April they raided eight nationalist houses in neighbouring Killybearn, blindfolded the male occupants and marched them several miles to a field, where mock executions were carried out. Francis Neill was seriously injured and John Corey bayoneted.[54] An ambush on a mixed patrol of RIC and USC by the Dunamore IRA on 29 June saw USC from Cookstown and Dungannon travel out to raid Dunamore village on 3 July.[55] They burned the parochial hall; shot John Monaghan, a 70-year-old farmer; destroyed several houses and threatened to shoot a young girl if she did not 'sign a document', testifying 'that no harm had been done'.[56] John McKenna claimed that the IRA ambush represented one of a number of fictitious incidents designed 'to do something to keep the B men quiet' but his cynicism appears misplaced.[57] The announcement of a truce on 11 July brought no immediate end to USC violence. When the RIC arrested a local man on 12 July for taking a sash from a Cookstown Orangeman, a loyalist crowd attacked the police to get the man, who fled to nationalist Orritor Street. That night there were two separate attacks on the area. Armed gangs fired into twelve Catholic houses and razed one to the ground.[58] The loyalists of Cookstown carried out a relentless campaign of intimidation against local nationalists, which continued long after the defeat of the local IRA in 1922.[59]

The USC represented a highly partisan, loyalist militia, hardened by the brutality of trench warfare, with official *carte blanche* to 'get on top' of nationalist neighbours. The level of violence depended on the concentration of unionists, the commander's disposition and whether the regular police obstructed, ignored or encouraged intimidation. Nationalist mid-Tyrone was relatively quiet as the RIC restrained the B men. James McElduff recalled that after the attack on Mountfield barracks on 5 May 1921, the local RIC sergeant overheard 'a couple of B men saying among themselves: "We are going to do a Dromore at the McElduff's. You will do no such thing, said he, I will arrest those men".'[60] Between June 1920 and July 1921, of the twenty-three people killed and wounded by Crown forces, only three resulted from military engagements. Eight were reprisals on known republicans but twelve were reprisals against nationalist civilians. The police also injured an IRA Volunteer during a round-up in

September 1920. All the reprisals occurred in strongly unionist areas such as Cookstown or in the isolated republican area around Fintona, Dromore and Trillick. Between June 1920 and July 1921, the IRA committed twenty-two incidents of violent intimidation compared to seventy-six by Crown forces. The USC essentially executed an indiscriminate, terrorist campaign against the entire nationalist population, something acknowledged by its own leaders such as Stevenson.

If the IRA were struggling militarily, then politically republican prospects appeared similarly bleak as the British pushed ahead with elections to the Belfast parliament. On his return from America, de Valera secured £2,000 for propaganda purposes, half provided from Dáil funds and half from the SF party fund.[61] He also promptly contacted Joseph MacRory, bishop of Down and Connor.[62] Despite professed non-sectarianism on northern matters, de Valera generally bowed to the Catholic Church. On 17 February he informed MacRory that, after vainly seeking Devlin's withdrawal, the two agreed on a joint abstentionist policy, giving 'the next preferences to the other Nationalist group of candidates'.[63] The SF standing committee confirmed, however, that only republicans would sit in Dáil Éireann.[64] SF's resolve over abstention and strength outside Belfast left the IPP with a choice between entering parliament 'with a ragged regiment of 6 or 8 Nationalists confronted by the Orangemen on one side, and with fire in the back from the Sinn Féiners on the other' or abstention.[65] T.P. O'Connor duly informed John Dillon that 'the Nationalists are determined not to give even the fig leaf of respectability to the whole rotten arrangement by attending the [northern] Parliament.'[66] Just before the poll Dillon observed that 'within the next six weeks, de Valera and his fighting crowd must ... either ... make peace on the basis of dropping the demand for a Republic, and leaving Ulster alone – or ... continue the war – in face of a greatly intensified military regime'.[67] His own party merely sought to survive. Across the six counties, the combined constitutional nationalist and SF vote reached just over thirty-two per cent. Under PR, both parties won six seats out of a total of fifty-two. SF received twenty per cent of the poll, the IPP eleven.[68] Carson claimed that 'it will take a very bold statesman after this demonstration to suggest putting the six counties under Home Rule in Dublin!'[69] The result confirmed de Valera's pre-election warning that 'Unless we are able to secure about say ten members ... it would be inadvisable to show up our weakness' as 'the British will use it in a world-wide way to make it appear that partition was justified'.[70]

Nationalists of all hues won four seats in the eight-seat Fermanagh and Tyrone constituency. With a combined vote of 33,927, Arthur Griffith, Seán Milroy and Seán O'Mahony were returned for SF.[71] The IPP won 12,681 votes; Harbison was elected on the tenth count, a relatively successful result given that Devlin could only muster 40 'mostly old men' out of an expected 400 at the UIL convention.[72] Unionists won the remaining four seats with a combined poll of 37,927. William Coote and Edward Archdale, elected MP North Fermanagh in 1918, polled strongly. William Miller represented north-west Tyrone and James Cooper, rural Fermanagh. The elections heralded the opening of the northern parliament on 22 June.[73] Increasingly, Tyrone constitutionalists looked to the Dáil ministry, not Joe Devlin in Belfast, for direction. In the Westminster elections in November 1922 the two seats in the Fermanagh and Tyrone constituency were won by Harbison and SF's Cahir Healy, both of whom accepted the direction of the emerging Free State government.

The Belfast parliament created a de facto unionist administration, which Lloyd George exploited during the Treaty negotiations in the autumn of 1921. In July T.P. O'Connor told Dillon that Lord Birkenhead was 'quite ready to be liberal to Ireland now that he and his friends had secured the safety of Orange Ulster.'[74] On the inauguration of the northern parliament, Hamar Greenwood congratulated Craig for 'making strong the cement of Empire'.[75] The king's speech at the opening of the parliament hastened the agreement of the July truce. The No. 1 Brigade responded to the news by burning Doon's creamery in Kildress. The IRA viewed the truce as a mere cessation and set about preparing for a fresh campaign for the Republic should the negotiations fail. Charlie Daly, for example, believed the truce 'was only a matter of a few weeks'.[76] The politicians in SF and their nationalist allies, however, hoped that any settlement would reassert the primacy of politics and strengthen their influence over events which had waned during the previous year.

In preparation for the Treaty negotiations the Dáil ministry consulted the SF leadership in Tyrone regarding partition but the Dáil's northern policy lacked coherence. A northern subcommittee had been established in August 1920 but, according to Seán Milroy, who was a member, it was ineffective.[77] Griffith suggested that its role was 'to organize the North and look after the civil side only. The IRA ... will look after the military side.' He contended that with a third of the population 'utterly opposed to Partition and thoroughly organized that Parliament could not function'.[78] The northern subcommittee met in the Mansion House in Dublin on 24 August and in St Mary's hall, Belfast on 6 September with Murnaghan presiding.[79] Milroy was concerned by 'an atmosphere of aloofness on the part of the Volunteers, and an implied attitude that the SF Clubs were not serving any useful purpose and that it was a waste of time and energy to trouble about them'.[80] However, Vincent Shields, the IRA's liaison officer, failed to have any Volunteers co-opted on the committee because politicians maintained that they should concentrate on the military side.[81] This military-political divide in SF was sharply exposed by the Anglo-Irish Treaty of December 1921. In September 1921 another northern advisory committee was established to gather information on partition for the Irish negotiating team in London; Eoin MacNeill was chairman and Milroy secretary.[82] Father

O'Doherty of Omagh betrayed his former political allegiance by recommending Tim Healy as the 'most reliable' authority on northern gerrymandering.[83] Cahir Healy advised a 'small commission of 3 or 4 experts', tasked with demonstrating 'how unworkable partition is from the local government standpoint'.[84] Milroy appointed George Murnaghan as the first expert.[85] He remained the SF and then pro-Treaty man in Tyrone for the next year and duly joined the negotiating team in London.[86]

In early October, just before departing for London, Milroy's committee met with northern nationalists, but not with Devlin. Concerns regarding control of local government and education dominated the discussions. Harbison claimed that the Belfast administration's control over the franchise left nationalists at its mercy. He sought a guarantee to protect PR, the only 'chance of retaining the power we have'. The clergy feared losing control over education. Fr O'Doherty of Strabane, for example, claimed that partition 'would mean the placing of the Catholic schools under the management of the Ulster bigots'.[87] Little now distinguished Hibernians from constitutional separatist Sinn Féiners. A year later Dillon dismissed Harbison as 'an utterly worthless, selfish person completely in the hands of the Murnaghan gang', who represented a 'poisonous little faction' in Tyrone.[88] This grouping's objectives reflected its constituent elements: middle-class politicians hungry for local government patronage and Catholic clergy obsessed with denominational education. Their political allegiance fluctuated, depending on prevailing circumstances, yet class interests remained constant: to preserve their dominant role within Catholic society.

During the autumn the wider nationalist community suffered concerted attacks from the demobilized USC.[89] James Mayne of Cookstown wrote to Austin Stack to propose a co-ordinated SF chapel gate 'memorial' against Tyrone's inclusion in NI.[90] Instead de Valera suggested a deputation 'from the whole Northern area', on 'a national' rather than 'sectarian basis', which would operate through Milroy's committee.[91] He then sought Dr James Gillespie's advice. Replying on 23 November, Gillespie reassured de Valera that northerners would stand by any London agreement and recommended Eoin MacNeill, Bishops McHugh and MacRory and, interestingly, Joe Devlin as delegates, adding that 'it is a religious matter in the N.E.'[92] In a direct reference to the ongoing Treaty negotiations, he expressed astonishment 'that the Orange Cabinet in Belfast' received security powers before 'the negotiations ... ended one way or the other'.[93] His remarks on the transfer of security powers indicated the increasing disquiet in west Ulster that the Irish negotiating team had been outmanoeuvred, an opinion confirmed by salacious rumours of Michael Collins's conduct in London, which Eoin MacNeill encountered on his tour of Fermanagh.[94] De Valera then agreed to Mayne's request to meet representatives of nationalist opinion on 8 December, with T.J. Harbison and Dr Gillespie acting for Tyrone.[95] The delegation did not mention partition and instead concentrated on 'Education – the danger of secularizing it – and the question of the Franchise, so that local governing bodies should not have the power of gerry-mandering the Franchise'.[96] These represented the limits of the group's aspirations.

From the outset, Tyrone's 'Sinn Féin' county council prevaricated on non-recognition of Craig's new administration and shuffled pragmatically between the Dáil and Belfast. This changed during the Treaty negotiations. Murnaghan's main task was to collate maps based on local electoral districts for Griffith and Collins, whom de Valera had instructed to break negotiations, if necessary, on partition.[97] Therefore, in order to strengthen the negotiating position, on 28 November nationalist-controlled councils in Tyrone and Fermanagh 'decided … to cut all connection with the Belfast Parliament' in favour of the Dáil.[98] At Fermanagh County Council in November 1921 unionist councillors objected to this, claiming that 'Mr Healy's Sinn Fein majority' came from 'the servant boys and herds who came in from other counties to get a living and work for farmers who were Protestants'.[99] The Dáil, through MacNeill, proposed that northern nationalists follow a policy of passive resistance and non-recognition. This characterized Dublin's approach for the next two years.[100] Accordingly, on 3 December Tyrone County Council rejected the 'arbitrary, new-fangled, and universally unnatural boundary', pledging 'to oppose it steadfastly and to make the fullest use of our rights to nullify it'.[101]

Two days earlier, however, the Belfast cabinet had decided to disband 'recal-citrant' councils in Fermanagh and Tyrone.[102] The transfer of security powers enabled the MHA to execute this decree even before the signing of the Treaty. On 5 December the police raided Omagh courthouse and suspended the county council. Faced with suspension, the ever pragmatic nationalist politicians, temporarily and under protest, accepted the northern government.[103] When Cosgrave's Dáil ministry queried the volte-face, the council replied that 'in view of the altered political situation, and with a desire to promote a peaceful settle-ment', all communication would 'for the present', be sent 'to the Northern Minister of Local Government', thereby nominally recognizing its authority.[104] Cosgrave retorted that this 'at least has the merit of safety, and doubtless in six months' time' you 'will be able to judge more accurately, as to which of the contending parties is likely to emerge triumphant', with pragmatism 'the deciding factor rather than say any consideration of right or justice'.[105] In the meantime, however, the Treaty had been signed and Cosgrave's vote at the Dáil cabinet had proved decisive in its acceptance. Tyrone County Councillors were not alone in sacrificing principle on the altar of pragmatism.

While the political side of the revolution suffered death by committee, the military men appeared to resent the restraints placed on them by the talks in London. The Tyrone IRA honoured their interpretation of the truce by ceasing attacks on police, civilians and property but not drilling or training in arms. The

Belfast boycott also continued at a more concerted level. The truce period witnessed one case of republican intimidation when a Drumquin Volunteer was beaten and tied to the chapel gates with a sign round his neck announcing his expulsion.[106] Above all, the local IRA's preparation for future hostilities breached the spirit of the truce. Throughout the summer and autumn IRA veterans headed north to train local units. Dan Breen spent five weeks in Tyrone during August and September.[107] Donegal's Joe Sweeney recalled that Breen's party was 'chased out [by USC] one night in their shirts with their clothes under their arms'.[108] As in the south, the Tyrone IRA received an influx of Trucileers. Mick Gallagher wondered: 'Where did ye get all these men? I didn't think there was as many men in the whole division during the war'.[109] By October 1921 the 2nd ND had increased from less than 500 to 1,350 Volunteers: 399 in the No. 1 (Dungannon) Brigade, 432 in the No. 2 (Omagh) and 192 in the newly-formed Gortin Battalion.[110] The Cookstown RIC suggested this growth was based on a degree of compulsion.[111] The town's USC claimed however that recruitment relied on 'the fascination which their style of crime undoubtedly exercises over a certain type of Irish mind'.[112] Nonetheless, Seán Corr 'looked on the men who remained out of the Volunteers during the Tan War as wanting in national outlook and of little military use'.[113]

Daly oversaw IRA training at all levels. This culminated in the establishment of brigade camps on 11 September. One week later the IRA set up a divisional camp at Sperrin Lodge, where they mounted three machine-guns.[114] Daly sought to inculcate a spirit of self-reliance and reported 'a big improvement all round', the Volunteers 'at last, beginning to realise that they are soldiers and form part of an army'.[115] Nevertheless, the accidental death of James McNally led the Director of Training to complain that 'if Volunteers in training do not know sufficient about guns to keep them from pointing the barrel towards one's body, then they should not have guns'.[116] Securing sufficient arms remained a problem in Tyrone and little real progress was made during the truce period.[117] In September the 2nd ND had only 109 rifles with seventy bullet per weapon, 39 automatics with five bullets a piece, 153 revolvers with six bullets each, 204 shotguns and 92 grenades.[118] In October Daly claimed that the Cookstown IRA were completely 'unarmed'.[119] Even as late as the end of February 1922 the Carrickmore area had only 40 serviceable rifles, 300 shotguns and 100 revolvers.[120]

The British decision to negotiate with SF left many unionists fearful for the survival of the fledging NI state, or at least Tyrone's place in it. The British cabinet wanted the Treaty negotiations to hinge on the imperial question and believed that a breakdown over Fermanagh and Tyrone would be 'far less favourable to us than if the break came on the refusal to accept British sovereignty and Empire'.[121] It feigned impartiality on Ulster and partition to secure agreement. The B Specials were suspended and responsibility for northern security remained with Dublin Castle until the transfer of security powers on 22 November. The Tyrone IRA took advantage of this to test the new northern administration. The IRA regularly wore uniforms in unionist areas, where any republican activity was provocative. SF courts openly challenged the local petty sessions in Aughnacloy, Clogher and the Moy, while SF police patrolled the major towns and villages apart from Cookstown.[122] The IRA detained suspected criminals at an improvised prison at Cranagh Hall.[123] Wickham did not confine the RIC to barracks and so parallel systems of civil and military organization vied with one another. Dublin Castle directed complaints from the local RIC to Vincent Shields or Eoin O'Duffy, IRA liaison for Ulster, who had an office in St Mary's hall, Belfast. He advised that 'arrests should not be made in the first instance.'[124] One policeman complained that 'the so-called Liaison Officers are of the corner-boy type and could not enforce order even if they wished to do so'.[125] On 17 September McClintock requested of O'Duffy that Plumbridge barracks be re-opened because IRA activity in Cranagh had local loyalists 'in a great state of excitement'.[126] Daly objected because the barracks gave 'the enemy a strategic position', which 'would mean one more link in the chain of posts by which the most important area in the Division is encircled'.[127]

Loyalists and the RIC were disturbed that the authorities allowed the IRA to train and grow during the truce. Wickham warned Dublin Castle that 'if some action is not taken to put a stop to this drilling, the Unionists will take the law into their own hands.' Unionists could not understand 'the open preparation for hostilities by a rebel organization' in a county with 'its own elected Government … against which these preparations are primarily directed'.[128] This was exacerbated by the standing down of the B Specials. On 15 August a demobilized B Special fired into a passing republican band, killing John O'Neill of Coalisland and wounding another.[129] With a cortège of 'about 1,500 men', the local IRA used O'Neill's funeral 'to give a demonstration of strength and military efficiency'. DI Walshe admitted that the 'military precision' was 'a revelation' to him.[130] Complaints about firing a volley over O'Neill's grave were rebuffed by O'Duffy.[131] The coexistence of republican and Crown forces in the south during the truce was possible because a future 'police' war was implausible. That was not the case in Tyrone, where the republicans' counter-state merely fuelled unionist resentment.

The importance of restoring the USC as a means of restraining loyalism was voiced by Wilfrid Spender, head of the reconstituted UVF, during a visit to London in early August.[132] Efforts at reorganization were made in secret. This allowed Wickham to inform the northern cabinet in mid-August that 'they could, with the forces at their disposal, deal with any situation that may arise'.[133] The truce appeared to confirm unionist fears about the Dublin Castle administration. On 31 August the northern cabinet discussed the violence in Belfast. Bates blamed IRA activity, advocated internment and advised the remobilization of the USC because 'action would be taken by the Unionist element with disastrous results'.[134] Andy Cope, the principal British civil servant in Dublin, vetoed remobilization because the 'government would be presented as having taken a party side ... and both sides were shooting'.[135] For the first time the government had rejected unionist demands. In effect, British policy shifted from unconditional support for unionism to a balancing act between assuaging northern security concerns and attempting to split SF along lines conducive to a non-republican southern settlement.

In light of changed circumstances, Craig played a double game. He adhered to British requests on one hand, but gave unofficial sanction to the UVF's re-organization on the other.[136] This allowed him a degree of control over extreme loyalists. He informed Crawford, whom he tasked with the enterprise, that 'we must have as a force one that will do nothing illegal. When we call them out they must come out as forces of the Crown.'[137] On 20 October the *Courier* reported the reformation of the Ulster Volunteers because of 'the inactivity of the government to combat the actions of Sinn Feiners who by establishing camps in the middle of unionist districts and openly drilling with rifles and machine-guns are menacing the loyalist people.'[138] The remobilization of the UVF allowed Craig to use warnings of growing loyalist militancy in his petitions to the British government for an immediate transfer of security powers while publicly remaining on the side of law and order.[139] This is further discussed in the next chapter. As loyalist patience wore thin, however, the newly reformed UVF stepped up its activity and the intensity of unofficial intimidation continued. The Dungannon No. 7 mobile platoon carried out a series of provocative route marches to Omagh in October. The RIC suggested that nationalists regarded this 'as a recruiting march for the UVF'.[140] In 'retaliation for military manoeuvres gone through recently by the Platoon of Specials in Ranfurly Park', the IRA drilled and marched from Dungannon to Edendork on 23 November.[141]

Once again Cookstown witnessed concerted loyalist activity. When the IRA liaison officer complained, DI Hall sardonically replied that 'the UVF are not partner to the truce and hence this cannot be reckoned a breach'.[142] In what Hamar Greenwood called an 'incident of a somewhat sensational character', local B men, now Ulster Volunteers, attacked an IRA party outside Cookstown on 15 September. John Glackin was wounded, twenty-five were taken prisoner and eight loaded revolvers were seized.[143] The *Tyrone Courier*, unaware that Craig had sanctioned remobilization, blamed the northern administration, which dithered, while 'the young Protestant farmers in the neighbourhood' mostly B Specials Constables, had taken 'independent action'.[144] The following week 'Orange gunmen' ambushed a party of Cookstown GAA supporters returning from Ballinascreen.[145] In October disbanded B men launched a raiding campaign on republican houses.[146] Cookstown Sinn Féiners such as James Gillespie, Daniel Chambers and James Mayne called a meeting to protest at 'organized lawlessness and terrorism'.[147] In October Daly requested arms from GHQ because of 'Orange aggressiveness and cowardly attacks on defenceless people'. He stated that the 'position of our people in this district was always pretty bad but since the Truce it has become desprate [sic]'. Incidents had become so numerous and serious 'that Truce or no Truce the Volunteers must take action to protect themselves and their people'.[148] GHQ requested a report on the extent of loyalist forces and the location of 'the bad Orange centres' on a divisional map. This suggests that the Treaty negotiations took precedence over protecting local nationalists.[149]

In early December an impatient Daly ordered the drawing up of a blacklist of the 'most actively hostile Orange houses' throughout the divisional area in readiness for when hostilities recommenced. 'The intention is to do as much damage to property and inflict as many casualties as possible at the very outset'. Daly ordered his men to destroy the secret order once it had been read and noted.[150] He envisaged that 'each company … will be a self-contained unit', acting 'by itself and without any outside assistance' and ordered the creation of outposts to protect IRA positions from enemy reprisals.[151]

The Tyrone IRA had at best held its own in 1921. The differing nature of the IRA and USC campaigns would find further expression after the Anglo-Irish Treaty during the IRA's abortive and stop-start northern campaign of 1922. It was clear, however, that the IRA's prospects of overthrowing the new northern administration in Tyrone appeared bleak in terms of resources and organization, despite the relative progress made during the truce. Much would hinge on the outcome of the Treaty negotiations. The Tyrone example suggests that the Dáil plenipotentiaries entered the talks with a far from coherent northern policy. There was an obvious gap between Griffithite dogma regarding passive resistance and the reality of a divided political territory, where unionist intransigence and military prowess undermined SF's non-sectarian rhetoric.

In 1917 Fr Michael O'Flanagan told Sinn Féiners in Omagh that their demand for 'an Irish democracy, broad, tolerant and reasonably democratic' would entice 'all that was best in the Orange ranks to join their movement'.[152] But SF was built to defeat constitutional nationalism not to convert Ulster unionism. To that end its northern policy involved co-opting middle-class former constitutionalists, often with little interest in a genuinely popular movement, to facilitate electoral success in Ulster. The petit-bourgeois nationalist revolution never gave serious consideration to fulfilling the aims of the Dáil's Democratic Programme to attract working-class support. Neither was culturally-inspired separatism likely to attract middle- and upper-class unionism. In 1922 Lord Londonderry informed Hugh Kennedy, Irish Free State attorney-general, that he could not 'subscribe to the littleness of thought which envisages a tiny little island speaking a language which no one understands, self-centred, proud and unduly sensitive'.[153] The Dáil's campaign of passive resistance hardly met with universal success even in areas where it could claim unquestioned electoral support. Griffith's ruminations about a third of the population passively rendering a northern parliament, backed by a formidable military capacity financed from London, inoperative were naive. The dispassionate observer might suggest that the Treaty negotiations represented a case of men against boys.

8 Endgame in Tyrone

In Inverness on 7 September 1921 at a cabinet conference to discuss British strategy in the Treaty negotiations, Lloyd George quipped that 'men will die for Throne and empire. I do not know who will die for Tyrone and Fermanagh'.[1] Once again the dreary steeples of Tyrone had emerged at the level of high politics. The final consolidation of six-county partition took place in 1922. Although Article 12 of the Treaty proposed a Boundary Commission to adjudicate on the border, significant change was never likely. In Tyrone the moderate SF leadership and their constitutionalist allies believed the boundary would shift according to local nationalist majorities and supported the campaign of non-recognition advocated by the Free State. The republican grass roots and IRA stood on principle and, as late as April 1922, thirty-two out of thirty-four SF cumainn rejected the Treaty. Nevertheless, the wider nationalist community opposed partition rather than the Treaty *per se*. The 2nd ND's campaigns in March and May 1922 also sought to undermine partition militarily, efforts hindered by the emerging IRA split and the onset of civil war. From the beginning of 1922 until the end of 1923, the two communities faced new realities following the transfer of security powers to NI. The unionist government zealously deployed these powers to safeguard its territory and to consolidate its control over majority nationalist Tyrone.

The British government gradually realized that coercion in Ireland exceeded the limits of practical politics. While the approach changed, its basis did not. Whether policy vacillated between pinprick coercion, all-out repression and diplomacy, wider imperial interests remained paramount. Could a government whose representatives had redrawn the boundaries of Europe on the principle of the freedom of small nations ignore the clear mandate for Irish self-determination in Tyrone? Always mindful of public opinion, the British cabinet determined that, if the talks collapsed, empire versus republic rather than Ulster would constitute the primary issue.[2] The Treaty negotiations may be divided into three phases. The first from 11 October to 3 November consisted of seven plenary sessions and three sub-conferences. The Irish were willing to compromise on a range of issues for the sake of 'essential unity'. Then, from 5 to 16 November, Lloyd George vainly and disingenuously attempted to persuade Craig to compromise. The overture, nevertheless, engineered Griffith's acceptance of partition. Armed with this concession, the prime minister pressed a settlement on the Irish delegation and threatened war if an agreement was not reached.

Lloyd George manipulated his position as the Liberal head of a Conservative cabinet to dupe the Irish plenipotentiaries. The leading Conservatives, who dominated the cabinet, recognized that compromise with SF moderates would secure vital interests while a renewed military campaign might meet popular disapproval. The Tory die-hard element, however, viewed this as tantamount to surrender and unsuccessfully challenged the negotiations in parliament. They then scheduled another vote for the party conference in Liverpool on 19 November. Crucially, the government required Ulster Unionist support at the conference to survive. James Craig engineered tacit acceptance for the transfer of security powers, which had been withheld since the truce, in return for abstention in the conference vote.[3] Lloyd George duly agreed on 10 November. The next day he offered southern dominion status and loose essential Irish unity to Craig, who promptly rejected this, despite the bluff of 'civil war ... if the North did not follow this advice'.[4] The Prime Minister's gesture seemed to prove his good faith to Collins and Griffith but it outmanoeuvred them. His assertion that 'we do not care in the slightest degree where Irishmen put Tyrone and Fermanagh' contradicted his cabinet's previous determination not to break on the issue.[5] Later that month Erskine Childers, the Irish delegation's secretary, complained that the British had not made a concession since July.[6]

The Irish plenipotentiaries' analysis bore striking similarities to the British one: the coercion of Ulster unionists was impossible, compromise on the Republic inevitable and any break should be on Irish terms and principally on partition not the Empire. They were to relay any decision to the Dáil cabinet prior to signing; this they did not do. In addition, de Valera had instructed Griffith not to let Fermanagh and Tyrone go 'without a definite vote of the people'.[7] On 12 November, after Craig's rejection of essential unity, Griffith unilaterally gave a written promise not to obstruct the Boundary Commission idea. In one stroke he nullified the option of breaking on partition. Writing to de Valera, he believed that the commission would give 'us most of Tyrone, Fermanagh, and part of Armagh, Down'.[8] Lloyd George indicated significant territorial transfer. When the Dáil cabinet met in Dublin on 3 December, de Valera claimed that the proposed settlement required amendment on the oath and on Ulster. The Irish delegation was to return to London, 'prepared to face the consequences – war or no war'; Griffith left with instructions to 'try and put the blame on Ulster'.[9] At the crucial conference on 5 December, however, Lloyd George, 'with the air of a conjuror pulling a rabbit out of a hat',[10] revealed 'Griffith's earlier undertaking regarding the Boundary Commission' and the Irish negotiators caved in.[11] The Boundary Commission idea was both vague and delusionary, something Collins acknowledged. Arguably, he and Griffith shelved the partition issue in order to reach terms, a decision hastened by the threat of 'immediate and terrible war'. There is, therefore, an inexorable logic to John Regan's conclusion that

> Griffith and Collins became, through the advocacy of the treaty and the threat of renewed British violence, the arbiters of British policy in

Southern Ireland. The treatyite army fought the civil war as the proxy of the British state whatever about its aspirations towards a stepping-stone republic or freedom to achieve freedom.[12]

There was significant discrepancy between what Griffith agreed on 12 November, that the redrawn border be 'in accordance with the wishes of the inhabitants' and the actual proviso in Article 12 that such wishes be 'compatible with economic and geographic conditions'.[13] At a cabinet meeting on 6 December Lloyd George hailed 'Ulster – the rock upon which all previous efforts had been shattered' as the central triumph because 'the extremists had accepted a situation in which it was open to Ulster to contract out of a united Ireland'. Significantly, he suggested that the Boundary Commission 'would possibly give Ulster more than she would lose'.[14] The government then gave public and private assurances to outraged Ulster unionists that boundary change would not exceed minor rectification, especially after the Treaty had passed through Dáil Éireann.[15]

As the Treaty negotiations took place, the northern administration lost little time in consolidating its position in Tyrone. On 9 November Wickham, unbeknownst to Dublin Castle, announced 'a plan for the co-ordination into military units of unauthorised loyalist defence forces'.[16] The Wickham circular not only breached the GOIA but also predated the transfer of security powers on 22 November and the signing of the Treaty on 6 December. The re-mobilization of the USC represented the first step in unionist consolidation. The obliteration of the rival republican system, beginning with county councils, represented the second.[17] Wickham then ordered the suppression of all republican courts and IRA training camps.[18] On 21 December the USC broke up the IRA headquarters at Cranagh Hall.[19] On 6 January they arrested the officer corps of No. 2 Brigade in Dromore.[20] Bemoaning the 'loss of twenty important officers', Charlie Daly believed that the IRA was working under 'practically war conditions' and that the northern police offensive made it 'impossible to carry on.'[21] Within a month of the security transfer, the Belfast government had effectively neutralized one of Tyrone's two IRA brigades and destroyed any elements of a republican counter-state. Local government would henceforth be under unionist control. The IRA remained passive, honouring a truce the unionists never recognized.

Partition barely registered during the Treaty debates in the Dáil, primarily because few recognized the ambiguities contained in Article 12. Frank Aiken claimed that many republicans believed the Boundary Commission would reduce the northern area so as to render a functioning parliament 'impossible'.[22] Patrick McCartan, the sole Tyroneman in the house, spoke before the Christmas recess. His contribution epitomized northern confusion and inner turmoil. Standing 'uncompromisingly for an Irish Republic', he interrupted Seán

Milroy's speech to denounce the sell-out and betrayal of northern nationalists before incongruously supporting the Treaty: 'I as a Republican will not endorse it, but I will not vote for chaos. Then I will not vote against it.'[23] Seán MacEntee, the Belfast republican, perceptively argued that if the people were 'aware of the real effect of Article 12 … they would reject the Treaty' as they had IPP proposals in 1916 and 1918.'[24] When Dáil Éireann eventually voted on 7 January 1922, 64 supported the Treaty, 57 opposed it and 3 abstained. In Tyrone, the local government bodies, led by those who met de Valera on 8 December, sent a series of letters to Seán O'Mahony, the Tyrone anti-Treatyite TD, criticizing his position. The Murnaghanite Mid-Tyrone comhairle ceantair was 'satisfied that the Treaty confers practical Freedom on the Country, and that our interests in the North shall be safeguarded.'[25]

The week after the Dáil vote, Louis Walsh wrote to Bishop MacRory, a fellow Treatyite, outlining a definite northern policy. With force 'out of the question', he suggested that, the Provisional Government ought 'to admit that the Treaty virtually recognizes the Belfast Parliament' and obtain guarantees regarding civil liberties, Catholic education and an end to 'the reign of Terror in Belfast' in return for the termination of the Belfast boycott.[26] In London on 21 January Collins, the provisional government chairman, essentially agreed such arrangements with James Craig. Under the first 'pact', Collins promised to end the Belfast boycott and Craig to facilitate the return of expelled Catholic shipyard workers. There were also tentative moves by both men to come to a more acceptable version of the Council of Ireland proposed under the GOIA and the Treaty.[27] Ronald McNeill applauded Craig's 'stroke of real statesmanship', in obtaining 'an acknowledgement of Partition by the Sinn Fein representatives'.[28] Significantly, both also agreed to shelve the Boundary Commission and selected Tyronemen, George Murnaghan and William Miller, to prepare for bilateral negotiations on the border.[29] Collins still anticipated significant territorial transfer and ordered Murnaghan to get 'maps into proper shape'.[30] Collins wished to make the boundary issue 'one solely between Irishmen' and recognized that 'a generous financial gesture' on education would placate the Catholic Church.[31] Therefore, he detailed the payment of northern teachers, insisted that the 'peace policy should get a fair chance', but reaffirmed that 'non-recognition of the northern parliament was essential – otherwise they would have nothing to bargain on with Sir James Craig'.[32]

Nationalists in Tyrone now faced a three-way split, for in addition to the diminishing division between respectable Sinn Féiners and IPP adherents, the traditional republican community re-emerged from its self-imposed political exile. The pact did not meet with popular approval in Tyrone. On 1 February James Mayne complained to Collins of 'a strong feeling around here … that you are conceding too much to Sir James Craig', especially as life under the USC was 'hell'. He then warned Collins that 'the Irish Party were swept aside' because of partition and if Tyrone was thrown to the 'Ulster wolves an agitation will arise that will shake the foundation of the Free State.'[33] Mayne was secretary of the East and South Tyrone comhairle ceantair, which, under the influence of IRA members from the Thomas Clarke cumann in Dungannon, had rejected the Treaty.[34]

The pact collapsed on 2 February because Collins claimed that Lloyd George had promised the transfer of 'large territories not merely a boundary line as Sir James Craig was given to understand privately by several British Ministers' and by Lloyd George in parliament.[35] That night Collins told a northern delegation that, regarding partition, 'they were only trying to force an open door and using unnecessary energy in doing so'.[36] Griffith argued that 'the Treaty recognizes the essential unity of Ireland' and that government policy reflected de Valera's previous admission that 'he would not coerce Unionist Ulster, but equally we shall not permit Nationalist Ulster to be coerced'.[37] Nevertheless, Craig reaffirmed British assurances about 'a mere rectification', arguing that Collins had been 'driven by extremists to reverse his former policy of conciliation'. He then claimed that Murnaghan's maps demonstrated that Collins 'had already promised to bring into the Free State almost half of Northern Ireland, including the counties of Fermanagh, Tyrone, large parts of counties Armagh and Down, Derry City, Enniskillen and Newry'.[38] Similarly, John Dillon believed that 'Collins and Griffith are in a desperate difficulty ... If they give in, the Catholics of Tyrone, Fermanagh and Derry &c will be furious', but, 'if they commit themselves to a fight with Craig on this question, *it will destroy the Provisional Government and the Treaty*.' He concluded that 'their position is so weakened by the Republicans that they are afraid to quarrel with ... Tyrone and Fermanagh and their present proposals to Craig are preposterous'. Craig would, Dillon claimed, risk assassination, 'if he yielded to them'.[39]

SF organized an extraordinary ard fheis on 7 February 1922. A concerned Murnaghan and O'Shiel took a renewed interest in the SF standing committee, with O'Shiel seconding Collins's motion that delegates be elected by secret ballot.[40] The ard fheis sparked a republican challenge to the respectable Sinn Féiners, whom the Tyrone IRA had largely left to their own devices since 1919. The *Herald* reported that 'as far as we can learn practically all the clubs have appointed delegates who are opponents of the Treaty'. The Omagh cumann elected two Volunteers, Thomas Holland and former prisoner John Mackin. They defeated Murnaghan and Patrick Cunningham, a pro-Treaty county councillor.[41] Murnaghan criticized IRA dictation in the selection of delegates, yet his position on the Treaty did not reflect that of the majority of Tyrone republicans.[42] Eventually on 3 March 1922 the standing committee adjourned the ard fheis for three months 'to prevent a split within Sinn Féin', 'avert the danger' of 'an immediate election', and 'to give an opportunity to the signatories of the London agreement to draft a constitution'.[43]

The SF party did, however, establish yet another northern advisory committee made up of pro and anti-Treaty members. Griffith urged O'Shiel 'to put the point of view of the Provisional Government before our friends, that Clause 12 of the Treaty still stood' and they 'intended to extend economic tariffs against the north'.[44] The committee met in Belfast on 7 March and proposed an aggressive non-recognition policy, a reversal of Tyrone county council's previous recognition of Craig's government, the establishment of SF arbitration courts and a military offensive in the six counties. Clearly alarmed, O'Shiel proposed that the republican committee 'do not put into operation any resolution' until 'sanctioned by the Officer Board of the Sinn Féin organization'.[45] McCartan summarized the situation at the end of March: 'the IRA in the six counties are all anti-Treaty almost to a man. They, however, are out against partition rather than the Treaty. They feel they have been let down'.[46] As late as April 1922, 32 out of 34 SF branches came out against the Treaty, partly in reaction to the abortive second Craig–Collins pact. They also jettisoned the moderate Murnaghan as the county's representative at the ard fheis.[47] This mirrored the position of the Tyrone IRA, which acquired new influence in many cumainn. Of 60 in the county, only 2 backed the treaty and aligned themselves with the Murnaghanite Mid-Tyrone comhairle ceantair.[48] The East/South Tyrone and North Tyrone comhairlí ceantair opposed the agreement. But, the northern security clamp-down meant that this defiance of the Treaty represented the dying kick of republican politics in Tyrone.

Despite the input of Tyrone moderates like O'Shiel and Murnaghan, the establishment of the provisional government relied on its chairman's ability to convince sufficient republicans in order to win the Dáil vote and then negate an immediate IRA split, for which the fledgling Free State army was ill-prepared. Collins headed a government composed mainly of conservatives such as Griffith, Cosgrave and Kevin O'Higgins. They were distinctly uncomfortable with his overt military power and, more pertinently, his conspiratorial role within the IRB. But Collins's influence and, ultimately, the pro-Treaty majority in Dáil Éireann relied on his non-political roles. He convinced many TDs, who were fellow members of the IRB, to endorse the Treaty. In March John Dillon perceptively stated that 'without Collins, Griffith would not last a fortnight'.[49] In essence, Collins secured treatyite support by arguing that it provided the freedom to achieve freedom, by espousing a pessimistic assessment of the IRA's chances under 'immediate and terrible war', by promising a republican Free State constitution and by engaging in a covert northern offensive with anti-Treatyites.[50]

The Free State's 'political' policy, however, relied on MacNeill's plan for passive resistance and non-recognition of Craig's administration, especially in education. This led to northern schoolteachers being subsidized by the Dáil. In essence, the pro-Treaty element within the Dáil formalized the same approach to northern affairs that had been apparent since the beginning of 1921. Contact was maintained with moderate northern leaders, constitutional and SF, while the opinion of the grass roots tended to be ignored.[51] Dr Gillespie believed that the 'policy given to us would have been good had the Boundary Commission met in the time set out in the Treaty', but that the civil war 'destroyed that policy'.[52] Collins's co-operation with republicans sought to stave off this internecine conflict, yet it also contradicted stated policy.

The analysis of the IRA concentrates on the 2nd ND, which unlike surrounding divisions contained no Free State territory. Neighbouring divisions, however, had a profound effect on Tyrone because of Collins's incongruous attempts to achieve a middle ground between the Treaty and the republic through the abortive joint-IRA northern campaign of 1922. Frank Aiken recounted how on the night the Treaty was signed, the most important northern commanders met O'Duffy, who claimed 'the signing of the Treaty was only a trick; that he would never take that oath and that no one would be asked to take it. He told us that it had been signed with the approval of GHQ in order to get arms to continue the fight'. Aiken agreed to head a joint-IRA Ulster Council with his division operating under GHQ but on a neutral footing. Although he was 'against the treaty', he acquiesced due to 'promises then being made about the Irish interpretation of the treaty and the elimination of the oath and partition'.[53] Therefore, the 4th ND remained 'neutral and on good terms with both sides', before GHQ essentially drove it into the anti-Treatyite camp in July.[54] The 4th ND contained a small area around Benburb and the Moy. The local brigade actually attended the IRA Executive, against Aiken's orders, which reflected its association with the strongly anti-Treaty East Tyrone Brigade.[55] The Moy IRA wounded two special constables in an ambush at Charlemont in April.[56] Despite another ambush at Benburb in June, most operations took place in Aiken's South Armagh heartland.[57]

While Collins negotiated the first pact with Craig, he agreed to a northern offensive should it fail. GHQ would supply the northern IRA through an exchange of weapons with Liam Lynch's anti-Treaty southern division. The Ulster Council set up its headquarters in Clones, inside O'Duffy's 5th ND. On 8 February 1922, less than a week after the breakdown of the first Craig–Collins pact, the IRA, crossing from the south, kidnapped over forty unionists in Tyrone and Fermanagh. The Monaghan units kidnapped twenty-one prominent Tyrone unionists in the Clogher Valley alone.[58] Tension was high after the arrest of five prominent IRA men, including Dan Hogan, O'Duffy's successor in Monaghan, in Dromore in mid-January. The 'Monaghan footballers' were using an Ulster championship match as cover for the planned jail break of three Volunteers sentenced to death in Derry jail on 9 February. On 30 January O'Duffy, now Chief of Staff, told Collins that he had 'arranged the kidnapping of one hundred prominent Orangemen'. Alluding to local pressure over partition, he explained that 'there are 54 affiliated [Sinn Féin] clubs in Co. Monaghan', which, if the necessary action were taken, should translate into '108 votes … for the Treaty'.[59] Events took a further twist after the shooting of A Specials in Clones on 11 February. This provoked an 'inevitable sequel' in Belfast, where 'twenty-four persons, including six children' were killed and seventy wounded.[60] Two days later two specials constables from Caledon encountered heavy machine-gun fire near the Monaghan border.[61] The Monaghan IRA continued to snipe in Tyrone until June 1922. These incidents caused the death of Robert Scott, a unionist civilian, and provoked the clearance of nationalist families from Caledon.[62] As with the kidnappings, the actions served no real military purpose beyond appeasing the Monaghan IRA and indicating that GHQ had an active northern policy.

The situation led to the establishment of a border commission composed of two British officers stationed at Clogher and two USC officers, with a parallel body established in Monaghan on 20 February.[63] In June Special Constable Thomas Sheridan was killed by cross-border sniping.[64] Dr Con Ward, the Monaghan IRA's representative on the commission, claimed that the sniping resulted from the continued imprisonment of northern republicans and the destruction by the USC of bridges linking Tyrone and Monaghan, particularly Ballagh and Burn's bridge in the Aughnacloy and Caledon areas.[65] On the day of the kidnappings, John Fulton wrote to Bates that 'there will be serious reprisals' in Caledon, urging the deployment of extra troops 'as those in responsible positions here cannot guarantee that the peace will be kept'.[66] Reports of the expulsion of unionists on the Free State side of the border provoked a sharp reaction in Caledon, where Fulton had previously manipulated sectarian animosity to defeat trade unionism.

The Monaghan IRA took 'pleasure' in commandeering the Orange hall at Glaslough, a majority unionist village on the border.[67] On 12 March two UVF men from Glaslough, Johnston and Elliott, fired into the house of Mr McGuire of Tynan in retaliation for their treatment by IRA police. Another nationalist house was riddled with bullets and on 14 March three nationalists sustained injuries when a bomb was thrown at Caledon chapel.[68] The next day a prominent IRA volunteer, John Garvey, and Patrick McPhillips were shot by B Specials as they returned home to Benburb.[69] On 18 March five nationalist families were forcibly evicted from their homes in Caledon by armed B men, 'as a reprisal for the eviction of five Protestant families from their houses in Glaslough'.[70] Charles Wickham claimed that Caledon loyalists 'demand that action be taken to protect their co-religionists in Co. Monaghan or else that such treatment as is given to them should be given to the S.F. sympathisers on their side of the Border'.[71]

In fact, on 27 March the British border commissioner, Colonel Sutton, revealed that Elliot and Johnston 'now state they left Glaslough voluntarily through fear of remaining there'.[72] Elliot continued to work in Glaslough and Sutton reported his arrest in May by Free State troops who had 'good cause for detaining him' as he had orchestrated the expulsions in Caledon.[73] Elliot's inaccurate accounts of expulsion had sparked the clearance of numerous Catholic families from Caledon. Some were clearly Sinn Féin sympathizers; James Doran allegedly took part in an ambush of Specials on 22 March.[74] However, these attacks targeted anyone of a nationalist disposition.[75] On the 18 April Frank Riley of Rahoney was shot dead 'by "B" patrol ... when returning with others from cockfight at Glaslough'. Although the driver of the car, Patrick Maguire, was a Sinn Féiner, the other two passengers, William Moore and William Irvine, were Protestant labourers.[76] Sutton was clear that 'the leadership of the "B" Class Special Constabulary in Caledon has got into the wrong hands'.[77] Writing to Bates again on 22 March, John Fulton claimed that union-ists were experiencing a state of terror due to IRA activity.[78] In fact, the USC commander, John McClintock, reported that the 'only place where Unionists can't work is Ballagh Bridge'.[79] Con Ward reiterated that the sniping would cease 'provided the Northern Authorities would guarantee not to demolish the bridge'.[80] The weight of evidence suggests that there had been some intimida-tion of southern unionists, but, by early March, as the northern border commission admitted, 'the Unionist population were not being interfered with' and 'the Irish Army had actually protected them'.[81]

Similarly on the border with Donegal, some unionists had moved eastwards, but the British army reported that this was 'grossly exaggerated' by the Belfast media 'for political purposes'.[82] The western periphery of Tyrone operated within the 1st ND. Although several prominent Donegal republicans, such as Peadar O'Donnell, later attended the IRA executive in March 1922, the majority remained loyal to GHQ and local TD, Joe Sweeney. The British army identified about '400 I.R.A. in the neighbourhood of Clady', a small nationalist village between Strabane and Castlederg. The IRA seized two Clady unionists, John Baird and Albert Yorke, as part of the February kidnappings, which provoked reprisals on 10 February. Elsewhere, the Donegal IRA ambushed the No. 5 USC Platoon Strabane at Clady, killing Constable Charles McFadden. The USC responded by indiscriminately attacking nationalist houses in Castlederg.[83] The GHQ faction took little offensive action, rather Mulcahy tasked Sweeney with consolidating border positions.[84] Accordingly, the IRA unsuccessfully attempted to burn Strabane workhouse, which British troops then occupied.[85] Before March 1922 IRA operations on the border appeared more geared towards guaranteeing support for GHQ in O'Duffy's division than challenging partition militarily.

Arguably, Collins, Mulcahy and O'Duffy supported the offensive to avoid conflict in early 1922 when republicans were militarily stronger than the nascent Free State army. Within the IRA, the pro-Treaty GHQ faced an anti-Treaty majority, which established an IRA executive on 26 March. It emerged when Mulcahy banned the proposed Army Convention, which both factions had organized at a joint meeting on 18 January 1922. The role of the Ulster Council was crucial in the interim, as pro- and anti-Treaty IRA agreed to co-operate in a northern campaign to avoid a breach.[86] Therefore, Collins vacillated between a conciliatory, political policy with Craig and aggressive co-operation with southern republicans. This promised co-operation assuaged Charlie Daly, who bitterly criticized the Treaty on 18 January and he sent O'Duffy a detailed plan of operations on 25 January. He required weapons and proposed 'dumping places … outside the Northern Frontier from which they could be smuggled in'. Daly suggested the creation of a full-time brigade staff and that ASUs travel south to receive two weeks' intensive training while the guns were in transit.[87] The IRA in Tyrone was clearly in earnest.

The acceptance and ratification of the Treaty ultimately obliged Collins to abide by its terms. His northern policy suggests that he realized this from an early date. If the anti-Treaty IRA could not be reconciled then its threat should be minimized. O'Duffy diverted arms intended for Tyrone to Monaghan under the arms exchange of 17 February and then manipulated the issue to replace Charlie Daly as O/C 2nd ND with Tom Morris.[88] Daly alleged that Mulcahy had ordered his removal because of his opposition to the Treaty on 18 January.[89] Certainly, Mulcahy and O'Duffy had planned his removal since February, with Collins's sanction.[90] This represented one in a series of moves to replace republican northern commanders. The pro-Treaty IRA could not risk uncontrolled ATIRA activity in the North. Arguably, the Ulster Council represented an attempt to avert such an outcome rather than instigate a concerted military campaign against the Belfast administration.

Tyrone witnessed a number of minor operations in the joint IRA offensive of March 1922. On 19 March a twenty-five strong IRA party raided Pomeroy barracks with help from a sympathetic policeman from Mayo.[91] The garrison was tied up and the arsenal removed. Frank Ward was almost left behind, sitting in the kitchen with a Thompson machine gun on his knee drinking tea with the head constable.[92] Daly, who deemed this 'a very successful job', had also planned reprisals against the homes of USC in No. 2 Brigade.[93] On 20 March the Dromore IRA killed Samuel Laird in a raid on the home of John Allingham, the local B commander.[94] The homes of four other USC were burned. Three nights later the IRA renewed attacks at Trillick. George Chittick, a local B man, was shot dead outside his house.[95] Retribution was swift. On 24 March the USC summarily executed Edward McLoughlin, Francis Kelly and William Cassidy, all Trillick nationalists.[96] These killings formed part of 'a state of terror' that lasted until June. The police conceded that the abduction of T.J. Gallagher was in reprisal for the death of Chittick.[97] In December they claimed Gallagher was fighting with the Irregulars in Donegal, alongside his cousin, Mick.

Nevertheless, the police unsuccessfully dredged several local loughs searching for his body.[98] The IRA alleged that Gallagher was 'taken from his bed and after being tortured … thrown into a limekiln and cremated alive'.[99]

The following case illustrates the official attitude to these events. John Rodgers's house was one of several attacked on 3 April, allegedly 'to prevent his children from criticizing recent shootings in Trillick'.[100] In November 1924 the *Ulster Herald* claimed that loyalists bombed his home, two years after warning Rodgers to leave the area.[101] The RUC contended that rather than this being an explosion, a 'string of onions' hanging from a rafter had fallen and took the central beam of the house with it![102] The MHA then took proceedings against the newspaper for spreading republican propaganda.[103] A Trillick RUC report about 12 June 1922 confirmed that loyalists 'ordered him and family to leave the district', one event in a series of twenty, in which drunken B men raided nationalist houses.[104] This counter-insurgency campaign devastated the No. 2 IRA Brigade and general nationalist morale. The brigade area witnessed no IRA activity during the May offensive. After the Pomeroy raid, the Crown forces concentrated operations in republican areas of No. 1 Brigade.[105] On 31 March a party of USC ambushed an IRA unit which was destroying a bridge at Dunamore. Frank Ward, who had sipped tea in Pomeroy barracks a fortnight earlier, was killed. In response, the ASUs from the three East Tyrone battalions went on the run in the vicinity of Carrickmore.

Collins connived in the March offensive. He then agreed a second pact with Craig on 30 March, which had by mid-April descended into acrimony due to bad faith on both sides.[106] The agreement reflected the terms of the earlier pact. It also proposed nationalist recruitment into the USC in Belfast and mixed patrols to police nationalist areas. A conciliation committee with alternating chairmen would handle complaints about intimidation. Meanwhile all IRA activities would cease and the Belfast arrangements would gradually extend across the six counties.[107] Collins's duplicity became even harder to maintain when a faction of the IRA executive, under Rory O'Connor and Liam Mellows, seized control of the Four Courts on 14 April. They envisaged British offensive action, which would unify the IRA and wreck the Treaty. Prior to the seizure, the British had warned Collins that they 'could not allow the Republican flag to fly in Ireland' and were prepared to take action if the Provisional government did not. Both Collins and Griffith stressed that it was 'vital and indispensable to the success of the policy of the Treaty to avoid striking the first blow against the Republicans'.[108] The failure of the second Craig–Collins pact formed the backdrop to the Tyrone IRA's final offensive in May 1922.

Despite controversy regarding the financing and direction of the IRA's 25 May offensive, both pro- and anti-Treaty southern IRA units planned the attack for 3 May 1922, but a request from the Belfast Brigade led to its postponement.[109] The 2nd ND was directed to carry on, however.[110] The anti-Treaty No. 1 Division under Lehane and Daly on the Donegal/Tyrone border was the only southern unit to engage in any fighting during the May offensive. An attempt on Derry on 3 May led by degrees to an altercation with Sweeney's Free State forces at Newtowncunningham.[111] The cross-border campaign also provoked violent reprisals against the nationalist population in Castlederg and Strabane.[112] The pro-Treaty 5th Northern, under Hogan, and the 1st Northern, under Sweeney, as well as Mac Eoin's Midland Division took no action. Ernest Blythe later stated that 'a decision appears to have been taken that there would be no fighting on the Border'.[113] Despite extensive preparation, Aiken, still co-operating on a neutral basis with GHQ, cancelled the offensive in South Armagh and 'remained in Dundalk barracks inactive and remote from his command and so petered out this latest, and maybe the last, rising in the Ulster area'.[114] Writing in late May, Daly claimed that Sweeney 'was intent on frustrating republican efforts in Donegal'.[115] Sweeney later claimed that he 'had no use for the North for I thought they were no good. *I got no encouragement from Collins or from G.H.Q. about helping the North, nor had I any instructions to back them up*'.[116]

The decision not to engage combined with permission for an early offensive in Tyrone indicates that GHQ had no intention of a genuine offensive, a point reinforced by Liam Lynch's allegations regarding the movement of arms.[117] This had catastrophic consequences for the East Tyrone Brigade, which staged two military attacks on 3 May.[118] The anti-Treaty IRA in Coalisland attacked the town's barracks. In line with the March offensive, this included a reprisal element. After the attack, the IRA set fire to Special Constable McClung's house and then shot dead Constable Cecil Caldwell as he attempted to put out the fire.[119] A party of USC, two of them 'unable to stand, they were so drunk', went to the house of James McGrath of Annaghboe and took away his two sons.[120] While the McGrath brothers knelt on the road, Thomas Hagan, the local postman, and his friend, Charles Lavelle came along on bicycles. The USC shot both men and mutilated their dead bodies. Displaying what the local police described as 'undoubted presence of mind, the McGrath brothers bolted, zigzagging across nearby fields'.[121] Appalled by the event, Stevenson, who commanded the B force in Coalisland, issued a public statement, claiming that 'the persons who are responsible for the death of the two innocent Roman Catholics should suffer the full penalty of the law'.[122] There were no subsequent arrests.

The second IRA attack took place in Dunamore and led to the death of Constable William T. McKnight. In reprisal, a party of USC shot John McCracken in the doorway of his pub in Dungate.[123] Charlie Daly wrote ''twas in his house I was brought when I had the flu. He was a fine old man and we were great friends. The poor man was about 80'.[124] Throughout May and June, and as had been the case in March, the IRA had little response, with the exception of the Dungannon Battalion's reprisal attack on the USC at Castlecaulfield.[125] The May offensive also witnessed the execution by the IRA of an alleged British spy in Tyrone. A Dungannon Cumann na mBan member provided evidence about an Englishman masquerading as a *Daily Mail* journalist.[126] The police recovered the body of Israel Sagarsky, aka John Erin, an ex-serviceman and native of Manchester, on a road near Gortin on 6 May 1922, with a label tied to his wrist bearing the words – 'Convicted Spy'. Certainly, local unionists took it for granted that Sagarsky was a spy and Tom Morris later claimed that Sagarsky admitted as much under interrogation, although no evidence had yet been uncovered in British archives.[127]

There is some debate regarding the allegiance of the 2nd ND in this period. It sent representatives to the anti-Treaty IRA convention on 26 March. Tyrone was represented by Frank McGurk of Dunamore and Mick Gallagher of Dromore.[128] By April, however, O'Duffy reported that No. 1 and 2 brigades in Tyrone 'went with the Four Courts due to a misunderstanding' but were 'returning just as rapidly'.[129] What were the grounds for this conversion? Immediately after replacing Daly, O'Duffy cleared the 2nd ND's debts and secured a shipment of arms from Liam Lynch's republican forces in Cork.[130] That month, Collins told the Tyrone IRA that 'Partition would never be recognized even though it might mean the smashing of the Treaty'.[131] In fact, the majority of Tyrone IRA stayed with the executive until May when Corr claimed that No.1 Brigade asked Daly, then in Donegal, for money and weapons. Tom Morris was contacted only after Daly failed to deliver.[132] Daly claimed that the Tyrone IRA switched sides to obtain arms and would return to the anti-Treatyite fold 'because it is well known that Beggar's Bush will not risk the Treaty by carrying on the fight in Ulster.'[133]

Morris, who always believed Collins's pledge regarding partition, played a central role in frustrating Daly's hopes.[134] In early June he moved the nominally neutral 2nd ND to Donegal. O'Duffy provided Morris with barracks in Donegal 'for the purpose of training some hundreds of men with the intention of an invasion of the six counties in the late summer'.[135] Lehane claimed that despite Morris's 'assurance of neutrality he later co-operated with the Staters'.[136] At the beginning of July Daly publicly challenged Morris, who 'without the least shadow of a doubt ... made up his mind not to fight for, or protect, his own and your people in the "Six Counties". He means to fight against the Republic'.[137] Morris's position in Donegal siphoned off potential republican forces fleeing west after the general round-up in May.[138] Having achieved this, and following the abandonment of the supposed northern invasion, he then took his men to Keane Barracks, Curragh, under camouflaged internment.[139] This coincided with a Provisional government decision to adopt a policy of peaceful obstruction towards the unionist administration.[140]

Following the May offensive, the unionist administration introduced internment and rounded up those Volunteers who had not already moved west to fight with Daly. On 22 May 1922, 282 nationalists were interned across the six counties. Thirty or forty prisoners, unconnected with SF, availed of the chance to appear before the MHA Advisory Committee. By July Bates had transferred many prisoners to the *Argenta*, a 'floating gulag' on Belfast Lough.[141] The Free State government directed its prisoners to maintain the policy of non-recognition.[142] The republican, Treatyite and neutral internees formed a joint council under the chairmanship of James Mayne in September 1922.[143] But tensions over the Civil War divided the three groups. The Free State supporters claimed that the 'neutral' commandant, Mayne, favoured the republican position.[144] The May offensive marked the end of IRA operations in Tyrone. In June and July 1922 the 2nd ND's pro-GHQ rump reported no operations by either Free State or ATIRA in the northern area.[145]

This was hardly surprising as the attack on the Four Courts on 28 June precipitated civil war in the south. Between May and early June, Collins still sought to avoid internecine conflict. On 20 May he and de Valera announced an election pact ahead of the June general election, which would result in a pro- and anti-Treaty SF panel, with representation proportionate to the Dáil vote on 7 January. Collins also chaired the committee that proposed a thinly veiled republican constitution to the British, while complaining of a pogrom against Belfast Catholics. He believed that by writing out the Crown there was a possibility that de Valera and his supporters might be reconciled to the pro-Treaty majority. For the British cabinet such an arrangement would breach the Treaty as the four envisaged republican ministers would not take the oath. Churchill then developed contingency plans for the reoccupation of Ireland, using Ulster as a base.[146] In effect, the British government, again under the threat of violence, outlawed any attempt to include anti-Treatyite opinion in the new Free State government.

Churchill then intimated what this violence would entail when British forces attacked a largely pro-Treaty installation in the Belleck–Pettigo triangle on 5 June. Three Tyrone Volunteers – William Kearney and Bernard McCanny from Drumquin and William Deasley from Dromore – were killed.[147] By 13 June the British, as Churchill put it had brought Collins 'to heel'.[148] Collins was compelled to retain the oath and the office of the governor-general. The following day he repudiated the election pact in Cork. Further complications emerged with the assassination of Henry Wilson on 22 June, which Collins apparently ordered, but for which the British cabinet, increasingly alarmed at the Four Courts defiance, chose to blame the ATIRA. By 24 June the British government ordered its own attack on the Four Courts' republican garrison, only withdrawing under advice from Macready that this was what the garrison, which was planning to launch its own northern offensive, actually desired. Four days later, Free State forces attacked the Four Courts with British artillery.[149] By the first week of July Churchill felt confident in assuaging Craig's fears regarding his administration's security now that 'Collins had definitely drawn the sword against the enemies of the British Empire'.[150]

While the IRA engaged in no military operations, the USC intensified activity in June. The figures for violent intimidation fell the following month and remained constant until the end of 1922. In June 1922 the British civil servant, Stephen Tallents, arrived in Ulster to enquire into outrages against northern nationalists. Ricardo admitted that the A Specials 'contained a large leaven of a bad type', had serious problems with 'drink and consequent indiscipline' and represented a 'distinctly partisan force'. The B Specials were 'drawn from the Protestant section of the population and mainly from the more extreme side'. In Catholics areas, Ricardo claimed that commandants approached the leading nationalist with a list featuring 'his name at the top and he is told that if any B man is touched the list will be attended from the top'. Ricardo then stated that the 'N. Govt. is a very strict party machine which is influenced at the present time entirely by Belfast views of extreme type' and concluded that 'the 26 counties [govt.] are not the only one that would benefit by a return to the Union and to impartial govt by the Imperial Govt.'[151]

Both Ricardo and Stevenson preferred to appeal to the 'impartial' imperial government. Yet, their faith appeared groundless. In spite of his contemptible opinion of Bates and his violently partisan secretaries, Megaw and Watt, Tallents's report represented a whitewash. Lloyd George may have described Mussolini's *Fascisti* as an exact analogy for the USC, but the British government paid for the paramilitary force for the next two years to the tune of over £6 million, when there was little or no violence in the north.[152] Ricardo hinted that the Specials partially solved the problem of chronic unemployment: 'every man in N.I. who has lost his job or who is at a loose end has endeavoured to get into the "A"s and in many cases has succeeded.'[153] In September DI Gorman of Omagh claimed that continued republican outrages were 'found to be the work of a few half-hearted isolated irresponsibles, or in some cases to be of very doubtful origins'.[154] Gordon alluded to the USC faking ambushes to justify their continued existence.[155] Raids, intimidation and provocation peppered the daily life of nationalists. In 1923 Bernard Mallon removed a Union Jack from a tree outside his house near Ardboe. The Specials beat Mallon, who was almost eighty, unconscious, breaking his ribs and knocking out his teeth.[156] That summer Specials interned Joseph Campbell for ripping down a flag near Stewartstown. When asked about the proportionality of the police response, Megaw wrote that 'no-one can justify (in Northern Ireland at any rate) taking offence at the country's flag. My view is the police were quite entitled to arrest for the insult to the flag.'[157]

In the two-year period from June 1920 the Crown forces killed seventeen people, the same number as the IRA 2nd ND. The combined figure for Crown forces casualties and fatalities stood at 46, compared with a figure of 41 for the IRA. Over four-fifths of killings and casualties committed by the Crown forces represented either reprisals against republicans or civilians, with the latter twice as prominent. Half of IRA killings constituted military casualties, while less than a third represented reprisals on combatants or civilians; reprisals against combatants were almost twice as prominent. The vast majority of republican reprisals took place between March and May 1922. Of the total number of casualties, over two-thirds were military in nature, with reprisals comprising only seventeen per cent. The IRA carried out forty-two counts of violent intimidation; the Crown forces committed 211. This partially emerged from superior resources and reflected general British counter-insurgency policy across Ireland from the second half of 1920 up until the truce. Ricardo reported that 'today the feeling against the Specials … is more bitter than against the Black & Tans – with this great difference – on the removal of the Black & Tans one side of the contending parties was removed'. In Tyrone many killers had known their victims since childhood, establishing what Ricardo termed 'a group of personal blood feuds which will last for generations to come'.[158]

Why were unionists more likely to carry out indiscriminate reprisals? Ideology provides some answers. This is not a case of good people against bad people; rather, is it a case of people acting on the basis of how they made sense of the world. The inclusive republican ideal appears to have actually checked retaliation. Clearly, there was animosity, an outlook Charlie Daly, in particular, gradually adopted after experiencing Tyrone loyalists at first hand. Nonetheless, the stated objectives driving republican violence were more egalitarian and inclusive than unionism or loyalism. A supremacist dimension formed part of the internal logic of loyalism and, rather than restraining this tendency from 'running amok', the structures of the unionist bloc in fact encouraged conceptions of Protestant superiority and Catholic inferiority, thereby justifying violence. Separate republican and Free State intelligence reports in 1924 claimed that several Specials in Tyrone had formed branches of the Ku Klux Klan.[159] The payoff for preferential treatment in employment, whether a position in the A Specials, a job in a linen mill or a local government post, was that working-class Protestantism was 'stripped of' its 'progressive elements'.[160] Local Catholics were not entirely passive victims; neither were the Protestant lower class, but the unionist élite represented the net beneficiaries. To ignore this crucial structural reality is as grave if not more serious than paying scant regard to the internal dynamics of the unionist bloc, or indeed for that matter the agency of the unionist working class.

The unionist administration quickly neutered nationalist politics in Tyrone. The Belfast government established the Leech Commission, which gerrymandered electoral boundaries, abolished PR and inserted a rateable valuation clause in the Local Government Act (1922), guaranteeing unionist control of the county council and local bodies, and the crucial patronage that went with them. Nationalist leaders hardly helped their case by withholding recognition and looking in vain to the Boundary Commission.[161] The evidence of unionist gerrymandering, discrimination and opposition to proportional representation prior to 1920, as outlined in this book, suggests that nationalist non-recognition merely facilitated a process that unionists would implement regardless of the consequences. Above all, the unionist claim to Tyrone rested on force, a position articulated by successive politicians. On 15 March 1922 Bates introduced the Civil Authorities (Special Powers) bill, which permitted search, arrest and detention without warrant, flogging and capital punishment for arms offences and the suspension of civil liberties.

Furthermore, despite the internal dynamics of Ulster unionist politics, the British state underwrote this entire relationship through financial, political and military support.[162] During the Treaty negotiations, Lloyd George gestured on essential unity to extract concessions from the Irish delegation. The Tory-dominated cabinet had already decided that a breakdown of negotiations 'with regard to Ulster, and in particular our policy with regard to the Counties of Tyrone and Fermanagh … would be one far less favourable' than an Irish 'refusal to accept British sovereignty and Empire', which would 'command universal acceptance' from the British public.[163] Therefore, the government concocted the Boundary Commission to extricate Ulster from the equation. This permitted British statesmen to dictate terms and remain confident that they would not receive a reprimand at the polls.

While the provisional government prevaricated on attacking the Four Courts' garrison and sought a compromise with republicans, Ulster still remained a live issue. The British military admitted that 'Arthur Griffith was the only genuine Free Stater' and that the remainder 'merely accepted the treaty as a stepping-stone to the … republic' and in response to the 'universal desire' for peace.[164] The manipulation of the northern issue by Collins helped gain support for the Treaty and pressurize the British during negotiations over the Free State constitution. After one particularly heated exchange, Lionel Curtis compared negotiating with Collins to 'writing on water', to which Lloyd George dismissively replied, 'Shallow and agitated water'.[165] The British cabinet effectively encouraged civil war by rubbishing the Free State constitution and forbidding the SF electoral pact. It then ordered the attack on the Four Courts, before relenting and providing the Free State with the arms to do so. The Civil War precluded any military challenge to unionist rule in Tyrone. With Collins's clandestine machinations at an end, the Free State reverted to a futile and contradictory policy of non-recognition, in vain expectation of the Boundary Commission.

The leaders of Tyrone constitutionalism, the county's nationalist middle class, returned to their natural environ, somewhat bruised by their brief flirtation with republicanism. The latter had fared even worse and its traditional working-class supporters faced unionist repression and the condemnation of the nationalist middle class and clergy. In addition, partition was now an unavoidable fact.

Tyrone unionists, with the assistance of their Tory allies, had successfully defeated all-Ireland home rule. It was a strange victory, however, for they accepted their own version of home rule and the abandonment of covenanters in three Ulster counties. Moreover, it established a peculiar new type of government; not a state, as Westminster still retained sovereignty; not a country or even the most northerly part of Ireland; not a province, as inclusion of nationalist, west Ulster threatened unionist hegemony over a nine-county parliament. Rather this was a one-party regime, prejudiced by a deliberate six-county boundary, backed by considerable coercive legislation and by British-financed military capability. In due course, unionists implemented and oversaw discrimination on the basis of religion and subverted the rights of citizenship through coercion and blatant interference in democratic procedure. It also suffered slow and inexorable economic decline as the traditional industries that distinguished Ireland's north-east corner withered against international competition and only survived on British subventions. Ironically, the nationalist third of the population, whom the Northern government viewed at best with suspicion, endured the fate that unionists themselves had envisaged under a Dublin parliament. The Ulster unionists were right: home rule had led to the tyranny of the majority.

9 Continuity and change

Everything changes and nothing changes. Before the onset of the Irish revolution, the struggle between constitutional nationalism and unionism dominated Tyrone politics. This contest revolved around control of local government, which the unionist élite held and the nationalist middle class, through the auspices of constitutionalism, in whatever guise, sought to usurp. By 1923 unionist dominance was incontestable and the nationalist bourgeoisie, after a flirtation with separatism, were rapidly returning to their constitutional roots. The Catholic Church's eventual control of education only consolidated this trend, helping to create 'a state within a state ... equipped with its own social infrastructure of Catholic, schools, hospitals, sporting activities, newspapers, businesses, and the sectarian' AOH.[1] Having petitioned de Valera to secure their class interests in December 1921, nationalists then pledged allegiance to the Free State and the delusional Boundary Commission. After 1925 the church and middle class came to terms with the unionist administration; retention of denominational control of education remained paramount.

The northern government that emerged from the revolutionary period reflected the socio-economic and political relationships within unionist civil society, which pre-dated the unsuccessful revolution. While James Craig famously told Stormont that 'All I boast is that we are a Protestant Parliament and a Protestant State', he merely echoed remarks made in 1906, when he claimed to be 'an Orangeman first and a Member of Parliament afterwards'.[2] Orangeism underpinned the unionist campaign against home rule and the subsequent consolidation of the northern government. Tyrone unionists accepted the lead provided by Belfast and élite British circles not only because they shared ideological assumptions, but also out of self-interest. A paramilitary police force, a gerrymandered electoral system, preferential economic treatment in government and private employment explained the devotion of Tyrone unionists to the Belfast regime.

Nationalist civil society, which existed in parallel, harnessed many of the same social divisions. It also registered a long list of grievances against the Stormont administration. By 1923 the middle class once more coalesced around a Devlinite brand of Hibernian nationalism, arguably just as sectarian in ethos as its Orange counterpart. In Dungannon respectable nationalist businessmen and priests joined the Knights of Columbanus, and included Joe Stewart, the Devlinite urban councillor and draper.[3] The gravitational pull of these sectarian forces generally succeeded in maintaining a strange equilibrium. Writing in 1939, Stewart, then NI MP for East Tyrone, claimed that during elections, although the Hibernians appeared unenthusiastic, 'young men and women with republican tendencies were my best workers and supporters' and 'all the priests without exception took a leading part'. He did admit, however, that the 'Kelly gang' had proved a disruptive influence.[4] This was a reference to the Kelly family from Dungannon, which had played an active part in republican politics for generations past and would continue to do so.

The parallel societies predated partition, which merely reinforced them. The Catholic, nationalist middle class and clergy carved out a niche to protect their mutual interests, and acted as a check against any radical attempt to challenge the status quo. Dejected by their revolutionary experience, they formed a surrogate establishment, which largely rendered on to Caesar, and rejected republicanism as a viable political alternative. Alice Donnelly described the machinations of the 'old gang' of clergyman and Hibernian in 1924, when Mary MacSwiney electioneered for SF in Cookstown. Harbison employed 'his whole battery', while clerical condemnation meant that 'even those who have sons in jail say they'd be afraid to vote'. Hibernians and priests warned that anyone who supported SF would have their names sent to the MHA and would 'be arrested if not killed in their beds and their houses burnt out'.[5] SF's poor showing in the October 1924 general election and subsequent northern elections demonstrated that republicanism was, once again, the preserve of a minority, the creed of significant numbers of the nationalist working class.[6]

The obstinate militarism of some, though not all, of those who took the republican side accelerated this eclipse. This mentality can be traced to the rejection of the perceived political hypocrisy and self-interest apparent in the Devlinite machine. However, the subordination of politics during the emergence of SF weakened republicanism. The primacy of the trench-coated flying columns in mythology ignores the reality of guerrilla warfare. As the case of Tyrone demonstrates, without a critical mass of support within the local populace, the revolutionary, to invert Mao's analogy, is a fish out of water. Across most of Ireland, the republican demand took root and facilitated guerrilla warfare because, as the correspondent for the British left-wing *Daily Herald* noted, 'the invisible Republic exists in the hearts of the men and women of Ireland and wields a moral authority which all the tanks and machine guns of King George cannot command'.[7] The British government had the military capacity to conquer Ireland; it lacked the ideological resources. The general desire for peace and the manner in which Collins, in particular, articulated the Treaty drastically reduced popular republican support. In the south other avenues were pursued, such as the electoral panel or even parliamentary attendance without taking the oath, but the British government blocked any concessions and militarized the question. This was apparent in the North even before the Treaty. As Charlie Daly wrote to his brother in the wake of the meeting with Dick Mulcahy on 18 January 1922, 'it seems curious we must risk our lives for the sake of a cause that has been handed over to the enemy. Of

course the Northerners must fight for their existence under whatever government is in power'.[8]

The two predominant blocs in Tyrone society before 1912 still held sway at the
end of the period. But much had changed. Before 1912 Ireland was a unitary
component of the United Kingdom. By 1923 the island had two parliaments. The
Dublin parliament ruled twenty-six counties as a British dominion with powers
approaching an independent state. In May 1922 Lloyd George emphasized that
unlike the Free State, NI was not a dominion.[9] The six-county administration
controlled internal affairs, most significantly, security matters, which underpinned wholesale discrimination against the sizeable nationalist minority. This
study has been chiefly concerned with the cause of partition and why Tyrone,
with its nationalist majority, found itself on the northern, unionist side of the
border. Partition, in its final form, relied primarily on the actions of the British
state, whether unilaterally through the GOIA or, in the case of the Anglo-Irish
Treaty, in concert with the majority element of the revolutionary Dáil.

SF represented a nationalist, bourgeois revolution, not dissimilar to
numerous independence struggles across the globe in the twentieth century. Its
ideology, as understood in its founding document, the 1916 Proclamation, was
both secular and republican. It also spoke of social equality and laid the blame
for the schism between North and South at the door of British imperialism.
Nevertheless, many who sheltered under the SF umbrella were socially conservative and lukewarm on the republic, including Arthur Griffith himself. The
first attempt to implement SF policy ended in acrimony before the 1910
elections, when the IRB criticized Griffith's monarchism and attempted
rapprochement with the Healyite AFIL.[10] The Anglo-Irish Treaty constituted
the foundation document of the Irish counter-revolution, for it consummated
the Healyite–Griffithite alliance. The Healyites eventually dominated Tyrone
separatism, as they did the new Free State, after the purge of 'revolutionaries,
Irish-Irelanders and most especially the militarist-republicans' from the government.[11] Tim Healy, the first Governor General of the Irish Free State, remarked
that SF 'won in three years what we did not win in forty … in broad outline, they
have got what was denied us by Gladstone, Asquith and Bannerman'.[12] Kevin
O'Higgins, the dominant member of the Free State cabinet after August 1922,
boasted how 'we were the most conservative-minded revolutionaries that ever
put through a successful revolution'.[13] Clearly, SF achieved a level of southern
autonomy unimaginable, or even unappealing, to the IPP. Nevertheless, the
revolution also reinvigorated a wider republican demand, which resonated in
Tyrone long after the period of study and to which even Cosgrave's Cumann na
nGaedheal government had to pay lip service.

An examination of Free State policy on two key issues relevant to Tyrone,
internment and the Boundary Commission, demonstrates Treatyite shortcom-
ings. The Free State government had proposed non-recognition in the North,

provided, but later withdrew, financial support to national schoolteachers, and let several hundred internees remain incarcerated on the *Argenta*. Yet, their entire strategy since June 1922 had recognized the northern administration.[14] Many Free State supporters in Tyrone recognized the obvious inconsistency of this position.[15] By 1923 the *Argenta* prison ship held 263 men, with a similar number interned across Belfast prison, Larne workhouse and Derry jail.[16] Matters came to a head in January when six of the nine schoolteachers on board decided to appear before the Advisory Committee. Four withdrew after a collective meeting of internees, but Frank Crummey, a Free State supporter from Belfast who claimed to have Eoin MacNeill's consent, persevered.[17] Mayne proposed an 'immediate boycott and ostracization of the teachers', attacked Cosgrave's government and refused to let Cahir Healy speak in its defence. In response, Kevin O'Shiel, who handled northern affairs for the Free State government, reaffirmed the non-recognition policy.[18]

When the Civil War ended in May 1923, Free State supporters anticipated renewed efforts on behalf of Treatyite internees, who constituted half of the inmates.[19] O'Shiel merely reaffirmed non-recognition prior to the Boundary Commission.[20] Clearly frustrated, the internees started a futile hunger strike directed by Tyrone republican and veterinarian, Mack McCartan.[21] By 29 June 1923 SF had organized itself on the ship and the majority of Tyrone internees took the republican position.[22] They formed a new council and rejected the joint body under Mayne.[23] The following month O'Shiel admitted that internment had 'done a good deal towards prejudicing our supporters in the Six Counties against us'. Notably, he urged action on the internees' behalf to secure 'very strong propaganda' for upcoming elections.[24] Acting on Cahir Healy's advice, O'Shiel immediately petitioned the British for the release of Free State supporters.[25] Bates, with whom authority rested, refused to differentiate between Free Staters and republicans.[26] In October 1923 the prisoners started another hunger strike. Healy reported that only about twenty Treatyites took part.[27] The MHA transferred the leaders to Belfast prison and subsequently sent twenty more, including Mayne, to Derry to break the strike.[28] By the first week of November 1923 there were 131 hunger strikers in Belfast, 70 in Derry and 40 in Larne.[29] When challenged by O'Shiel, Bates retorted that the 'women's weapon of hunger strike ... must reap the full consequences' and he reminded the southern government of its attitude to republican hunger strikers during the Civil War.[30] The strike ended on 10 November and the last prisoners were released at the end of 1924. The internment issue demonstrated that the Free State still played the game of non-recognition not merely in anticipation of the Boundary Commission, but because it fitted with popular southern attitudes to partition and the unionist government.

In May 1924 while convalescing in Derry jail, James Mayne, the former neutral commandant of internees on board the *Argenta*, conceded that he had 'no opinion on the Boundary Commission; all parties concerned over it are frauds. We seem to be pawns in a miserable game'.[31] The suppression of the findings, after they were leaked to the *Morning Post* in November 1925, dashed any remaining hopes and marked the denouement of growing border nationalist disenchantment with the Free State.[32] Such an outcome was always likely. Indeed, the British promised to veto any findings unsatisfactory to the unionist administration. Furthermore, the appointment of Richard Feetham, the conservative, South African chairman indicated that Britain was not a 'neural arbitrator'.[33] As early as July 1924 Cosgrave privately conceded that the findings would result in mere 'rectification' of the border.[34] On 3 December 1925 his government agreed to keep the existing boundaries in return for the cancellation of its contribution to the British war debt. As de Valera put it, the Free State 'sold Ulster natives for four pound a head', to clear 'a debt we did not owe'.[35] Cosgrave's government also singularly failed to exact any concessions from Craig in terms of reducing discrimination against the northern minority.[36] By 1929, in line with local government in 1924, the unionists abolished PR and gerrymandered the northern parliamentary constituencies.[37]

The middle-class leaders of Tyrone nationalism received scant reward for their steadfast loyalty to the Free State and its policy of non-recognition. In 1926 Cahir Healy claimed that 'when the time of trial came they cut our cable and launched us rudderless, into the hurricane, without guarantee or security even for our ordinary civic rights'.[38] By this stage Healy was an abstentionist member of Stormont; he took his seat, with Harbison, in 1927.[39] He had already attended Westminster soon after his release from the *Argenta* in February 1924. The ground had been prepared for reconciliation with Devlinism at the April 1925 elections to the northern parliament when Devlinites and Pro-Treaty Sinn Féiners, standing simply as 'Nationalists', received twenty-four per cent of the vote, winning ten seats. SF won five per cent and returned two candidates, including de Valera.[40] Yet the Free State's existence and the emergence of its conservative, post-colonial élite relied on the actions of Britain, as did the failure to fulfil the provisions of Article XII as understood by the Irish plenipotentiaries.

To understand Tyrone's history in the period, one must acknowledge the paramount influence of British policy. Britain's role in Ireland was shaped by her global position and the pressure felt by government due to increased democratic and social demands. In the words of Laffan, 'Lloyd George's government changed its policy more in response to international hostility, and to the shame and revulsion felt by British public opinion, than as a consequence of military weakness or defeat'.[41] Obviously, 'prime ministers refused to embrace policies that might result in their losing office', but this scarcely constitutes the 'bottom line'.[42] It hardly begins to explain why Lloyd George, the Welsh-speaking son of a Baptist shoemaker's daughter, led a coalition dominated by Tory plutocrats. Neither does it recognize the structural restraints in which he operated. The

Tories, who dominated the coalition cabinet, were the very same men who challenged parliament's sovereignty, openly supported the Curragh 'Mutiny' and funded the Larne gun-running in 1914.[43] While in office, they steadfastly reinforced partition through legislation and enormous financial support for the northern regime's security apparatus.

The rationale was clear: the British political élite supported Ulster unionists in order to subvert home rule and, failing that, handicap any independent Irish state to the extent that it remained a virtual British possession. During the Buckingham Palace Conference of 1914, Lord Milner, the British 'race patriot' and arch-imperialist, advised Carson to 'stick out for the six counties as a minimum', although he added, 'There is no particular virtue in counties … as long as the excluded area is one solid block'.[44] Tory opposition to home rule was expedient, but it operated within a definite framework. During the home rule crisis, Milner formed the Ulster Union Defence League to rescue 'the white settler colony of Ulster from submersion in a sea of inferior Celts'.[45] His chief ally in this venture was Walter Long, whose parliamentary committee drew up the plans for six-county partition after Belfast Town Hall informed him that they could not control nine. Again, this policy revolved on an imperial pivot which operated globally. In November 1917 the Balfour Declaration promised a Jewish homeland in Palestine. Sir Ronald Storrs, the first military governor of Jerusalem, argued that such a state 'would form for England "a little loyal Jewish Ulster" in a sea of hostile Arabism'.[46] In Ireland, Tyrone unionists viewed NI as 'an impregnable, Protestant and Unionist Pale', which would serve as 'a bridge head for the re-conquest of Ireland' in the event of the declaration of a Republic.[47]

The partition of Ireland did not rely on the existence of two nations or on fears of religious persecution, but rather on the determination of a Tory political elite, which included the Ulster unionist leaders, to preserve imperial interests. When asked why he did not espouse the two nations theory to the Irish Convention, Montgomery remarked that Ulster unionists should 'take firmer ground as loyal subjects and Denizens of the British Empire'.[48] Six counties rather than nine represented the largest area unionists felt that they could control, in line with the UVF contingency plan of 1914 – self-determination for an Ulster nation was meaningless; the enterprise was designed to subvert self-determination. The task of government was to manage this process as effectively as possible. At a notable cabinet meeting on 31 May 1922 Lloyd George revealed that a breach on Ulster 'would be a bad case' because it was 'very important' to carry British and international opinion as 'democratic communities were sentimental communities and that was why a policy of repression could not be carried through'. The government, therefore, sought to 'eliminate the Ulster question and leave a clean issue of "Republic versus British empire".'[49]

British government policy may have been subject to democratic pressure but democratic principle did not lie at its heart. The British had the military capacity to defeat SF and applied it for a period. However, their control of Britain itself relied on sufficient support from the 'sentimental community' they claimed to represent. The republican movement's greatest success arguably lay in articulating a demand that exposed the hypocrisy of a great imperial power with democratic pretensions. Churchill himself encapsulated the British position when he told a pre-war cabinet meeting that

> We [the British] are not a young people with innocent record and a scanty inheritance. We have engrossed to ourselves [an] altogether disproportionate share of wealth and traffic of the world. We have got all we want in territory, and our claim to be left in an unmolested enjoyment of vast and splendid possessions, mainly acquired by violence, largely maintained by force, often seems less reasonable to others than to us.[50]

Lloyd George recognized that the British people might not accept further military involvement in Ireland over partition, or Tyrone's inclusion therein, as he admitted himself 'our Ulster case is not a good one'.[51] He was fortunate that Michael Collins initiated a proxy war in the south in support of the empire, armed with British artillery. Within the British cabinet Churchill, who had been driven from Ulster Hall in February 1912, had become the Ulster Unionists' chief ally a decade later. Indeed, in September 1922 Lord Londonderry confided that Churchill 'fought our battle courageously from beginning to end'.[52]

At a cabinet meeting in July 1920 W.E. Wylie, the legal advisor to Dublin Castle, argued that charging unionists with 'maintaining law and order' in Ulster would have 'disastrous' results and forecast that 'in Belfast, the Protestants would reduce the Catholics to a state of terror', while 'in Tyrone there would be an unceasing and unending civil war'.[53] Although the resulting level of violence in Belfast largely conformed to Wylie's grave forecast, his prediction regarding Tyrone did not transpire. This partly rested on Ulster unionists' insurmountable military capacity. In effect, the IRA, even when inclined to do so, was incapable of extending its campaign into Ulster. By August 1922 Lord Londonderry, the most moderate member of the northern cabinet, responded to complaints from Hugh Kennedy about a pogrom against Catholics with the minatory remark: 'You talked to me about Lisburn, and I can retort by showing you many districts in the six counties in which there is such a preponderance of Protestants that the extermination of the Catholics would be a very easy matter indeed'.[54] In effect, sizeable IRA actions in Ulster, or on Ulstermen serving elsewhere in Ireland, sparked largely indiscriminate attacks on Belfast's nationalist community. The USC replicated this reprisal element, admittedly on a smaller scale, in Tyrone, where unionist dominance had to be adapted in the face of nationalist confidence and demands for equality. Supremacy, once challenged, re-emerged through force and within this equation the intimidation of the nationalist community became the *modus operandi* of the consolidation of unionist control in Tyrone.

Tyrone's eventual inclusion in the northern administration also owed a significant debt to the ineptitude of Dáil Éireann's plenipotentiaries in 1921, particularly the chief negotiator, Arthur Griffith. 'Their dealings with the Boundary Commission Article betray a surprising lack of due diligence', which reflected 'a deep-seated indifference to the problems posed by the north east, soon to be displayed in the Treaty debates'.[55] Lloyd George's threat of immediate and terrible war represented an elaborate bluff given the British cabinet's determination in September to avoid a breakdown on Ulster and consequent adverse public opinion.[56] The failure to go back to the country without agreement, however, betrayed a distinct lack of faith in the Irish people's resolve. De Valera admitted as much at the end of the Civil War, stating that although 'there is no love in the hearts of the people for the F.S. having got the lead, the majority probably would accept the Free State rather than face the possibility of the renewal of the war with England.'[57] Furthermore, Tyrone's accession into the Free State would still have left the question of partition unresolved. The Treaty negotiations represented a brief window of opportunity for some form of Irish unity; their mishandling on the Irish side ended the already remote prospect of overturning partition.

Everything changes and nothing changes. The two governments that emerged from the unsuccessful SF revolution pointed to change but little had changed in terms of the demand for an all-Ireland republic, as proclaimed in 1916 and mandated in 1918. Similarly, the unionist desire to maintain control led to obvious discrimination in Tyrone, in line with the area's pre-revolutionary history. The legacy of the failed revolution resonated in the muddy by-ways of Tyrone. A half-century later it provided the rationale and motivation for another challenge to unionist and then British control of the county.

Notes

CHAPTER ONE *County Tyrone in 1912*

1   Michael and Eleanor Brock (eds), H.H. Asquith, *Letters to Venetia Stanley* (Oxford, 1982), p. 109.
2   Eamon Phoenix, *Northern nationalism: nationalist politics and the Catholic minority in Northern Ireland, 1890–1940* (Belfast, 1994), p. 85; Jeremy Smith, 'Federalism, devolution and partition: Sir Edward Carson and the search for a compromise on the third home rule bill, 1913–14', *IHS*, 35:140 (2007), 499.
3   Cabinet conclusions, 7 Sept. 1921 (TNA, CAB 23/27).
4   *Hansard (Commons)*, 16 Feb. 1922, vol. 150, c. 1271.
5   *Report of the 1911 census: province of Ulster, County Tyrone* (London, 1911), pp 68–72.
6   Philip Robinson, *The plantation of Ulster* (Belfast, 1994), pp 84–94, 119.
7   Michael Laffan, *The partition of Ireland, 1911–1925* (Dundalk, 1983), p. 5.
8   CI Tyrone, July 1913 (TNA, CO 904/90).   9 Kevin O'Shiel (BMH WS 1770/1, p. 26).
10   *1911 census for Tyrone*, pp 68–72.
11   David Fitzpatrick, 'The geography of Irish Nationalism 1910–1921', *Past & Present*, 78 (1978), 138–9.
12   T. C. Kennedy, 'War, patriotism, and the UUC, 1914–18', *Éire-Ireland*, 40 (2005), 189–211.
13   *Dungannon News* (hereafter *DN*), 7 Feb. 1907.
14   Montgomery to Farnham, 25 Mar. 1919 (PRONI, Montgomery papers, D627/437/62).
15   Jim Smyth, 'Men of no popery: the origins of the Orange Order', *History Ireland*, 3:3 (1995), 53.
16   David Fitzpatrick, *The two Irelands, 1912–39* (Oxford, 1998), p. 11.
17   Fergal McCluskey, *Fenians & Ribbonmen: the development of republican politics in East Tyrone, 1898–1918* (Manchester, 2011), p. 45.
18   A.C. Hepburn, 'Liberal policies and Nationalist politics in Ireland' (PhD, University of Kent, 1968), p. 835.
19   D.C. Savage, 'The origins of the Ulster Unionist Party, 1885–6', *IHS*, 12:47 (1961), 189–90.
20   Andrew Gailey, 'Unionist rhetoric and Irish local government reform, 1895–9', *IHS*, 24:93 (1984), 54.
21   Castlederg RDC had 5,668 Catholics in a population of 11,161. The corresponding figures for the other RDCs were: Clogher (6,982/13,744), Cookstown (9,966/18,831), Dungannon (13,748/26,420), Omagh (19,552/31,604), Strabane (10,586/19,532), and Trillick (2,302/3,915), *1911 census for Tyrone*, pp 115–32.
22   Cookstown UDC had 1,523 Catholics in a population of 3,685. The corresponding figures for the other UDCs were: Dungannon UDC (2,120/3,830), Omagh (2,818/4,836/), Strabane (3,750/5,107), *1911 Census for Tyrone*, p. 114.
23   O'Shiel (BMH WS 1770/1, p. 24).   24 *Hansard (Commons)*, 24 Mar. 1919, vol. 114, c. 145.
25   Miller to Abercorn, 3 May 1915 (PRONI, Abercorn papers, D623/A/348/4).
26   O'Shiel (BMH WS 1770/1), p. 12.   27 *TC*, 5 Jan. 1911.
28   Owen McGee, *The IRB: the Irish Republican Brotherhood, from the Land League to Sinn Féin* (Dublin, 2005), p. 24.
29   Précis, 3 Nov. 1905 (TNA, CO 904/117).
30   McCluskey, *Fenians & Ribbonmen*, pp 11–12.
31   CI Armagh, Oct. 1913 (TNA, CO 904/91).
32   See CI Tyrone, Jan. 1915 (TNA, CO 904/96).   33 *DN*, 5 Jan. 1899.

34 John D. Brewer, *The Royal Irish Constabulary: an oral history* (Belfast, 1990), p. 7.
35 CI Tyrone, Oct. 1913 (TNA, CO 904/91).
36 Eamon Phoenix, 'Nationalism in Tyrone, 1890–1972' in Charles Dillon & Henry A. Jefferies (eds), *Tyrone: history and society* (Dublin, 2000), pp 765–71.
37 Tom Garvin, *Nationalist revolutionaries in Ireland, 1891–1922* (Oxford, 1987), p. 127.
38 Bridget Hourican, 'Murnaghan, George', *DIB*.
39 McCluskey, *Fenians & Ribbonmen*, p. 39.   40 *Tyrone Constitution*, 31 Dec. 1909.
41 O'Shiel (BMH WS 1770/1, p. 60).   42 CI Donegal, Jan. 1916 (TNA, CO 904/99).
43 Ibid., June 1914 (TNA, CO 904/93).
44 Eugenio Biagini, *British democracy and Irish nationalism* (Cambridge, 2010), p. 266.
45 *TC*, 14 Aug. 1913.
46 Johan Galtung, 'A structural theory of imperialism', *Journal of Peace Research*, 8:2 (1971), 81–117.
47 John Darwin, *The empire project: the rise and fall of the British world-system, 1830–1970* (Cambridge, 2009), p. 299.
48 Carson–Londonderry correspondence, Dec. 1921 (PRONI, Londonderry papers, D3099/3/17/1–13).
49 James Stronge to Montgomery, 12 Mar. 1920 (PRONI, Montgomery papers, D627/435/9).

CHAPTER TWO *No home rule and no surrender!*

1   The inscription on the Orange banner at Baronscourt on 12 July 1912.
2   IG Jan. 1913 (TNA, CO 904/89).
3   Alvin Jackson, *Home rule: an Irish history, 1800–2000* (London, 2004), p. 142.
4   Carson to Bonar Law, 20 Sept. 1913, cited in Jackson, *Home rule*, p. 144.
5   Patrick Buckland, *Irish unionism, 1885–1923: a documentary history* (Belfast, 1973), p. xii.
6   *Tyrone Constitution*, 19 Apr. 1907.
7   W. Sinclair, 'Minute book of North Tyrone Women's Unionist Association', 1907 (PRONI, D1098/2/1/1).
8   Diane Urquhart, '"The female of the species is more deadly than the male?": the Ulster Women's Unionist Council, 1911–40' in Janice Holmes & Diane Urquhart (eds), *Coming into the light: work, politics and religion of women in Ulster, 1840–1940* (Belfast, 1994), pp 93–125.
9   *TC*, 18 Jan. 1912.
10 For the Unionist Clubs in the South and East Tyrone Executive area, see *TC*, 21 Dec. 1911, 18 Jan. 1912, 22 Feb. 1912, 7 Mar. 1912; for the Mid-Tyrone club, Omagh, see *Tyrone Constitution*, 9 Feb. 1912.
11 Urquhart, 'The female of the species', p. 100.   12 Jackson, *Ireland*, p. 235.
13 Leah Levenson & Jerry H. Natterstad, *Hanna Sheehy-Skeffington: Irish feminist* (Syracuse, 1989), p. 24.
14 *TC*, 8 Nov. 1911.
15 Ibid., 13 Feb. 1913; Dungannon pillar boxes interfered with by suffragettes, 1913 (NAI, CSORP, 1913/327); *TC*, 18 Dec. 1913.
16 Alan O'Day, *Irish home rule, 1867–1921* (Manchester, 1998), pp 230–5.
17 A.C. Hepburn, *The conflict of nationality in modern Ireland* (London, 1980), p. 74.
18 *UH*, 27 Jan. 1912.   19 CI Tyrone, Oct. 1911 (TNA, CO 904/85).
20 Michael T. Foy, 'Ulster Unionism and the development of the Ulster Volunteer Force' in Jürgen Elvert (ed.), *Nordirland in gerschichte und gegenwart* (Stuttgart, 1994), p. 102.
21 CI Tyrone, Feb. 1911 (TNA, CO 904/83).
22 Terence Dooley, 'The organization of Unionist opposition to Home Rule in Counties Monaghan, Cavan and Donegal, 1885–1914', *Clogher Record*, 16:1 (1997), 52.
23 *DN*, 27 Apr. 1911.   24 *TC*, 28 Sept. 1911.

25 CI Derry, Aug. 1912 (TNA, CO 904/87). 26 Foy, 'Ulster Unionism', p. 102.

27 Ronald McNeill, *Ulster's stand for union* (London, 1922), pp 56–7; Bridget Hourican, 'McNeill, Ronald John Baron Cushendun', *DIB*.

28 CI Tyrone, Jan. 1911 (TNA, CO 904/83).

29 Ibid., Oct. 1911 (TNA, CO 904/85); Jan. 1912 (TNA, CO 904/86).

30 IG, Jan. 1912 (TNA, CO 904/86); CI Tyrone, Jan. 1912 (TNA, CO 904/86).

31 CI Donegal, CI Fermanagh, June 1912 (TNA, CO 904/87).

32 CI Tyrone, Dec. 1911 (TNA, CO 904/85).

33 'Report as to Dungannon rifle club', 1912 (NAI, CSORP, 1912/8598); *Mid-Ulster Mail*, 1 June 1912.

34 CI Tyrone, Mar. 1912 (TNA, CO 904/86), Feb. 1913 (TNA, CO 904/89).

35 Ibid., Jan. 1912 (TNA, CO 904/86). 36 Jalland, *The Liberals and Ireland*, p. 62.

37 Hepburn, *Catholic Belfast*, pp 139–40.

38 Paul Bew, *Ideology and the Irish question* (Oxford, 1994), p. 55.

39 J.B. Armour to W.S. Armour, Jan. 1912 (PRONI, J.B. Armour papers, D1792/A/3/3/5).

40 CI Tyrone, Apr. 1912 (TNA, CO 904/86). 41 *UH*, 13 Apr. 1912.

42 PRONI, http://applications.proni.gov.uk/UlsterCovenant/Search.aspx.

43 Daithí Ó Corráin, 'Resigned to take the bill with its defects: the Catholic Church and the third Home Rule bill', paper to Cork Studies in the Irish Revolution: the home rule crisis, 1912–14 (Oct. 2012).

44 Hepburn, *Catholic Belfast*, pp 129–31; Armour to W.S. Armour, 16 Mar. 1911 (PRONI, Armour papers, D1792/A/3/2/12).

45 Graham Walker, 'The Irish Presbyterian Anti-Home Rule Convention of 1912', *Studies: An Irish Quarterly Review*, 86:341 (1997), pp 71–2.

46 *TC*, 15 Feb. 1912. 47 *Irish Times*, 18 Nov. 1911.

48 Horner to Moutray, 16 Nov. 1911 (PRONI, Moutray papers, D2023/6/2/1); Crawford to Moutray, 24–7 Nov. 1911 (ibid.).

49 *Mid-Ulster Mail*, 9 Dec. 1911. 50 Ibid., 6 Jan. 1912.

51 CI Derry, June 1912 (TNA, CO 904/87); RIC Judicial Division report, 1912 (TNA, CO 903/17), p. 5.

52 *Hansard (Commons)*, 2 Jan. 1913, vol. 46, cc 500–3; *Tyrone Constitution*, 5 July 1912.

53 J. B. Armour to W.S. Armour, 3 July 1912 (PRONI, Armour papers, D1792/A/3/3/21).

54 Graham Walker, *A history of the Ulster Unionist Party: protest, pragmatism and pessimism* (Manchester, 2004), pp 31–2.

55 *Hansard (Commons)*, 31 July 1912, vol. 41, c. 2092; City Commissioner RIC Belfast, July 1912 (TNA, CO 904/87).

56 Michael Wheatley, *Nationalism and the Irish Party: provincial Ireland, 1910–1916* (Oxford, 2005), pp 167–9.

57 Bew, *Ideology*, p. 67. 58 CI Antrim, July 1912 (TNA, CO 904/87).

59 *TC*, 18 July 1912. 60 CI Tyrone, June 1909 (TNA, CO 904/78).

61 Précis, 6 Aug. 1910 (TNA, CO 904/119).

62 *Hansard (Commons)*, 16 Jan. 1913, vol. 46, c. 2255; Hepburn, *Catholic Belfast*, pp 132–4.

63 *Hansard (Commons)*, 14 Nov. 1911, vol. 31, cc 208–331.

64 Devlin to J.J. Horgan, 7 Nov. 1911 (NLI, J.J. Horgan papers, MS 18,271).

65 *DN*, 21 Mar. 1912. 66 *TC*, 26 Mar. 1914.

67 Andrew Scholes, *The Church of Ireland and the third home rule bill* (Dublin, 2010), p. 41.

68 *TC*, 3 Oct. 1912.

69 See Gordon Lucy, *The Ulster Covenant: an illustrated history of the 1912 home rule crisis* (Belfast, 2012).

70 PRONI, http://applications.proni.gov.uk/UlsterCovenant/Search.aspx.

71 David W. Miller, *Queen's rebels: Ulster loyalism in perspective* (Dublin, 1978), pp 114–21.

72 *TC*, 15 Aug. 1912, 21 Aug. 1913. 73 *TC*, 14 Aug. 1913.

74   *DN*, 11 Apr. 1912.   75 *Hansard (Commons)*, 7 May 1912, vol. 38, c. 302.

76   J.B. Armour to W.S. Armour, Oct. 1912 (PRONI, Armour papers, D1792/A/3/3/3).

77   Ibid., 12 Feb. 1913 (PRONI, D1792/A/3/4/7).

78   Scholes, *Church of Ireland*, p. 43.

79   *TC*, 30 May 1912.   80 Ibid., 20 Mar. 1913.   81 Ibid., 15 Aug. 1912.

82   Ibid., 11 Jan. 1912.   83 *DN*, 30 Mar. 1913.

84   Walker, 'The Irish Presbyterian Convention', pp 76–7.

85   *TC*, 8 Feb. 1912.   86 *TC*, 12 Feb. 1914.

87   Charles Townshend, *Political violence in Ireland: government and resistance since 1848* (Oxford, 1983), p. 225.

88   Gordon Scott to Lowry, 14 July 1913 (PRONI, Lowry papers, D1132/6/8).

89   CI Tyrone, Aug. 1912 (TNA, CO 904/87).

90   Scholes, *Church of Ireland*, p. 74.   91 *Hansard (Commons)*, 24 July 1913, vol. 55, c. 2199.

92   IG, Aug. 1913 (TNA, CO 904/90).   93 Jackson, *Ireland*, pp 236–7.

94   For general organizational structure, see 'Minute book of Fermanagh UVF', Dec. 1912 (PRONI, D1402/4); for early battalion structure in Tyrone, see 'Organization of sections and companies' [Jan.?] 1913 (PRONI, Lowry papers, D1132/6/1).

95   Intelligence notes, 1913 (TNA, CO 903/17), p. 110; provincial figure, Oct. 1913 (PRONI, UUC papers, D1327/1/2).

96   Intelligence notes, 1913 (TNA, CO 903/17), p. 124.

97   City Commissioner, Belfast, Jan.–Mar. 1914 (TNA, CO 904/92).

98   Timothy Bowman, *Carson's army: the Ulster Volunteer Force, 1910–22* (Manchester, 2007), p. 83.

99   E.C. Herdman, No. 1 Tyrone Regiment, Jan. 1913 (PRONI, D1414/30); William Miller, adjutant, 1st (North Tyrone) to O/C each Company, 1913 (PRONI, D1414/30); Northland to 4th Tyrone Regiment (PRONI, Lowry papers, D1132/6/7); Bowman, *Carson's army*, p. 47.

100 Cruickshank to Lowry, Oct. 1913 (PRONI, Lowry papers, D1132/6/1).

101 Intelligence notes, 1913 (TNA, CO 903/17).

102 Note on J Company, Dungannon Battalion (PRONI, Lowry papers, D1132/6/17).

103 John Sears's notebook, 23 Jan. 1914 (PRONI, Falls and Hanna papers, D1390/19/1); Bowman, *Carson's army*, p. 86.

104 Foy, 'Ulster Unionism', p. 108.

105 UVF circular, Aug. 1913 (PRONI, Lowry papers, D1132/6/1).

106 Dooley, 'The organization of Unionist opposition to Home Rule', p. 61.

107 Northland to Lowry, 13 Oct. 1913 (PRONI, Lowry papers, D1132/6/1).

108 Foy, 'Ulster Unionism', p. 108.   109 CI Tyrone, Oct. 1913 (TNA, CO 904/91).

110 *NL*, 3 Oct. 1913.

111 Minutes of meeting of committee, 4 Sept. 1913 (PRONI, Moutray papers, D2023/11/1B).

112 *TC*, 9 Jan. 1919.

113 Identified from PRONI, Lowry papers, D1132/5/5.

114 Bowman, *Carson's army*, pp 50–2.   115 Ibid., p. 6.

116 Officers identified in *Tyrone Courier and Tyrone Constitution* and PRONI, D1414; occupations, 1911 census, http://www.census.nationalarchives.ie/pages/1911/Tyrone/

117 For officer list, see *NL*, 12 Feb. 1914; occupations, 1911 census for County Tyrone.

118 Dooley, 'The organization of Unionist opposition to Home Rule', p. 52.

119 UVF 4th (Dungannon) Batt., 29 Oct. 1913 (PRONI, Lowry papers, D1132/6/1).

120 Jackson, *Home rule*, p. 134.   121 *DD*, 18 Feb. 1914.

122 CI Tyrone, Jan. 1914 (TNA, CO 904/92).

123 Dungannon Battalion manoeuvres, 25 Mar. 1914 (PRONI, Orange Order documents, D4246/3/3/1).

124 CI Tyrone, Mar. 1914 (TNA, CO 904/92).   125 Foy, 'Ulster Unionism', p. 115.

126 Miller to O/C each Company, 1913 (PRONI, D1414/30).

127 Bowman, *Carson's army*, p. 104.   128 George Berkeley (BMH WS 971, p. 27).
129 IG, June 1914 (TNA, CO 904/93).
130 Montgomery to John Ross, 17 Dec. 1921 (PRONI, Montgomery papers, D627/439/26).
131 A. Moutray [India] to Moutray, 13 Nov. 1913 (PRONI, Moutray papers, D2023/6/2/1).
132 Copeland Trimble to A. Moutray, 18 Apr. 1914; Edward Slater to A. Moutray, 25 July 1913
      (ibid.).
133 Refugee registers for three companies of 5th battalion, Cookstown, 1914 (PRONI,
      D4121/C/5/2).
134 Townshend, *Political violence*, p. 255.
135 Jackson, *Ireland*, p. 238.   136 *TC*, 15 Jan. 1914.
137 Ibid., 18 June 1914.   138 Jackson, *Home rule*, p. 141.

CHAPTER THREE *'Tyrone for Ulster, Ulster for Ireland ... up with home rule!'*

  1 *DN*, 3 Feb. 1910.   2 Ibid.
  3 *An tÉireannach*, 23 Bealtaine 1936, p. 6; Denis McCullough (BMH WS 915, p. 6).
  4 James McCullough (BMH WS 529, p. 2); CI Armagh, Jan. 1913 (TNA, CO 904/89).
  5 Précis, 22 Nov. 1910 (TNA, CO 904/119); Ernest Blythe (BMH WS 939, pp 17–18).
  6 McCluskey, *Fenians & Ribbonmen*, p. 60.   7 Précis, 23 June 1910 (TNA, CO 904/119).
  8 W.J. Kelly senior (BMH WS 226, p.1).   9 Précis, 15 Aug. 1909 (TNA, CO 904/119).
 10 *DD*, 21 July 1913; CI Armagh, Jan. 1914 (TNA, CO 904/92); *DD*, 23 Oct. 1913; CI Armagh,
      Sept. 1913 (TNA, CO 904/90).
 11 CI Tyrone, Mar. 1915 (TNA, CO 904/96).   12 McGee, *IRB*, p. 357.
 13 Ernest Blythe (BMH WS 939, pp 17–18).
 14 Patrick McCormack (BMH WS 339, pp 1–3); Seamus Reader (BMH WS 933, p. 13); James
      Byrne (BMH WS 828, p. 1).
 15 *TC*, 5 Dec. 1907; CI Armagh, Oct. 1913 (TNA, Co904/91); Mac Diarmada to McGarrity, 12
      Dec. 1913 (NLI, McGarrity papers, MS 17,618).
 16 McCartan to McGarrity, 21 Jan. 1910 (NLI, McGarrity papers, P8186).
 17 Précis, 13 Feb. 1910 (TNA, CO 904/119).   18 Précis, 13 Oct. 1909 (ibid.).
 19 Précis, 6 Aug. 1910 (ibid.).   20 Précis, 13 Jan. 1909 (TNA, CO 904/118).
 21 Précis, 13 Mar. 1909 (ibid.).   22 *DN*, 3 Feb. 1910.   23 *UH*, 30 Mar. 1907.
 24 McCluskey, *Fenians & Ribbonmen*, pp 58–94.
 25 CI Tyrone, Sept. 1911 (TNA, CO 904/85).
 26 Précis, Aug. 1911 (TNA, CO 904/119).
 27 McCartan to McGarrity, 2 Jan. 1911 (NLI, McGarrity papers, P8186).
 28 McGarrity to McCartan, 16 Apr. 1912 (ibid.).
 29 CI Tyrone, Oct. 1912 (TNA, CO 904/88).
 30 IG, July 1913 (TNA, CO 904/90); CI Tyrone, Aug. 1913 (ibid.).
 31 Précis, 18 Oct. 1914 (TNA, CO 904/120); McCartan (BMH WS 766, p. 28); Albert Tally
      (BMH WS 884, p. 2); Arthur McElvogue (BMH WS 221, p. 2).
 32 McCartan (BMH WS 776, p. 28).
 33 CI Tyrone, June 1909 (TNA, CO 904/78).
 34 McCluskey, *Fenians & Ribbonmen*, p. 38.
 35 McCartan to McGarrity, 1 May 1908 (NLI, McGarrity papers, P8186).
 36 IG, Dec. 1908 (NAI, CBS, IGCI, Box 15).
 37 Wheatley, *Nationalism & the Irish Party*, p. 75.
 38 O'Shiel (BMH WS 1770/2, p. 156).
 39 Patrick Maume, *The long gestation: Irish nationalist life, 1891–1918* (Dublin, 1999), p. 2.
 40 Phoenix, *Northern nationalism*, pp 5–6.
 41 *TC*, 1 Aug. 1911; *DD*, 4 Feb. 1913.

42 *DD*, 24 Sept. 1914; John Newsinger, *Rebel city: Larkin, Connolly and the Labour movement* (London, 2004), pp 63–4.
43 *DD*, 4 Mar. 1914.
44 F.J. O'Connor to James E. Dougherty, 11 Oct. 1912 (NAI, CSORP, 1912/18029); *Mid-Ulster Mail*, 12 Oct. 1912.
45 *Mid-Ulster Mail*, 14 Dec. 1912.
46 *UH*, 27 June 1914.   47 *TC*, 6 Mar. 1914.
48 CI Tyrone, 2 Apr. 1914 (NAI, CSORP, 1914/6076).
49 Ibid., May 1914 (TNA, CO 904/93).
50 *Mid-Ulster Mail*, 3 June 1911.
51 William O'Brien, *An olive branch in Ireland* (London, 1910), p. 418.
52 Devlin to Redmond, 15 July 1905 (NLI, Redmond papers, MS 15,181/1); O'Brien, *Olive branch*, p. 420.
53 *II*, 12 May 1909.   54 O'Shiel (BMH WS 1770/1, pp 139–48).
55 Précis, 30 July 1909 (TNA, CO 904/118).   56 O'Shiel (BMH WS 1770/1, p. 141).
57 Bew, *Conflict & conciliation*, p. 186.   58 *Northern Whig*, 20 Mar. 1910.
59 *Tyrone Constitution*, 31 Dec. 1909; Bew, *Conflict & conciliation*, p. 196.
60 *DN*, 6 Jan. 1910.   61 Ibid., 13 Jan. 1910.
62 Montgomery to John E. Walsh, 9 Nov. 1918 (PRONI, Montgomery papers, D627/436/53).
63 O'Shiel (BMH WS 1770/3, p. 420).   64 Hepburn, *Catholic Belfast*, p. 58.
65 CI Tyrone, May 1911 (TNA, CO 904/84).   66 *DN*, 8 June 1911.
67 CI Tyrone, Aug. 1911 (TNA, CO 904/84).
68 McCartan to McGarrity, 4 Apr. 1913 (NLI, McGarrity papers, P8186).
69 *UH*, 28 Apr. 1917.   70 Bridget Hourican, 'Murnaghan, George', *DIB*.
71 Patrick H. Arkinson, 'McHugh, Charles', *DIB*.
72 John Privilege, *Michael Logue and the Catholic Church in Ireland, 1879–1925* (Manchester, 2009), pp 89–90.
73 Oliver Rafferty, *Catholicism in Ulster: an interpretative history* (London, 1994), p. 189.
74 David W. Miller, *Church, state and nation in Ireland, 1898–1921* (Dublin, 1973), p. 496.
75 Logue to Beglie, 9 Feb. 1912 (CÓFLA, Logue papers, v).
76 Logue to Walsh, 22 Nov. 1912 (Dublin Diocesan Archives, Walsh papers, 383/5).
77 Logue to O'Donnell, 5 Nov. 1912 (CÓFLA, O'Donnell papers, III).
78 Ó Corráin, 'Resigned to take the bill', p. 11.   79 Phoenix, *Northern nationalism*, pp 10–13.
80 *Gaelic American*, 4 May 1907.   81 *DN*, 22 Dec. 1910; *TC*, 5 Jan., 12 Jan., 26 Jan. 1911.
82 See, for example, PRONI, Lowry papers, D1132/5/13–14.
83 W.J. Harbison to Redmond, 14 Apr. 1915 (NLI, Redmond papers, MS 15,261/3).
84 *DN*, 31 Mar. 1910.   85 Ibid., 6 Feb. 1913.
86 CI Derry, Jan. 1913 (TNA, CO 904/89).
87 J.B. Armour to W.S. Armour, 30 Jan. 1913 (PRONI, Armour papers, D1792/A/3/4/6).
88 *DD*, 14 May 1913.   89 McCluskey, *Fenians & Ribbonmen*, p. 75.
90 Ibid., p. 46.   91 O'Day, *Irish home rule*, p. 235.
92 *TC*, 1 June 1911.   93 Ibid., 10 Oct. 1912.
94 Wheatley, *Nationalism & the Irish Party*, p. 75.
95 *TC*, 30 Nov. 1911.   96 *IF*, Dec. 1910.
97 Senia Pašeta, *Before the revolution: nationalism, social change and Ireland's Catholic elite, 1879–1922* (Cork, 1999), pp 40–2.
98 *DN*, 8 Aug. 1912.   99 *DD*, 2 July 1913.
100 IG, July 1912 (TNA, CO 904/87).   101 IG, Sept. 1912 (TNA, CO 904/88).
102 CI Armagh, July 1913 (TNA, CO 904/90).
103 CI Derry, Aug. 1913; CI Tyrone, Aug. 1913 (ibid.).
104 Dungannon shots fired from an excursion train at Moy [?] C. McShane injured, Aug. 1913 (NAI, CSORP, 1913/14962).

105 CI Tyrone, Oct. 1913 (TNA, CO 904/91). 106 *DD*, 2 July 1913.
107 O'Shiel (BMH WS 1770/3, p. 416). 108 *UH*, 21 Feb. 1914.
109 Phoenix, *Northern nationalism*, pp 11–12.
110 Redmond to O'Neill [Feb.] 1914 (NLI, Redmond papers, MS 15,257/2).
111 Hepburn, *Catholic Belfast*, pp 149–51. 112 Phoenix, *Northern nationalism*, pp 12–13.
113 *DN*, 2 July 1914. 114 IG, May 1914 (TNA, CO 904/93).
115 *UH*, 20 June 1914. 116 *DD*, 29 July 1914.
117 William Redmond, 'Memorandum of six northern counties', 3 June 1914 (NLI, Redmond papers, MS 22,189).
118 *UH*, 20 June 1914.
119 Marnie Hay, *Bulmer Hobson and the nationalist movement in twentieth-century Ireland* (Manchester, 2009), p. 111.
120 *IV*, 7 Feb. 1914. 121 Ibid., 8 Apr. 1916.
122 M.J. Kelly, *The Fenian ideal and Irish nationalism, 1882–1916* (Woodbridge, 2006), p. 215.
123 *DD*, 27 May 1914. 124 IG, Mar. 1914 (TNA, CO 904/92).
125 J.D. Nugent, 'Private and confidential memo', May 1914 (NLI, Ceannt papers, MS 13,070/9).
126 CI, May 1914 (TNA, CO 904/93); Intelligence notes for Tyrone, 1914 (TNA, CO 903/18/51).
127 Précis, 22 Nov. 1913 (TNA, CO 904/119). 128 James Tomney (BMH WS 169, p. 1).
129 Précis, 21–4 Jan. 1914 and 19 Apr. 1914 (TNA, CO 904/120).
130 Précis, 21–2 Feb. 1914 (ibid.).
131 Arthur McElvogue (BMH WS 221, pp 1–2); Albert Tally (BMH WS, p. 3); Seán Corr (BMH WS 145, p. 1); James Hackett (BMH WS 228, p. 1); James Tomney (BMH WS 169, p. 1).
132 Tom Kelly (BMH WS 378, p. 1).
133 McCartan (BMH WS 776, pp 28–9). 134 Eugene Coyle (BMH WS 325, p. 2).
135 IG, Nov. 1914 (TNA, CO 904/95); *IV*, 29 Aug. 1914.
136 Coyle to Moore, 17 May 1915 (NLI, Maurice Moore papers, MS 10,561/6).
137 M.J. Kelly, 'The Irish Volunteers: a Machiavellian moment?' in D. George Boyce & Alan O'Day (eds), *The Ulster crisis* (London, 2005), p. 79.
138 IG, Jan. 1914; CI Tyrone, Feb. 1914 (TNA, CO 904/92).
139 CI Tyrone, Mar. 1914 (TNA, CO 904/92).
140 Phoenix, *Northern nationalism*, pp 13–4. 141 *IV*, 7 Feb. 1914.
142 *UH*, 24 May 1914; CI Tyrone, May 1914 (TNA CO 904/93).
143 CI Donegal, June 1914 (TNA, CO 904/93); James McMonagle (BMH WS, 1385, p. 1).
144 CI Donegal, Apr. – Mar. 1914 (TNA, CO 904/92).
145 CI Fermanagh, Dec. 1913 (TNA, CO 904/91); ibid., Apr. 1914 (TNA, CO 904/92).
146 CI Monaghan, Feb. – Mar. 1914 (TNA, CO 904/92).
147 CI Derry, Mar. 1914 (ibid.); Joost Augusteijn, *From public defiance to guerrilla warfare: the experience of ordinary volunteers in the Irish war of independence, 1916–1921* (Dublin, 2006), p. 46.
148 CI Armagh, June 1914 (TNA, CO 904/93); John Garvey (BMH WS 178, p. 1).
149 CI Armagh, Apr. 1914 (TNA, CO 904/93).
150 O'Shiel (BMH WS 1770/3, p. 429).
151 Annual intelligence notes for County Tyrone, 1914 (TNA, CO 903/18).
152 Précis, 5 Apr. 1914 (TNA, CO 904/120).
153 CI Tyrone, Apr. 1914 (TNA, CO 904/93).
154 Casement to Moore, 4 May 1914 (NLI, Moore papers, MS 10,561/3).
155 Casement to Moore, 2 June 1914 (ibid.).
156 *DD*, 10 June 1914; George Berkeley (BMH WS, 971, p. 84).
157 CI Tyrone, May 1914 (TNA, CO 904/93).
158 Kelly, 'The Irish Volunteers', p. 65.

159 Précis, 31 May 1914 (TNA, CO 904/120).

160 Clarke to Devoy, 25 June 1914 (NLI, Leon Ó Broin papers, MS 31,696).

161 Bulmer Hobson, *A short history of the Irish Volunteers* (Dublin, 1918), p. 101.

162 IG, May 1914 (TNA, CO 904/93).

163 *DD*, 17 June 1914; *FJ*, 10 June 1914.

164 Gerard MacAtasney, *Seán Mac Diarmada: the mind of the revolution* (Manorhamilton, 2004), pp 66–9.

165 Clarke to Devoy, 25 June 1914 (NLI, Ó Broin papers, MS 31,696).

166 *DD*, 17 June 1914.   167 *UH*, 6 June 1914.

168 CI Tyrone, July 1914 (TNA, CO 904/94); *UH*, 1 Aug. 1914.

169 *UH*, 21 July 1914.   170 Foy, 'Ulster Unionism', p. 117.

171 CI Tyrone, June 1914 (TNA, CO 904/93).

172 J.R. White to George Berkeley, 22 July 1914 (Cork City & County Archives, Berkeley papers, CCCA/PR12/77).

173 IG, Sept. 1914 (TNA, CO 904/94).   174 *IV*, 29 Aug. 1914.

175 Seán Corr (BMH WS 145, p. 2).   176 J.R. White, *Misfit* (London, 1930), pp 232–4.

177 *IN*, 7 Sept. 1914.   178 James O'Daly (BMH WS 235, p. 2).

179 Seamus Dobbyn, Belfast (BMH WS 279, p. 4).   180 Phoenix, *Northern nationalism*, p. 18.

181 *DN*, 17 Sept. 1914.   182 Ibid., 10 Sept. 1914.

183 White, *Misfit*, p. 319.   184 Kelly, *Fenian ideal*, p. 238.

185 Asquith to Bonar Law, 11 Sept. 1914 (House of Lords, Bonar Law Papers/34/5/34).

186 Police report, 31 Oct. 1914 (NLI, Redmond papers, MS 15,258).

CHAPTER FOUR *Empire or republic?*

1 Ian Chambers, *The Chamberlains, the Churchills and Ireland, 1874–1922* (New York, 2006), p. 215.

2 Bew, *Conflict & conciliation*, p. 213.   3 CI Tyrone, Aug. 1914 (TNA, CO 904/94).

4 *UH*, 29 Aug. 1914.   5 CI Tyrone, Aug. 1914 (TNA, CO 904/94).

6 Intelligence notes for Tyrone, 1914 (TNA, CO 903/18/11).

7 CI Fermanagh, Aug. 1914; CI Armagh, Aug. 1914; CI Tyrone, Aug. 1914 (TNA, CO 904/94).

8 Timothy Bowman, 'The UVF and the formation of the 36th (Ulster) division', *IHS*, 32:128 (2001), 505–6.

9 Intelligence notes for Tyrone, 1915 (TNA, CO 903/19/1).

10 Bowman, 'UVF', p. 507; David Fitzpatrick, 'The logic of collective sacrifice: Ireland and the British Army, 1914–18', *Historical Journal*, 38:4 (1995), 1026.

11 IG, Apr. 1915 (TNA, CO 904/96); *DD*, 28 Apr. 1915; *UH*, 1 May 1915.

12 *DD*, 21 Apr. 1915.

13 O'Connor to Moore, 10 Mar. 1915 (NLI, Moore papers, MS 10,551/1).

14 IG, Dec. 1915 (TNA, CO 904/98).   15 CI Tyrone, Nov. 1914 (TNA, CO 904/95).

16 CI Tyrone, Jan. 1915 (TNA, CO 904/96).

17 Montgomery to Charles Montgomery, 18 July 1916 (PRONI, Montgomery papers, D627/429/50).

18 Montgomery to Trimble, 1 Sept. 1916 (ibid., D627/429/55).

19 Report on recruiting in Ireland (1914–16), Cd 8168.

20 'Estimate of the number of recruits who have joined the army', 4 Aug. 1914–15 Jan. 1916 (NLI, Brennan papers, MS 26,191).

21 Report on the state of Donegal, 1916 (TNA, CO 904/120/3).

22 CI Tyrone, Sept. 1914 (CO 904/94).

23 'Estimate of the number of recruits who have joined the army', 4 Aug. 1914–15 Jan. 1916 (NLI, Brennan papers, MS 26,191).

24 Eric Mercer, 'For King, country and a shilling a day: Belfast recruiting patterns in the Great War', *History Ireland*, 11:4 (2003), 29–33.

25 Reports on the state of Fermanagh, Derry, Tyrone, 1916 (TNA, CO 904/120/3).
26 Ricardo to Montgomery, 29 Aug. 1918 (PRONI, Montgomery papers, D627/436/37).
27 Duchess of Abercorn to Carson, 10 Oct. 1916 (PRONI, Irish papers, D1507/A/19/9).
28 Montgomery to J.R. Fisher, 13 June 1918 (PRONI, Montgomery papers, D627/434/37A).
29 *Hansard (Commons)*, 31 Oct. 1916, vol. 86, c.1529.
30 Timothy Bowman, *Irish regiments in the Great War: discipline and morale* (Manchester, 2003), p. 63.
31 *TC*, 6 Aug. 1914.
32 Montgomery to 'My Dear Hugo', 27 June 1916 (PRONI, Montgomery papers, D627/429/48).
33 *Hansard (Commons)*, 23 Dec. 1915, vol. 77, cols 647–784.   34 *DD*, 24 Mar. 1915.
35 Horner to Carson, 3 Sept. 1915 (PRONI, Irish papers, D1507/A/13/22).
36 *UH*, 8 Sept. 1915; Tyrone County Council and National Registration Act, Aug. 1914 (NAI, CSORP, 1915/13755).
37 *UH*, 12 June 1915.
38 Montgomery to Fisher, 22 Apr. 1918 (PRONI, Montgomery papers, D627/433/132).
39 Montgomery to Bates, 21 Apr. 1918 (ibid., D627/433/129).
40 Augusteijn, *Public defiance*, pp 32–42.   41 Patrick McCartan (BMH WS 776, p. 30).
42 IG, Dec. 1914 (TNA, CO 904/95).   43 *IV*, 16 Jan. 1915.
44 'Note on the activities of Herbert M. Pim', 1915 (NLI, Ó Broin papers, MS 31,654).
45 *DN*, 15 Oct. 1914.
46 Albert Tally (BMH WS 884, pp 3–4); Tom Kelly (BMH WS 378, p. 1).
47 Intelligence notes for Tyrone, 1914 (TNA, CO 903/18), p. 51.
48 Proinsias de Búrca (BMH WS 105, p. 3); Report on the state of Monaghan, 1916 (TNA, CO 904/120/3).
49 IG & CI Donegal, Nov. 1914 (TNA, CO 904/95).   50 *UH*, 19 Feb. 1916.
51 Coyle to Moore, 17 May 1915 (NLI, Moore papers, MS 10,561/6).
52 IG, Jan. 1915 (TNA, CO 904/96).
53 Coalisland, Donaghmore and Dungannon, 21–3 Oct. 1914; Clogher, 21 Nov. 1914 (IG, Oct.–Dec. 1914, TNA CO 904/95); Omagh anti-enlistment campaign, Sept.–Dec. 1914 (NAI, CSORP, 1914/15689); Dungannon burning Union Jack (NAI, CSORP, 1914/16584).
54 Ben Novick, *Conceiving revolution: Irish nationalist propaganda during the First World War* (Dublin, 2001), p. 90.
55 *UH*, 14 Nov. 1914.
56 Edward O'Connor (Carrickmore), undated (NLI, McGarrity papers, P8191).
57 IG, Aug. 1915 (TNA, CO 904/97).
58 J.J. O'Connell, 'Autobiographical account of events leading to 1916: Irish Volunteers in Tyrone 1915' (NLI, O'Connell papers, MS 22,114/1).
59 Précis, 23 Jan. 1917 (TNA, CO 904/120).
60 Eckersley to National Volunteer HQ, 21 June 1915 (NLI, Moore papers, MS 10,551).
61 *IV*, 10 July 1915.
62 O'Connell, 'Irish Volunteers in Tyrone 1915' (NLI, O'Connell papers, MS 22,114/1).
63 Confidential police reports of May 1916, 25 May 1916, in Martin, 'McCartan documents', 55–65.
64 O'Connell, 'Irish Volunteers in Tyrone 1915' (NLI, O'Connell papers, MS 22,114/1).
65 Eskersley to Redmond, 14 June 1915 (NLI, Moore papers, MS 10,544/3).
66 Eskersley to National Volunteers HQ, 21 June 1915 (ibid., MS 10,551).
67 O'Connor to Diarmid Coffey, 15 July 1915 (NLI, Coffey & Chenevix Trench papers, MS 46,309/3).
68 IG, Oct. 1915 (TNA, CO 904/98).
69 O'Connell, 'Irish Volunteers in Tyrone 1915' (NLI, O'Connell papers, MS 22,114/1).
70 *IV*, 3 July 1915.   71 *DD*, 7 July 1915.

72 O'Connor to Eckersley, 16 July 1915 (NLI, Moore papers, MS 10,551/1).

73 CI Tyrone, Aug. 1914 (TNA, CO 904/97); *UH*, 28 Aug. 1915.

74 Kelly, *Fenian ideal*, p. 249.

75 Note on the activities of Herbert M. Pim, 1915 (NLI, Ó Broin papers, MS 31,654/4); Jack Shields (BMH WS 224, p. 1); *IV*, 31 July, 6 Nov. 1915.

76 McCartan (BMH WS 776, p. 31).

77 *TC*, 22 July 1915.   78 *IV*, 31 July 1915.

79 Confidential police report, 25 May 1916, in Martin, 'McCartan documents', pp 55–65.

80 McCartan to McCullough, 9 Jan. 1932 (NLI, Ó Broin papers, MS 31,653).

81 Denis McCullough (BMH WS 915, p. 15).

82 McCartan to McCullough, 9 Jan. 1932 (NLI, Ó Broin papers, MS 31,653).

83 Charles Townshend, *Easter 1916: the Irish rebellion* (London, 2006), p. 133.

84 Denis McCullough (BMH WS 915, pp 19–20); MacAtasney, *Mac Diarmada*, p. 108.

85 McCullough to P.J. McGinley, 2 Sept. 1932 (NLI, Ó Broin papers, MS 31,653); CI Tyrone, Apr.–May 1916 (TNA, CO 904/99).

86 James Hackett (BMH WS 228, p. 2).

87 McCartan to McGarrity, 2 June 1916 in Martin, 'McCartan documents', p. 42.

88 McCartan to McGarrity, 22 May 1916 in ibid., p. 30.

89 McCartan to McGarrity, 28 Apr. 1916 in F.X. Martin, 'Easter 1916: an inside report on Ulster', *Record*, 12:2 (1986), 202.

90 McCartan to McCullough, 9 Jan. 1932 (NLI, Ó Broin papers, MS 31,653).

91 Conlin, 'Report of occurrences during recent rebellion', 23 May 1916, p. 61.

92 McCartan to McGarrity, 28 Apr. 1916 in Martin, 'Easter 1916', p. 202.

93 James O'Daly (BMH WS 235, p. 3); Eugene Coyle (BMH WS 325, pp 6–7).

94 McCartan to McGarrity, 28 Apr. 1916 in Martin, 'Easter 1916', p. 202.

95 Ibid.   96 Jack Shields (BMH WS 224, p. 3).

97 McCullough to P.J. McGinley, 2 Sept. 1932 (NLI, Ó Broin papers, MS 31,653).

98 McCartan to McGarrity, 28 Apr. 1916 in Martin, 'Easter 1916', p. 204.

99 Ibid.; Canon McNelis (CÓFLA, O'Kane collection, II A, 22).

100 Conlin, 'Report of occurrences during recent rebellion', 23 May 1916, p. 62.

101 Proinsias de Búrca [Frank Burke] (BMH WS 105, p. 3).

102 Thomas Wilson (BMH WS 176, p. 12).

103 James Tomney (BMH WS 169, pp 3–4).   104 W.J. Kelly senior (BMH WS 226, pp 5–6).

105 Seán Corr (BMH WS 145, pp 6–7).   106 Thomas Hackett (BMH WS 228, p. 2).

107 McCullough to P. J. McGinley, 2 Sept. 1932 (NLI, Ó Broin papers, MS 31,653); W.J. Kelly senior (BMH WS 226, p. 6).

108 Jack Shields (BMH WS 224, p. 3).   109 Seán Corr (BMH WS 145, p. 7).

110 Nora Connolly O'Brien in Uinseann Mac Eoin, *Survivors*, p. 183.

111 Tom Kelly (BMH WS 378, p. 7).

112 Ina [Connolly] Heron (BMH WS 919, pp 110–11).

113 McCartan to McGarrity, 28 Apr. 1916 in 'Easter 1916', *Clogher Record*, 12:2, 205.

114 McCartan to McCullough, 9 Jan. 1932 (NLI, Ó Broin papers, MS 31,653).

115 McCartan to McGarrity, 28 Apr. 1916 in 'Easter 1916', *Clogher Record*, 12:2, 203.

116 Canon McNelis (CÓFLA, O'Kane collection, II A, 22).

117 Tom Kelly (BMH WS 378, pp 4–5).

118 Report on the state of Tyrone, 1916 Tyrone, 1916 (TNA, CO 904/120/3).

119 Joseph McCarthy (BMH WS 1497, p. 71).

120 Rory Haskins (BMH WS 223, p. 9).   121 Townshend, *Easter 1916*, pp 218–21.

122 CI Tyrone, Mar. 1916 (TNA, CO 904/99).   123 Seán Corr (BMH WS 145, p. 6).

124 W.J. Kelly senior (BMH WS 226, p. 5); James Tomney (BMH WS 169, pp 2–3); James Hackett (BMH WS 228, pp 2–3); Eugene Coyle (BMH WS 325, pp 5–7); IG, Nov. 1914 (TNA, CO 904/95); *IV*, 29 Aug. 1914; Fr Coyle to Moore, 17 May 1915 (NLI, Moore papers, MS 10,561/6); McCullough to P.J. McGinley, 2 Sept. 1932 (NLI, Ó Broin papers, MS 31,653); Police reports, Dec. 1915 (TNA, CO 904/120).

125 Townshend, *Easter 1916*, p. 227.   126 Bowman, *Carson's army*, p. 10.

127 W.J. Miller CI, 25 May 1916, 'Confidential police report of May 1916', in 'Easter 1916', 'The McCartan Documents', *Clogher Record*, 6:1 (1966), 55.

128 Annual intelligence notes for County Tyrone, 1916 (TNA, CO 903/19/2).

129 Phoenix, *Northern nationalism*, p. 26.

130 Montgomery to Charles Montgomery, 9 June 1916 (PRONI, Montgomery papers, D627/429/26).

131 Montgomery to Willis, 15 June 1916 (ibid., D627/429/35).

132 Ricardo to Montgomery, 11 Apr. 1920 (ibid., D627/435/28).

133 Montgomery to Sinclair, 20 Sept. 1916 (ibid., D627/429/66).

134 Phoenix, *Northern nationalism*, p. 26.

135 Miller, *Church, state & nation*, p. 27.

136 Devlin to Redmond, 3 June 1916 (NLI, Redmond papers, MS 15,181/3).

137 *UH*, 10 June 1916.   138 *DD*, 22 Mar. 1916.

139 T.J. Harbison to Redmond, 27 May 1916 (NLI, Redmond papers, MS 15,262/5).

140 *DD*, 14 June 1916; *UH*, 17 June 1916.

141 Devlin to Redmond, 3 June 1916 (NLI, Redmond papers, MS 15,181/3).

142 Dillon to T.P. O'Connor, 17 June 1916 (TCD, Dillon papers, MS 6741/320).

143 Hepburn, *Catholic Belfast*, p. 179.

144 Kevin O'Shiel, *The rise of the Irish Nation League* (Omagh, 1916), p. 4.

145 John Dooher, 'Tyrone nationalism and the question of partition, 1910–25' (MPhil, University of Ulster, 1986), p. 187.

146 *DD*, 23 Aug. 1916.   147 *IV*, 26 Sept. 1914.

148 Thomas Clarke, *Glimpses of an Irish felon's prison life* (Cork, 1922), p. xiii.

149 J.B. Lyons, 'Tom Kettle, 1880–1916', *Dublin Historical Record*, 43:2 (1990), 95.

CHAPTER FIVE *From St Mary's hall to the Dáil: Sinn Féin, 1916–18*

1 Annual intelligence notes for County Tyrone, 1918 (TNA, CO 903/19/4).

2 Michael Laffan, *The resurrection of Ireland: the Sinn Féin Party, 1916–1923* (Cambridge, 1999), p. 63.

3 CI Tyrone, Oct. 1916 (TNA, CO 904/101).

4 O'Connor to Gavan Duffy, 18 Oct. 1916 (NLI, Gavan Duffy papers, MS 5,581/81).

5 CI Tyrone, Aug. 1916 (TNA, CO 904/100).

6 Laffan, *Resurrection*, p. 64.   7 *UH*, 5 Aug. 1916.

8 McCartan to Gavan Duffy, 30 Mar. 1917 (NLI, Gavan Duffy papers, MS 5,581/108).

9 *UH*, 30 Dec. 1916.

10 O'Connor to Moore, 29 May 1917 (NLI, Moore papers, MS 10,561/24).

11 Small letter book of Kevin O'Shiel, May 1918 (NLI, MS 22,964).

12 O'Kelly to Gavan Duffy, 30 Mar. 1917 (NLI, Gavan Duffy papers, MS 5,581/105).

13 McCartan to Gavan Duffy, 1 Apr. 1917 (ibid., MS 5,581/110).

14 O'Connor to Gavan Duffy, 7 Mar. 1917 (ibid., MS 5,581/94).

15 Murnaghan to Gavan Duffy, 6 July 1917 (ibid., MS 5,581/170).

16 Dooher, 'Tyrone nationalism', p. 232.

17 CI Tyrone, July 1916 (TNA, CO 904/100).   18 CI Tyrone, July 1918 (TNA, CO 904/106).

19 Owen Rogers to Dillon, 16 Aug. 1916 (TCD, Dillon papers, MS 6784/582).

20 McGee, *IRB*, p. 317.

21 Jack Shields (BMH WS 928, p. 2).   22 Albert Tally (BMH WS 884, p. 5).

23 Séamus Dobbyn (BMH WS 279, p. 13).   24 Jack Shields (BMH WS 928, p. 10).

25 W.J. Kelly jnr. (BMH WS 893, p. 4).

26 IRA AG to Frank Dooris, 26 Nov. 1919 (IMA, A/0391/7).

27 Augusteijn, *Public defiance*, p. 86.
28 Dungannon, cock-fighting at Moygashel, 1917 (NAI, CSORP, 1917/15984).
29 Thomas 'Banba' Martin, 18 July 1967 (CÓFLA, O'Kane collection, IV.B.07 0002 09).
30 CI Tyrone, Mar. 1917 (TNA, CO 904/102).
31 *TC*, 8 Aug. 1918.   32 *DD*, 15 Aug. 1917.
33 CI Donegal, Aug. 1917 (TNA, CO 904/103).   34 Kelly, 'The Irish Volunteers', p. 75.
35 Augusteijn, *Public defiance*, p. 55.
36 IG, June 1916 (TNA, CO 904/100).
37 *DD*, 29 Nov. 1916.
38 Phoenix, *Northern nationalism*, p. 45.
39 *UH*, 23 Dec. 1916.   40 *DD*, 12 Dec. 1917.
41 Ibid., 13 June 1917.   42 Ibid., 8 Aug. 1918.
43 Fearghal McGarry, *Eoin O'Duffy: a self-made hero* (Oxford, 2005), p. 37.
44 *DD*, 20 Dec. 1916; *UH*, 23 Dec. 1916.
45 *UH*, 10 Aug. 1918.   46 *DD*, 8 Aug. 1917.
47 *UH*, 23 June 1917.   48 Ibid., 21 July 1917.
49 Marie Coleman, *County Longford and the Irish revolution* (Dublin, 2003), p. 76.
50 O'Shiel (BMH WS 1770/6, p. 778).
51 William Donnelly to Alice Donnelly, 17 July 1923 (CÓFLA, O'Kane collection, III, F, 1); *UH*,
    29 Apr. 1929; Alice McSloy, 21 June 1967 (CÓFLA, O'Kane collection, IV, A, 16); Memoirs
    of Eithne Coyle (NLI, MS 28,818/1).
52 Appointment of Dr Owens, Pomeroy, Co. Tyrone, Sinn Féiner, to Omagh No. 2 Dispensary
    District, 1923 (PRONI, HA/32/1/332); *UH*, 20 Sept. 2012.
53 Mallon, Michael, Coagh, Co. Tyrone: exclusion order, 1924–6 (PRONI, HA/5/2522); Alice
    McSloy, 21 June 1967 (CÓFLA, O'Kane collection, IV, A, 16); Donnelly, William, Cookstown,
    Co. Tyrone, 1922–4 (PRONI, HA/5/1797); Mallon, Alice, Coagh, Co. Tyrone, 1923–6
    (PRONI, HA/5/2342).
54 Coleman, *Longford*, p. 56.
55 Omagh, Dr Patrick McCartan Sinn Féin elected dispensary doctor, Apr. 1917 (NAI, CSORP,
    1917/10159).
56 Carrickmore Creamery, dispute regarding managership [sic.], Feb. 1917 (NAI, CSORP,
    1917/8153).
57 Stronge to Montgomery, 27 June 1917 (PRONI, Montgomery papers, D627/430/60).
58 Murley Orangemen to Montgomery, 18 July 1917 (ibid., D627/430/68).
59 Montgomery to Coote, 19 July 1917 (ibid., D627/430/71).
60 Laffan, *Resurrection*, p. 95.
61 CI Tyrone, July 1917 (TNA, CO 904/103); *UH*, 30 June 1917; *UH*, 28 July 1917.
62 CI Tyrone, Sept. 1917 (TNA, CO 904/104).
63 *UH*, 16 Sept. 1917.   64 *DD*, 12 Sept. 1917.
65 CI Tyrone, Sept. 1917 (TNA, CO 904/104).
66 CI Derry and Donegal, Sept. 1917 (ibid.).
67 CI Fermanagh and Monaghan, Sept. 1917 (ibid.).   68 *UH*, 6 Oct. 1917.
69 Albert Tally (BMH WS 884, p. 5).
70 Secretaries report to the National executive Sinn Féin, 19 Dec. 1917 (NLI, Count Plunkett
    papers, MS 11,405); the police figure for the same month was 36 clubs with 2,135 members (CI
    Tyrone, Dec. 1917, TNA, CO 904/104); cumainn would only rise by a further 25%, with the
    RIC estimate for the County in December 1918, 50 cumainn and 3,585 members (CI Tyrone,
    Dec. 1918, TNA, CO 904/107); Fitzpatrick, *Politics*, p. 133.
71 Dooher, 'Tyrone nationalism', p. 235. 72 CI Armagh, Dec. 1917 (TNA, CO 904/104).
73 CI Derry, Dec. 1917 (ibid.).   74 CI Donegal, Dec. 1917 (ibid.).
75 CI Monaghan, Dec. 1917 (ibid.); McGarry, *Eoin O'Duffy*, pp 28–9.
76 Dooher, 'Tyrone nationalism', p. 236.   77 Phoenix, *Northern nationalism*, p. 24.

78 *UH*, 23 Feb., 9 Mar. 1918.   79 Hepburn, *Catholic Belfast*, p. 184.
80 Montgomery to Dicey, 16 July 1917 (PRONI, Montgomery papers, D627/430/66).
81 Jackson, *Home rule*, p. 208.   82 Laffan, *Resurrection*, p. 128.
83 Dillon to Redmond, 25 June 1917 (NLI, Redmond papers, MS 15,182/24).
84 *DD*, 27 Mar. 1918.   85 Miller, *Church, state & nation*, p. 399.
86 *II*, 1 Apr. 1918; O'Shiel (BMH WS 1770/6, p. 758).
87 O'Shiel (BMH WS 1770/6, p. 752).   88 *TC*, 4 Apr. 1918.
89 Roll book of Pomeroy battalion IRA (CÓFLA, O'Kane collection, I.E. box 1, folder 6).
90 *TC*, 25 Mar. 1918.   91 O'Shiel (BMH WS 1770/6, pp 756–7).
92 *II*, 4 Apr. 1918.   93 CI Tyrone, Jan. 1918 (TNA, CO 904/105).
94 Alice McSloy, 21 June 1967 (CÓFLA, O'Kane collection, IV.B.10 0002 09 Ee.4.4).
95 Phoenix, *Northern nationalism*, p. 47.
96 *DD*, 10 Apr. 1918.   97 *II*, 5 Apr. 1918.
98 CI Tyrone, Apr. 1918 (TNA, CO 904/105). 99 *DD*, 10 Apr. 1918.
100 W.J. Kelly Junior (BMH WS 893, p. 5).   101 Séan Corr (BMH WS 458, p. 3).
102 Alice Cashel (BMH WS 366, p. 3); McCarthy, *Cumann na mBan*, pp 109–10; Dromore (*UH*,
     16 Apr. 1921); Strabane (*UH*, 22 Mar. 1919; CI Tyrone, Jan. 1919, TNA CO 904/108);
     Glenelly (*II*, 6 June 1918); Coalisland (CI Tyrone, July 1918, TNA CO 904/106); Trillick,
     Mountfield, Gortin (*UH*, 26 July 1920); Omagh (*UH*, 28 May 1921); Dungannon (*UH*, 26
     June 1920; CI Tyrone, June 1920, TNA CO 904/112); Fintona, Rock, Cookstown (CI Tyrone,
     May 1918, TNA CO 904/106).
103 *UH*, 13 Apr. 1918.   104 Nicholas Smyth (BMH WS 721, p. 2).
105 CI Tyrone, Apr. 1918 (TNA, CO 904/105). 106 Nicholas Smyth (BMH WS 721, p. 2).
107 CI Tyrone, Apr. 1918 (TNA, CO 904/105).
108 Mrs M.E. Sinclair to Montgomery, 4 May 1918 (PRONI, Montgomery papers,
     D627/434/8).
109 J. Gunning Moore to Montgomery, 19 Apr. 1918 (ibid., D627/433/122).
110 *UH*, 2 Mar. 1918.   111 Ibid., 25 May 1918.
112 Augusteijn, *Public defiance*, p. 74.   113 *UH*, 21 Sept. 1918.
114 CI Tyrone, Apr. 1918 (TNA, CO 904/105).
115 O'Shiel (BMH WS 1770/6, pp 769–70).   116 Jack Shields (BMH WS 224, p. 6).
117 Anon. to Frank Dooris, 29 May 1923 (PRONI, HA/5/1573).
118 W.J. Kelly junior (BMH WS 893, p. 8).
119 *UH*, 25 May 1918; Michael Doherty (BMH WS 1583, p. 3).
120 Ricardo to Montgomery, 29 Aug. 1918 (PRONI, Montgomery papers, D627/436/37).
121 Nicholas Smyth (BMH WS 721, p. 3).
122 O'Shiel (BMH WS 1770/6, p. 771).
123 Montgomery to Fisher, 22 Apr. 1918 (PRONI, Montgomery papers, D627/433/132).
124 Dawson Bates to Montgomery, 19 Apr. 1918 (ibid., D627/433/123).
125 Montgomery to Bates, 21 Apr. 1918 (ibid., D627/433/129).
126 Barrie to Montgomery, 23 Apr. 1918 (ibid., D627/433/133).
127 Laffan, *Resurrection*, pp 142–4.   128 *UH*, 29 June 1918.
129 CI Tyrone, June 1918 (TNA, CO 904/106).
130 CI Tyrone, Sept. 1918 (TNA, CO 904/107).
131 Privilege, *Michael Logue*, p. 131.   132 John McCoy (BMH WS 492, p. 42).
133 Griffith to Murnaghan, 30 Nov. 1918 (PRONI, Arthur Griffith documents, T1635/1).
134 PRONI, Wilson & Simms papers, D2298/17/1.
135 Harbison to John Dillon, 28 Nov. 1918 (TCD, Dillon papers, MS 6755/612).
136 Walker, *Parliamentary election results*, p. 397.
137 *TC*, 12 Dec. 1918.   138 *DD*, 7 Mar. 1917.
139 Ibid., 19 Sept. 1917.   140 *UH*, 7 Dec. 1918.
141 Fisher to Montgomery, 17 Nov. 1918 (PRONI, Montgomery papers, D627/436/58).

142 Coote to Montgomery, 1917 (ibid., D627/430/18).
143 Fisher to Montgomery, 4 Mar. 1918 (ibid., D627/433/68).

CHAPTER SIX *Ulster Pale or Irish Republic, 1919–20*

1   *Irish Times*, 19 Jan. 1920.
2   Montgomery to Farnham, 25 Mar. 1919 (PRONI, Montgomery papers, D627/437/62).
3   Louis J. Walsh to MacRory, 29 May 1919 (CÓFLA, MacRory papers, folder 14).
4   *UH*, 17 May 1919.   5   CI Tyrone, Jan. 1919 (TNA, CO 904/108).
6   CI Tyrone Mar. 1919 (ibid.).   7   Laffan, *Resurrection*, p. 297.
8   *UH*, 17 May 1919.   9   CI Tyrone Aug. 1919 (TNA, CO 904/109).
10 *UH*, 20 Sept. 1919.   11 *Donegal News*, 4 Oct. 1919.
12 *UH*, 4 Oct. 1919.   13 Ibid., 6 Sept. 1919.
14 Arthur Mitchell, *Revolutionary government in Ireland: Dáil Éireann, 1919–22* (Dublin, 1995),
    p. 54.
15 IG, 13 May 1919 (TNA, CAB 24/79).
16 Dáil Loan net amounts at head office, 27 Sept. 1920 (NAI, DE/27).
17 GOC Ireland, 15 May 1919 (TNA, CAB 24/79).
18 CI Tyrone, Nov. 1919 (TNA, CO 904/110).
19 Augusteijn, *Public defiance*, pp 336–7.   20 *DD*, 26 June 1918.
21 CI Tyrone, Nov. 1919 (TNA, CO 904/110).
22 *UH*, 19 June 1920.   23 Ibid., 17 Apr. 1920.
24 Ibid., 15 May 1920.   25 CI Tyrone, Oct. 1920 (TNA CO 904/113).
26 *Hansard (Commons)*, 27 May 1919, vol. 116, cols 1082–8.
27 Ibid., 24 Mar. 1919, vol. 114, cols 144–6.
28 Stronge to Montgomery, 24 Mar. 1919 (PRONI, Montgomery papers, D627/437/61).
29 Montgomery to Farnham, 25 Mar. 1919 (ibid., D627/437/62).
30 *UH*, 1 May 1920.   31 Ibid., 15 May 1920.   32 Ibid., 5 June 1920.
33 Ibid., 19 June 1920, 23 Oct. 1920; CI Tyrone, June 1920 (TNA, CO 904/112).
34 *UH*, 26 June 1920; CI Tyrone, June 1920 (ibid.).
35 CI Tyrone, Nov. 1920 (CO 904/113).   36 CI Tyrone, June 1920 (CO 904/112).
37 *UH*, 8 Nov. 1919.   38 O'Shiel (BMH WS 1770/7, p. 933).
39 Mitchel, *Revolutionary government*, p. 139.
40 Augusteijn, *Public defiance*, p. 28; *UH*, 3 July 1920.
41 *UH*, 14 Aug. 1920.   42 Mitchel, *Revolutionary government*, p. 141.
43 *UH*, 17 July 1910.   44 *Irish Bulletin*, 27 Aug. 1920.
45 Weekly survey of the state of Ireland, 27 Dec. 1920 (TNA, CAB 24/117); Seán McElwee, IRA
    MSP (CÓFLA, O'Kane collection, I.B.17 0001 04 Ee.4.4).
46 Mitchel, *Revolutionary government*, p. 236.
47 *UH*, 25 Dec. 1920.   48 Phoenix, *Northern nationalism*, pp 90–1.
49 Sergeant A. Emerson, 27 Oct. 1921 (TNA, CO 904/156A).
50 Sergeant H. Gilroy, 15 Oct. 1921 (ibid.).   51 Sergeant J. Crawford, 6 Oct. 1921 (ibid.).
52 Suppression of SF arbitration court in Dungannon, 11 Jan. 1922 (PRONI, HA/32/1/8).
53 DCO, 31 Dec. 1921 (PRONI, HA/5/152).
54 DI Marshall, 13 Sept. 1921 (TNA, CO 904/156A).
55 AG to Department of Defence, 12 Oct. 1921 (NAI, DÉ 11/70); DI Walshe Dungannon, 24
    Sept. 1921 (TNA CO 904/156A).
56 Mary Kotsonouris, *Retreat from revolution: the Dáil courts, 1920–24* (Dublin, 1994), pp 54–5.
57 Fitzpatrick, *Politics*, p. 134.
58 Cookstown – Adair's and McCann's linen mills, CI Tyrone, Jan. 1918 (TNA, CO 904/105);
    Dungannon – Stevenson's and Dickson's (*DD*, 13 Feb. 1918; *TC*, 21 Feb. 1918); Coalisland
    spoke factory, CI Tyrone, Mar. 1918 (TNA, CO 904/105); ibid., Apr. 1918 (TNA, CO

904/106); Apr.–May, Donaghmore soap works (*DD*, 22 May 1918; *TC*, 25 Apr. 1918; July, Coalisland Roan spinning Mill, CI Tyrone, July 1918 (TNA, CO 904/107).

59 Strabane (*TC*, 25 Sept. 1918); Omagh, Carrickmore quarry, Clanabogan farm labourers, CI Tyrone, Aug. 1918 (TNA, CO 904/107).

60 CI Tyrone, Jan. 1919 (TNA, CO 904/108).

61 Donaghmore, strike at Brown's Soap Works, 1918 (NAI, CSORP, 1918/13567).

62 *DD*, 4 July 1917; *TC*, 5 Nov. 1917; *TC*, 15 Nov. 1917; CI Tyrone, July 1918 (TNA, CO 904/106); Annual intelligence notes for County Tyrone, 1918 (TNA, CO903/19/4); *DD*, 30 Oct. 1918; Omagh, Gas Works Strike, as to posn [sic.] of strikers and UDC under Conspiracy and Protection of Property Act 1875 (NAI, CSORP, 1918/33122); CI Tyrone, Mar. 1918 (TNA, CO 904/105); ibid., Apr. 1918 (TNA, CO 904/105); *DD*, 15 May 1918.

63 *DD*, 15 May 1918; Donaghmore, strike at Brown's Soap Works, May 1918 (NAI, CSORP, 1918/13567).

64 Henry Patterson, *Class, conflict and sectarianism: the Protestant working class and the Belfast labour movement, 1868–1920* (Belfast, 1980), p. 124.

65 CI Tyrone, Jan. 1919 (TNA, CO 904/108).

66 Mary T. McVeigh, 'Lock out? Caledon 1919', *Dúiche Néill*, 9 (1990), 98.

67 Wickham to S.J. Watt, 30 Mar. 1922 (PRONI, HA/5/905).

68 Crawford diary, 28 Sept. 1920 (PRONI, Crawford papers, D640/11/1).

69 McVeigh, 'Lock out?', pp 98–102.   70 Ibid., p. 108.

71 IG, July 1919 (TNA, CO 904/109).   72 CI Tyrone, Aug. 1920 (TNA, CO 904/112).

73 CI Tyrone, Feb. 1919 (TNA, CO 904/108).   74 CI Tyrone, Mar. 1919 (ibid.).

75 CI Tyrone, May 1919 (TNA, CO 904/109).   76 CI Tyrone, June, July 1919 (ibid.).

77 *UH*, 15 Mar. 1919.

78 CI Tyrone, Aug. 1918 (TNA, CO 904/106); Carrickmore, strike at County Council quarry, Apr. 1918 (NAI, CSORP, 1918/23292).

79 Internment file of Michael McMahon, 1922–4 (PRONI, HA/5/1681).

80 *UH*, 9 Aug. 1919.   81 Laffan, *Resurrection*, p. 253.

82 Mitchell, *Revolutionary government*, p. 166.

83 CI Tyrone, July 1920 (TNA, CO 904/112); *UH*, 24 July 1920.

84 CI Tyrone, Dec. 1920 (TNA, CO 904/113).

85 Peter Hart, *The IRA at war, 1916–1923* (Oxford, 2003), p. 21.

86 Fergus Campbell, *Land and revolution: nationalist politics in the west of Ireland, 1891–1921* (Oxford, 2005), p. 284.

87 *TC*, 23 June 1894; *DN*, 15 Feb. 1894; *DN*, 16 Aug. 1894; *TC*, 1 Sept. 1894; *DN*, 20 Jan. 1898; *TC*, 20 Jan. 1898; *DN*, 23 Dec. 1897.

88 IG, Apr. 1918 (TNA, CO 904/105); *UH*, 27 Apr. 1918.

89 CI Tyrone, Feb. 1920 (TNA, CO 904/111).

90 Rosanne Laury to Joseph Quinn, 8 Sept. 1924 (PRONI, HA/5/1837); strike at Tyrone Brick Works, Dungannon, Co. Tyrone, 1924 (PRONI, HA/5/1361); strike at Annagher Colliery, Coalisland, Co. Tyrone (PRONI, HA/5/1349).

91 W. McKenna to Cavanagh, 12 Aug. 1924 (PRONI, HA/5/1556).

92 *Northern Whig*, 13 July 1920.

93 Alan F. Parkinson, *Belfast's unholy war* (Dublin, 2004), pp 36–7.

94 Phoenix, *Northern nationalism*, p. 251.   95 Parkinson, *Unholy war*, pp 12–13.

96 Mitchell, *Revolutionary government*, p. 170.   97 *UH*, 21 Aug. 1920.

98 CI Tyrone, Aug. 1920 (TNA, CO 904/112).

99 SFSC, 10 Aug. 1920 (UCDAD, Minute books of Sinn Féin, P163/2/139–40).

100 Mitchell, *Revolutionary government*, pp 244–5.

101 Belfast boycott Circular, Dungannon, Aug. 1921 (TNA, CO 904/156A).

102 Constable P.J. Craword, 17 Oct. 1921 (TNA, CO 904/156A).

103 File relating to boycott of Belfast goods in Co. Tyrone, 1922 (PRONI, HA/5/111); Aughnacloy (PRONI, HA/5/108); Dromore (PRONI, HA/5/107); the Moy (PRONI,

HA/5/109); Castlederg (PRONI, HA/5/112); Strabane (PRONI, HA/5/113); Boycott of
J.J. Fleming, JP Gortin (PRONI, HA/5/116).
104 Murray to Bates, 28 Dec. 1921 (PRONI, HA/5/109).
105 J.J. Fleming to MHA, 21 Feb. 1922 (PRONI, HA/5/116).
106 Report of Monaghan Brigade, Apr. 1921 (UCDAD, Richard Mulcahy papers, P7a/39).
107 Augusteijn, *Public defiance*, p. 303.   108 *UH*, 4 Dec. 1920.
109 CI Tyrone, Nov. 1920 (TNA, CO 904/113).
110 SFSC, 12 Aug. 1921 (UCDAD, Minute books of Sinn Féin, P163/174).
111 Draft for the bill for the Government of Ireland, May 1917 (TNA, CAB 24/89).
112 Carson to Craig, 12 Jan. 1919 (PRONI, Craigavon papers, T3775/2/16).
113 Carson to Montgomery, 15 Aug. 1919 (PRONI, Montgomery papers, D627/434/53A).
114 Devlin to Archbishop Gilmartin of Tuam, Mar. 1920 (CÓFLA, O'Donnell papers,
     ARCH/10/4/14/19).
115 Devlin to O'Donnell, 23 Jan. 1919 (ibid., ARCH/10/4/14/10).
116 Devlin to O'Donnell, 13 Feb. 1920 (ibid., ARCH/10/4/14/13).
117 Devlin to O'Donnell, 2 Apr. 1920 (ibid., ARCH/10/4/14/22).
118 Stronge to Montgomery, 12 Mar. 1920 (PRONI, Montgomery papers, D627/435/9).
119 Bates to Montgomery, 8 May 1918 (ibid., D627/432/79); Craig to Montgomery, 13 May 1918
     (ibid., D627/434/14).
120 Stronge to Montgomery, 10 May 1918 (ibid., D627/434/11).
121 Jackson, *Home rule*, pp 198–9.
122 John Scott to Montgomery, 31 Mar. 1920 (PRONI, Montgomery papers, D627/435/13).
123 Ricardo to Montgomery, 8 Apr. 1920 (ibid., D627/435/23).
124 Ricardo to Montgomery, 11 Apr. 1920 (ibid., D627/435/28); Ricardo to Montgomery, 21 Apr.
     1920 (ibid., D627/435/47).
125 Gunning-Moore to Montgomery [?] Apr. 1920 (ibid., D627/435/57B).
126 Montgomery to Gunning-Moore, 26 Apr. 1920 (ibid., D627/435/58).
127 Montgomery to Stronge, 5 May 1920 (ibid., D627/435/72).
128 Jackson, *Ireland*, p. 242.
129 Stronge to Montgomery, 30 May 1920 (PRONI, Montgomery papers, D627/435/94).
130 Charles Townshend, 'The Irish Republican Army and the development of guerrilla warfare,
     1916–1921', *English Historical Review*, 94:371 (1979), 324–30.
131 Michael Hopkinson, *The Irish War of Independence* (Dublin, 2002), p. 16.
132 Mulcahy to O'Duffy, 21 Apr. 1921 (UCDAD, Mulcahy papers, P7a/4/220–1).
133 CI Tyrone, Dec. 1919 (TNA, CO 904/109).
134 *UH*, 25 Oct. 1919.   135 Jack Shields (BMH WS 224, p. 10).
136 Ibid., p. 20.
137 In March 1921 Clogher Company was transferred to No. 1 Brigade, 5th ND in Monaghan.
138 James Hackett (BMH WS 228, p. 3).
139 Albert Tally (BMH WS 884, p. 6).
140 Liam Ó Duibhir, *The Donegal awakening: Donegal and the War of Independence* (Cork, 2009),
     pp 115–17.
141 Pearse Lawlor, *The outrages, 1920–1922: the IRA and the Ulster Special Constabulary in the
     border campaign* (Cork, 2011), pp 19–23.
142 Jack Shields (BMH WS 224, p. 9).   143 Nicholas Smyth (BMH WS 721, p. 4).
144 Augusteijn, *Public defiance*, p. 95.
145 Patrick J. Colton, IRA MSP (CÓFLA, O'Kane collection, I.B.12 0001 04 Ee.4.4); Albert
     Tally (BMH WS 884, p. 6); *TC*, 20 May 1920.
146 W.J. Kelly junior (BMH WS 893, p. 13).   147 Augusteijn, *Public defiance*, p. 109.
148 *TC*, 10 June 1920.
149 CI Tyrone, July 1920 (TNA, CO 904/112); *TC*, 22 July, 5 Aug. 1920.
150 Weekly summaries of outrages, Aug.–Dec. 1920 (TNA, CO 904/149); *TC*, 2 Sept. 1920.

151 *TC*, 2 Sept. 1920.
152 Elizabeth and Nell Corr (BMH WS 179, p. 4); account of Nellie McGrath's notebook (*UH*, 20 Sept. 2012).
153 Ó Duibhir, *Donegal awakening*, pp 162–5; John McKenna, *A beleaguered station: the memoir of Head Constable John McKenna* (Belfast, 2009), pp 92–5.
154 Albert Tally (BMH WS 884, pp 7–8). 155 *TC*, 17 June 1920.
156 Albert Tally (BMH WS 884, p. 9). 157 *TC*, 23 Sept. 1920.
158 IRA memo to full time organizers, Aug. 1920 (NLI, Plunkett papers, MS 11,410/11).
159 CI Tyrone, Aug. 1920 (TNA, CO 904/112).
160 Crawford diary, 27 Sept. 1920 (PRONI, Crawford papers, D640/11/1).
161 Montgomery to Major Robert Lyon Moore, 22 May 1920 (PRONI, Montgomery papers, D627/439/13).
162 *TC*, 17 June 1920. 163 Crawford to Carson, 14 May 1920 (PRONI, Crawford papers, D640/7/7).
164 Craig to Crawford, 20 May 1920 (ibid., D640/7/9).
165 Michael Farrell, *Arming the Protestants: the formation of the Ulster Special Constabulary, 1920–27* (London, 1983), p. 15.
166 Ricardo to Greer, 28 July 1920 (PRONI, D4121/C/5/3/8).
167 British Cabinet Conference, 23 July 1920 (TNA, CAB 24/109).
168 CI Tyrone, Aug. 1920 (TNA, CO 904/112). 169 CI Tyrone, June 1920 (ibid.).
170 Murray to Craig, 2 Aug. 1922 (PRONI, HA/5/62–73).
171 Murray to Bates, 28 Dec. 1921 (ibid., HA/5/109).
172 Cabinet conclusions, 30 May 1922 (TNA, CAB 23/30).
173 McClintock, Ricardo and Stevenson to Tyrone UVF Battalion commanders, Sept. 1920 (PRONI, D1678/6/1).
174 Ibid.
175 Brooke to Co. Fermanagh USC, 23 Nov. 1920 (PRONI, Falls & Hanna papers, D1390/19).
176 Crawford diary, 27 Sept. 1920 (PRONI, Crawford papers, D640/11/1).
177 Nicholas Smyth (BMH WS 721, p. 4).
178 *UH*, 25 Sept. 1920. 179 *TC*, 23 Sept. 1920.
180 John Devlin's statement to the Advisory Committee, 12 Dec. 1922 (PRONI, HA/5/2224); *UH*, 18 Sept. 1920.
181 Nicholas Smyth (BMH WS 721, p. 5). 182 *UH*, 25 Sept. 1920.
183 Weekly summaries of outrages, Aug.–Dec. 1920 (TNA, CO 904/149/119).
184 Patrick J. Colton; Charles McGurk, IRA MSP (CÓFLA, O'Kane collection, I.B.12 0001 04 Ee.4.4); WSO, Aug.–Dec. 1920 (TNA, CO 904/149/191).
185 CI Tyrone, Nov. 1920 (TNA, CO 904/113); *II*, 2 Nov. 1920.
186 *Hansard (Commons)*, 3 Nov. 1920 vol. 134, cols 353–4. 187 *TC*, 4 Nov. 1920.
188 WSO, Aug.–Dec. 1920 (TNA, CO 904/149/268).
189 James McElduff in Mac Eoin, *Survivors*, pp 172–82.
190 Seán Corr (BMH WS 458, pp 7–9). 191 *TC*, 2 Dec. 1920.
192 Seán Corr (BMH WS 458, p. 8).
193 *Hansard (Commons)*, 11 Nov. 1920, vol. 134 col. 1344.
194 *TC*, 25 Nov. 1921. 195 CI Tyrone, Dec. 1920 (TNA, CO 904/113).
196 Seán Corr (BMH WS 458, pp 9–12). 197 CI Tyrone, Jan. 1921 (TNA, CO 904/114).
198 Miller, *Church, state & nation*, p. 2. 199 Mitchell, *Revolutionary government*, p. 79.
200 Ronan Fanning, 'Anglo-Irish relations: partition and the British dimension in historical perspective', *Irish Studies in International Affairs*, 2:1 (1985), 13.
201 Farrell, *Arming the Protestants*, pp 43–4.

CHAPTER SEVEN *Parliament, peace and partition, 1921*

1 *Hansard (Commons)*, 11 Nov. 1920, vol. 134, cols 1460–5.
2 Phoenix, *Northern nationalism*, p. 98.
3 Robert Lynch, *The Northern IRA and the early years of partition, 1920–1922* (Dublin, 2006), p. 47.
4 Augusteijn, *Public defiance*, p. 180.   5 W.J. Kelly, junior (BMH WS 893, p. 26).
6 Mulcahy to O'Duffy, 14 Mar. 1921 (UCDAD, Mulcahy papers, P7a/17/111).
7 Mulcahy to O'Duffy, 21 Apr. 1921 (ibid., P7a/4/220–1).
8 GHQ memo to ND Commandants, 24 Mar. 1921 (ibid., P7a/17/173).
9 McGarry, *Eoin O'Duffy*, pp 74–5.
10 Mulcahy to O'Duffy, 14 Mar. 1921 (UCDAD, Mulcahy papers, P7a/17/111); Mulcahy to O'Duffy, 21 Apr. 1921 (ibid., P7a/17/216).
11 O'Duffy to Mulcahy, 24 Nov. 1921 (ibid., P7a/5).
12 Seán Corr (BMH WS 458, pp 12–13).
13 W.J. Kelly junior (BMH WS 893, p. 7).
14 O'Duffy to Bob Price, 28 Apr. 1924 (UCDAD, Mulcahy papers, P7a/18/104–7).
15 McGarry, *Eoin O'Duffy*, p. 75.   16 Augusteijn, *Public defiance*, p. 41.
17 Seán Corr (BMH WS 458, p. 13); James McElduff in Mac Eoin (ed.), *Survivors*, pp 172–82; Mountfield Barracks, Apr. 1921 (CÓFLA, O'Kane collection, I.C.07 0001 05 Ee.4.4); Carrickmore ambush, Apr. 1921 (CÓFLA, O'Kane collection, I.C.10 0001 05 Ee.4.4); Pomeroy ambush, Apr. 1921 (CÓFLA, O'Kane collection, I.C.06 0001 05 Ee.4.4).
18 CI Tyrone, Apr. 1921 (TNA, CO 904/115); *TC*, 7 Apr. 1921.
19 See Lynch, *Northern IRA*, p. 53.
20 Nicholas Smyth (BMH WS 721, p. 13); 2nd ND report on atrocities, 21 Oct. 1921 (IMA, A/0664/24).
21 CI Tyrone, Nov. 1920 (TNA, CO 904/113); *UH*, 27 Nov. 1920.
22 CI Tyrone, Oct. 1920 & Dec. 1920 (ibid.).
23 CI Tyrone, Apr. 1921 (TNA, CO 904/115); *TC*, 18 Apr. 1921; *UH*, 30 Apr. 1921.
24 CI Tyrone, Apr. 1921 (TNA, CO 904/115).
25 O'Duffy to Price, 28 Apr. 1924 (UCDAD, Mulcahy papers, P7a/18/104–7).
26 W.J. Kelly junior (BMH WS 893, pp 19–20).   27 Townshend, 'IRA', pp 336–40.
28 WSO, Jan.–Dec. 1921 (TNA, CO 904/150).
29 W.J. Kelly junior (BMH WS 893, p. 22).   30 Townshend, 'IRA', p. 330.
31 Daly to O'Duffy, 8 Mar. 1922 (UCDAD, O'Malley papers, P17a/184).
32 Peter Hart, 'The geography of revolution in Ireland, 1917–1923', *Past and Present*, 155 (1997), 142–76.
33 Farrell, *Arming the Protestants*, p. 58.
34 Roll books of No. 1 brigade 2nd ND (CÓFLA, O'Kane collection) set against a detailed break-down of all IRA operations and where they took place.
35 Mobilization of special constables, Apr. 1922 (PRONI, FIN 18/1/361).
36 Irish Command, part 1, section B, July 1921 (TNA, WO 73/14), p. 101.
37 Cabinet conclusions, 2 June 1921 (TNA, CAB 23/26).
38 2nd ND, memo regarding pensions (IMA, A/0664/23).
39 CI Tyrone, Dec. 1920 (TNA, CO 904/113).
40 Daly to director of training, 24 Aug. 1921 (IMA, A/0664/7).
41 Hart, 'Geography of revolution', p. 151.   42 W.J. Kelly, junior (BMH WS 893, p. 23).
43 'Report of Dr Henry Owens of Pomeroy', 19 May 1921 (PRONI, HA/5/161).
44 Wickham to McClintock, 28 May 1921 (ibid.).
45 McKenna, *Beleaguered station*, pp 57–8.
46 MHA to Colonel Spender, 11 Jan. 1922 (PRONI, HA/5/161).
47 Statement of Rose Ann Gallagher, 28 Oct. 1921 (PRONI, HA/5/157); see also 2nd ND report on atrocities, 21 Oct. 1921 (IMA, A/0664/24); file on the Gallagher brother and sisters, 1922 (NAI, NEBB, 1/4/2).

48 Special Constabulary papers including list of names of A Company, Dungannon, giving ages and occupations, 1923 (PRONI, Newton papers, D1678/6/1).
49 'Return of barracks and other premises held in the Co. Tyrone', 20 Feb. 1922 (PRONI, HA/5/802).
50 Tyrone Special Constabulary, Dungannon, 25 Feb. 1915–6 Apr. 1923 (PRONI, Orange Order documents, D4246/3/3).
51 Major Robert Stevenson, 30 June 1922 (TNA, CO 906/27).
52 *TC*, 30 June 1921; *UH*, 11 June 1921.
53 *IN*, 1 Mar. 1922.   54 *UH*, 7 May 1921.
55 Patrick J. Colton, IRA MSP *c.* 1950 (CÓFLA, O'Kane collection, I.B.12 0001 04 Ee.4.4).
56 CI Tyrone, July 1921 (TNA, CO 904/116/15); *TC*, 7 July 1921; *TC*, 14 July 1921; *UH*, 16 July 1921.
57 McKenna, *Beleaguered station*, pp 77–82.
58 CI Tyrone, July 1921 (TNA, CO 904/116/15); *TC*, 25 Aug., 29 Sept. 1921; *UH*, 23 July 1921.
59 Alice to William Donnelly, Feb. 1923 (PRONI, HA/32/1/92).
60 McElduff in Mac Eoin, *Survivors*, pp 172–82.
61 SFSC, 13 Apr. 1921 (NAI, 999/40).
62 De Valera to MacRory, 17 Jan. 1921 (CÓFLA, MacRory papers, folder 8).
63 De Valera to MacRory, 17 Feb. 1921 (ibid.).
64 SFSC, 10 Feb. 1920 (NAI, 999/40).
65 T.P. O'Connor to John Dillon, 12 Mar. 1921 (TCD, Dillon papers, MS 6744/821).
66 O'Connor to Dillon, 18 Feb. 1921 (ibid., MS 6744/815).
67 Dillon to O'Connor, 19 May 1921 (ibid., MS 6744/836).
68 *II*, 28 May 1921.
69 Carson to Craig, 29 May 1921 (PRONI, Craigavon papers, T3775/2/17).
70 De Valera to Dáil ministry, 17 Jan. 1921 (UCDAD, de Valera papers, P150/1380).
71 Ibid.; SFSC, 12 May 1921 (NAI, 999/40); Éamon Donnelly to P. Ó Caoimhe, 24 May 1921 (UCDAD, de Valera papers, P150/1380).
72 Phoenix, *Northern nationalism*, p. 122.
73 Sydney Elliott, *Northern Ireland parliamentary election results, 1921–1972* (Chichester, 1973), p. 8.
74 O'Connor to Dillon, 29 July 1921 (TCD, Dillon papers, MS 6744/848).
75 Greenwood to Craig, 10 June 1921 (PRONI, Craigavon papers, T3775/14/2).
76 Charlie Daly, 'General report of training, 2nd ND', Sept. 1921 (IMA, A/0664/8); Daly to battn commandants, 13 Aug. 1921 (IMA, A/066/9); Daly to each brigade O/C, 27 Aug. 1921 (IMA, A/066/10); Daly to each brigade adjt., 30 Aug. 1921 (IMA, A/066/11) Daly to each brigade QM, 30 Aug. 1921 (IMA, A/066/12); Daly, Training syllabus, Aug. 1921 (IMA, A/066/13).
77 Milroy to rúnaí, 28 Nov. 1921 (UCDAD, de Valera papers, P150/1492).
78 SFSC, 12 Aug. 1921 (ibid.).
79 Vincent Shields to O'Keeffe, 9 Sept. 1921 (ibid.).
80 Milroy to Brugha, 22 Sept. 1922 (ibid.).
81 O'Keefe to Shields, 4 Oct. 1921 (ibid.).
82 Milroy to Bishop O'Donnell, 4 Oct. 1921 (NAI, DÉ 4/9).
83 O'Doherty to Milroy, 1 Oct. 1921 (ibid., 4/9/5).
84 Healy to Cosgrave, 16 Oct. 1921 (ibid., 4/9/25).
85 Cosgrave to Milroy, 10 Oct. 1921 (ibid., 4/9).
86 Murnaghan to Milroy, 14 Oct. 1921 (ibid., 4/9/25).
87 Milroy to Cosgrave, 11 Oct. 1921 (ibid., 4/9/25); Fr J. Doherty Strabane to Milroy, 8 Oct. 1921 (NAI, DÉ 4/9).
88 Dillon to O'Connor, 29 Sept. 1922 (TCD, Dillon papers, MS 6744).
89 *UH*, 29 Sept. 1921.

90   Mayne to Stack, 14 Nov. 1921 (NAI, DÉ 4/9).
91   Patrick O'Keefe to Milroy, 18 Nov. 1921 (ibid.).
92   Phoenix, *Northern nationalism*, p. 152.
93   Gillespie to de Valera, 23 Nov. 1921 (UCDAD, de Valera papers, P150/1492).
94   MacNeill to de Valera, 1 Dec. 1921 (ibid.).
95   Ó Caoimhe to de Valera, 6 Dec. 1921 (ibid.).
96   Meeting with northern delegation, 8 Dec. 1921 (ibid.).
97   Hoey to Milroy, 22 Nov. 1921 (NAI, DÉ 4/9).
98   Cosgrave to Milroy, 29 Nov. 1921; Hoey to Milroy, 30 Nov. 1921 (NAI, DÉ 4/9).
99   *TC*, 24 Nov. 1921.
100 MacNeill to de Valera, 1 Dec. 1921 (UCDAD, de Valera papers, P150/1492).
101 Tyrone County Council, 3 Dec. 1921, post-dated Bradley, 10 Dec. 1921 (NAI, DÉLG, 28/10).
102 NI Cabinet conclusions, 1 Dec. 1921 (PRONI, CAB 4/14/28).
103 *TC*, 8 Dec. 1921; *UH*, 10 Dec. 1921; *TC*, 15 Dec. 1921.
104 Patrick Gormley to Cosgrave, 16 Dec. 1921 (NAI, DÉLG, 28/10).
105 Cosgrave to Gormley, 17 Dec. 1921 (ibid.).
106 *UH*, 3 Sept. 1921.
107 Dan Breen, *My fight for Irish freedom* (Tralee, 1964), pp 160–1.
108 Joe Sweeny, 1949 (UCDAD, O'Malley notebooks, P17b/97/44–50).
109 Nicholas Smyth (BMH WS 721, p. 16).
110 Report of divisional and brigade strengths, Oct. 1921 (UCDAD, Mulcahy papers, P7a/18).
111 Hall to CI Hildebrand, 9 Oct. 1921 (TNA, CO 904/156A/20).
112 Commandant J. McIlwaine, 21 Apr. 1923 (PRONI, HA/5/2387).
113 Seán Corr (BMH WS 458, p. 15).
114 Daly to adjt. gen, 2nd ND report for Sept. 1921', 18 Oct. 1921 (IMA, A/0664/4); breaches of the truce, Co. Tyrone (TNA, CO 904/156A/22).
115 Daly to adjt. gen, 2nd ND report for Sept. 1921', 18 Oct. 1921 (IMA, A/0664/4).
116 Director of training to Daly, 14 Oct. 1921 (IMA, A/0664/16).
117 Seán Corr (BMH WS 458, p. 16).
118 Returns for each army division, brigade and battalion, Sept. 1921 (UCDAD, Mulcahy papers, P7a/17/29).
119 Daly to QM General, 14 Oct. 1921 (ibid., P7/A/26/75–7).
120 Seán Corr (BMH WS 458, p. 16).
121 Cabinet conclusions, 7 Sept. 1921 (TNA, CAB 23/27).
122 Breaches of the truce, Co. Tyrone, 1921 (TNA, CO 904/156A); interview with Hugh Breen, Frank MacMahon, John James McKee, Aloysius McKee and Roddy O'Kane, Feb. 1966 (CÓFLA, O'Kane collection, IV.A.072 0007, Ee.4.7); SF Court in the Moy, 1921 (TNA, CO 904/15A/148); Clogher, 1921 (TNA, CO 904/15A/150); Aughnacloy, 1921 (TNA, CO 904/15A/56).
123 Breaches of the truce, Co. Tyrone, 1921 (TNA, CO 904/156A/75–94); Liaison officer's reports on breach of truce by Sinn Féin, 1921 (PRONI, HA/32/1/4); SF arbitration 'court' in Dungannon, 11 Jan. 1922 (PRONI, HA/32/1/8).
124 RIC Dublin Castle to DIs, CIs, county commandants and senior DC, Cork, 23 July 1921 (TNA, CO 904/15A/129).
125 Report on SF court at Strabane, 27 Aug. 1921 (TNA, CO 904/156A).
126 McClintock to Wickham, 17 Sept. 1921 (TNA, CO 904/15A/19).
127 Daly to O'Duffy, 7 Nov. 1921 (PRONI, HA/32/1/130).
128 Wickham to Dublin Castle, 19 Sept. 1921 (TNA, CO 904/156A/18).
129 CI Tyrone, Aug. 1921 (TNA, CO 904/116/367).
130 DI Walshe, 18 Aug. 1921 (TNA, CO 904/15A/8).
131 O'Duffy to Wickham, 26 Aug. 1921 (TNA, CO 904/15A/8).

132 Spender to the cabinet, 10 Aug. 1921 (PRONI, CAB 4/14/15).
133 NI cabinet conclusions, 16 Aug. 1921 (ibid., CAB 4/14/23).
134 Ibid., 31 Aug. 1921 (ibid., CAB 4/17/7).
135 Ibid., 1 Sept. 1921 (ibid., CAB 4/17/2/7–8).
136 Crawford diary, 27 Oct. 1921 (PRONI, Crawford papers, D640/11/1).   137 Ibid.
138 *TC*, 20 Oct. 1921.   139 Farrell, *Arming the Protestants*, p. 74.
140 H.J. Walshe, 24 Oct. 1921 (TNA, CO 904/156A/33).
141 Constable Hallinan, 24 Nov. 1921 (TNA, CO 904/156A/41).
142 RIC memo, 28 Oct. 1921 (TNA, CO 904/156A/32).
143 Weekly survey of the state of Ireland, 19 Sept. 1921 (TNA, CAB 24/128); *TC*, 29 Sept. 1921;
     breaches of the truce, 1921 (TNA, CO 904/156A).
144 *TC*, 29 Sept. 1921.   145 *UH*, 25 Sept. 1921.   146 Ibid., 15 Oct. 1921.
147 Ibid., 29 Sept. 1921.
148 Daly to QMG, 14 Oct. 1921 (UCDAD, Mulcahy papers, P7a/26/75–7).
149 Divisional adjutant 2nd ND to CS, 23 Dec. 1921 (ibid, P7a/33/262).
150 Daly, Secret order, No. 1, 3 Dec. 1921 (IMA, A/0664/20).
151 Daly, Divisional order, No. 13, 3 Dec. 1921 (IMA, A/0664/3); No. 15, 6 Dec. 1921 (IMA,
     A/0664/22).
152 *UH*, 8 Sept. 1917.
153 Londonderry to Kennedy, 5 Aug. 1922 (UCDAD, Hugh Kennedy papers, P4/415/4).

CHAPTER EIGHT *Endgame in Tyrone*

1   Laffan, *Partition*, p. 78.   2 Cabinet conclusions, 7 Sept. 1921 (TNA, CAB 23/27).
3   Farrell, *Arming the Protestants*, p. 74.
4   Hopkinson, *Green against green: the Irish Civil War* (Dublin, 1988), p. 28.
5   Paul Bew, Peter Gibson, Henry Patterson, *Northern Ireland 1921–2001, political forces and social
    classes* (London, 2002), p. 21.
6   Memorandum by Erskine Childers, 23 Nov. 1921 (NAI, DÉ 2/304/1).
7   De Valera to Griffith, 26 Oct. 1921 (ibid.).
8   Griffith to de Valera, 8 Nov. 1921 (UCDAD, de Valera papers, P150/1914/8).
9   Meeting of Dáil cabinet, 3 Dec. 1921 (ibid., P150/1371/179–82).
10 Ronan Fanning, *The fatal path: British government and Irish revolution, 1910–1922* (London,
    2013), p. 308.
11 Hopkinson, *Green against Green*, p. 32.
12 John M. Regan, *The Irish counter-revolution, 1921–1936* (Dublin, 2001), p. 374.
13 '"Tentative suggestions" for a Treaty presented by Thomas Jones to Arthur Griffith', 16 Nov.
    1921 (NAI, DÉ 2/304/1); Anglo-Irish Treaty, 5 Dec. 1921 (TNA, CAB 24/131).
14 Cabinet conclusions, 6 Dec. 1921 (TNA, CAB 23/27/17).
15 *Hansard (Commons)*, 8 Feb. 1922, vol. 150, c. 205; *An Phoblacht*, 14 Feb. 1922.
16 Weekly survey of the state of Ireland, 21 Dec. 1921 (TNA, CAB 24/131).
17 *TC*, 8 Dec. 1921.
18 DCO, 29 Dec. 1921 (PRONI, HA/32/1/4).   19 Ibid., 31 Dec. 1921 (PRONI, HA/5/152).
20 Ibid., 16 Jan. 1922 (PRONI, HA/5/1520).
21 Daly to O'Duffy, 8 Mar. 1922 (UCDAD, O'Malley papers, P17a/184).
22 Frank Aiken (ibid., O'Malley notebooks P17b/193/4).
23 Dáil Éireann debates, 20 Dec. 1921, vol. T, no. 7, cc 74–81.
24 *An Phoblacht*, 10 Jan. 1922.
25 Mid-Tyrone Comhairle Ceantair to O'Mahony, Jan. 1922 (NLI, Seán O'Mahony papers, MS
    24,468).
26 Walshe to MacRory, 14 Jan. 1922 (CÓFLA, MacRory papers, folder 14).
27 Craig-Collins agreement, 23 Jan. 1922 (NAI, DT, S1801A).

28 *Morning Post*, 24 Jan. 1922.   29 Michael Collins, Feb. 1922 (NAI, NEBB, 1/4/1).

30 Murnaghan to Collins, 24 Jan. 1922 (NAI, DÉ 4/9); for Craig's view of the 'tighter' agreement, see James Craig's report to northern cabinet, 21 Jan. 1922 (PRONI, Craigavon papers, T3775/15/4).

31 Collins to McCullough, 26 Jan. 1922 (NLI, Ó Broin papers, MS 31,653); McCullough to Collins, 30 Jan. 1922 (NAI, NEBB, 1/4/2).

32 Michael Hopkinson, 'The Craig-Collins pacts of 1922: two attempted reforms of the NI government', *IHS*, 27:106 (1990), 149.

33 Mayne to Collins, 1 Feb. 1922 (NAI, NEBB, 1/4/2).   34 *TC*, 22 Dec. 1921.

35 Memo of Craig-Collins meeting, 2 Feb. 1922 (NAI, NEBB, 1/4/1).

36 *FJ*, 2 Feb. 1922; Newry/South Armagh delegation, 1 Feb. 1922 (PRONI, J.H. Collins papers, D921/2/2/85).

37 *FJ*, 3 Feb. 1922.   38 Ibid., 4 Feb. 1922.

39 Dillon to O'Connor, 6 Feb. 1922 (TCD, Dillon papers, MS 6744/871).

40 SFSC, 31 Jan. 1922 (NAI, 999/40).

41 *UH*, 4 Feb. 1922.   42 SFSC, 20 Feb. 1922 (ibid.).

43 SFSC, 3 Mar. 1922 (ibid.).

44 Griffith to Joseph McGrath, 6 Mar. 1922 (NAI, NEBB, 1/4/1).

45 SFSC, 10 Mar. 1922 (NAI, 999/40).

46 McCartan to Maloney, 31 Mar. 1921 (NLI, McGarrity papers, MS 17645).

47 *IN*, 28 Apr. 1922.   48 *UH*, 4 Feb. 1922.

49 Dillon to O'Connor, 23 Mar. 1922 (TCD, Dillon papers, MS 6744/880).

50 Frank Aiken (UCDAD, O'Malley notebooks, P17b/193/3–4).

51 Robert Kelly (BMH WS 549, p. 5).

52 Gillespie to Blythe, 6 June 1923 (NAI, NEBB, 1/1/14).

53 Frank Aiken (UCDAD, O'Malley notebooks, P17b/193/3–4).

54 Henry McGorm to his mother, 24 July 1922 (PRONI, HA/32/257).

55 DCO, Belfast, 31 Jan. 1922 (PRONI, HA/5/152).

56 Summary of outrages in NI, Mar.–Apr. 1922 (PRONI, HA/5/699).

57 Summary of outrages in NI, May–Sep. 1922 (PRONI, HA/5/700); *TC*, 24 June 1922.

58 O'Duffy to Collins, 10 Mar. 1922 (NAI, DT, S 1801/A).

59 O'Duffy to Collins, 30 Jan. 1922 (ibid.).

60 Weekly survey of the state of Ireland, 13 Feb. 1922 (TNA, CAB 24/133).

61 Summary of outrages in NI, 1921–22 (PRONI, HA/5/698).

62 Compensation claim of Mrs Robert Scott, 1922 (TNA, HO 144/2235).

63 GOC Ireland, 18 Feb. 1922 (TNA, CAB 24/133).

64 Summary of outrages in NI, May–Sept. 1922 (PRONI, HA/5/700).

65 Northern Border Commission, Feb.–June 1922 (PRONI, HA/32/1/16).

66 Fulton to Bates, 8 Feb. 1922 (PRONI, HA/5/165).

67 James McKenna, 1970 (CÓFLA, O'Kane collection, IV.D.11 0003 05 Ee.4.5).

68 Northern Border Commission (PRONI, HA/32/1/16); DCO, Belfast, 15 Mar. 1922 (PRONI, HA/5/152); Summary of outrages in NI, Mar.–Apr. 1922 (PRONI, HA/5/699).

69 Summary of outrages in NI, Mar.–Apr. 1922 (PRONI, HA/5/699).

70 Ibid.; DCO, Belfast, 31 Mar. 1922 (PRONI, HA/5/152); Northern Border Commission, 19 Mar. 1922 (PRONI, HA/32/1/16).

71 DCO report on the political situation at Caledon, 19 Mar. 1922 (PRONI, HA/5/903).

72 Northern Border Commission, 27 Mar. 1922 (PRONI, HA/32/1/16).

73 Northern Border Commission, 29 May 1922 (ibid.).

74 PRONI, HA/5/2232; DCO, Belfast, 18 Apr. 1922 (PRONI, HA/5/152).

75 DCO, Belfast, 31 Mar., 18 Apr. 1922 (PRONI, HA/5/152).

76 Telegram Fintona, 18 Apr. 1922 (PRONI, HA/5/205); persons killed or wounded since 6 Dec. 1921 in NI (PRONI, HA/5/219); *TC*, 27 Apr. 1922.

77 Northern Border Commission (PRONI, HA/32/1/16).

78   Fulton to Bates, 22 Mar. 1922 (PRONI, HA/5/905).
79   J.K. McClintock, 29 Mar. 1922 (ibid.).
80   Northern Border Commission, 28 Mar. 1922 (PRONI, HA/32/1/16).
81   *II*, 10 Mar. 1922.   82   GOC Ireland, 3 June 1922 (TNA, CAB 24/137).
83   *TC*, 16 Feb. 1922.   84   Sweeney to Mulcahy, 16 Feb. 1922 (IMA, A/0663/4).
85   GOC Ireland, 18 Feb. 1922 (TNA, CAB 24/133).
86   Lehane to Military Pensions Board, 7 Mar. 1935 (NLI, O'Donoghue papers, MS 31,340).
87   Daly to O'Duffy, 25 Jan. 1922 (IMA, A/0664/2).
88   O'Duffy to Mulcahy, 21 Feb. 1922 (IMA, A/0664/2).
89   Daly to O'Duffy, 22 Mar. 1922 (UCDAD, O'Malley papers, P17a/184).
90   Micheal Collins diary, 16 Mar. 1922 (UCDAD, Mulcahy papers, P7a/62); O'Duffy to Collins, 10 Mar. 1922 (NAI, DT, S1801/A); O'Duffy to Mulcahy, 21 Feb. 1922 (IMA, A/0664/2); Mulcahy to O'Duffy, 27 Feb. 1922 (IMA, A/0664/2).
91   Seán Corr (BMH WS 458, p. 17).
92   James McElduff in Mac Eoin, *Survivors*, pp 172–82.
93   Daly to Tom Daly, 20 Mar. 1922 (UCDAD, O'Malley notebooks, P17b/132/24–27); Nicholas Smyth (BMH WS 721, pp 19–20).
94   RIC Trillick to MHA, Mar. 1922 (PRONI, HA/5/194).
95   DCO, Belfast, 31 Mar. 1922 (PRONI, HA/5/152).
96   DCO, 3 Apr. 1922 (PRONI, HA/5/192).
97   CI to MHA, 18 June 1922 (PRONI, HA/5/243).
98   DI Omagh, 30 Dec. 1922; IG RUC, 8 June 1923 (PRONI, HA/5/243).
99   2nd ND, memo regarding pensions, undated (IMA, A/0664/23); File on John T. Gallagher, Aug. 1922 (NAI, DT, S5750/16).
100 DCO bi-monthly report, 18 Apr. 1922 (PRONI, HA/5/152); Summary of outrages in NI, Mar.–Apr. 1922 (PRONI, HA/5/699).
101 *UH*, 15 Nov. 1924.   102   CI Tyrone, 13 Nov. 1924 (PRONI, HA/5/489).
103 RUC Report, 21 Nov. 1924 (ibid.).
104 Summary of outrages in NI, May–Sept. 1922 (PRONI, HA/5/700); *UH*, 24 June 1922.
105 Summary of outrages in NI, Mar.–Apr. 1922 (PRONI, HA/5/699); DCO, 31 Mar. 1922 (PRONI, HA/5/152); *TC*, 30 Mar. 1922; McElduff in Mac Eoin, *Survivors*, pp 172–82.
106 Phoenix, *Northern nationalism*, pp 213–14.
107 Hopkinson, 'The Craig-Collins pacts', p. 151.   108   Cabinet minutes, 5 Apr. 1922 (TNA, CAB 23/30).
109 Regan, *Counter-revolution*, p. 63; Lynch, *Northern IRA*, p. 136.
110 Woods to Mulcahy, 27 July 1922 (UCDAD, Mulcahy papers, P7b/77).
111 Charlie Daly, Dublin Monday [15?] May 1922 (UCDAD, O'Malley notebooks, P17b/132/24–7).
112 *UH*, 3 June 1922.
113 Memo on north-east Ulster, 9 Aug. 1922 (UCDAD, Blythe papers, P24/554).
114 Patrick Casey (BMH WS 1148, p. 33).
115 Daly [15?] May 1922 (UCDAD, O'Malley notebooks, P17b/132/24–7).
116 Joe Sweeney and Peadar O'Donnell, 3 June 1949 (ibid., P17b/98/7).
117 Hopkinson, *Green against green*, p. 84.
118 Summary of outrages in NI, May–Aug. 1922 (PRONI, HA/5/700).
119 DCO, 16 May 1922 (PRONI, HA/5/152).   120   *TC*, 11 May 1922.
121 DI Dungannon, 6 May 1922 (PRONI, HA/5/921).
122 Stevenson statement, 9 May 1922 (PRONI, Orange Order documents, D4246/3/3/1).
123 Summary of outrages in NI, May–Aug. 1922 (PRONI, HA/5/700).
124 Daly to Tom Daly, May 1922 (UCDAD, O'Malley notebooks, P17b/132/24–7).
125 DI Dungannon, 8 May 1922 (PRONI, HA/5/923) raid on specials Castlecaulfield, May 1922 (CÓFLA, O'Kane collection, I.C.04 0001 05 Ee.4.4).

126 Interview Thomas Morris, 30 Oct. 1967 (CÓFLA, O'Kane collection, IV, A, 9).
127 DCO, Belfast, 16 May 1922 (PRONI HA/5/152); Summary of outrages in NI, May-Aug. 1922 (PRONI, HA/5/700); J.J. Fleming, to MHA, 24 May 1922 (PRONI, HA/5/268).
128 List of divisions, brigades, batts, 11 July 1921; Typescript list of army commands, 17 Jan. 1923 (NLI, O'Donoghue papers, MS 31,424); Memo on north-east Ulster, 11 Aug. 1922 (UCDAD, Blythe papers, P24/554).
129 Enda Staunton, *The Nationalists of Northern Ireland, 1918–1973* (Dublin, 2001), p. 53.
130 O'Duffy to Mulcahy, 4 Mar. 1922 (IMA, A/0664/2).
131 2nd ND report (NLI, Thomas Johnson papers, MS 17,143).
132 Seán Corr (BMH WS 458, p. 21).
133 HQ 1st ND Raphoe, 20 May 1922 (UCDAD, O'Malley notebooks, P17b/132/24–27).
134 Thomas Morris interview, 30 Oct. 1967 (CÓFLA, O'Kane collection, IV.A.009 0006 n.a. Ee.4.6).
135 Position of 2nd ND in 1922 (NLI, Johnson papers, MS 17,143).
136 1st ND report, 19 Sept. 1922 (UCDAD, O'Malley papers, P17a/63).
137 'Charlie Daly's call to arms for Ireland's full freedom' in *The story of the Drumboe martyrs – 80th anniversary* edition (Donegal, 2003), pp 30–4.
138 James McElduff in Mac Eoin, *Survivors*, pp 172–82.
139 Mulcahy to Morris, 17 Aug. 1922 (NLI, Johnson papers, MS 17,143).
140 PG minute, 3 June 1922 (NAI, DT, S1801/A).
141 Craig's Convict ship, Aug. 1922 (UCDAD, Hayes papers, P53/199/3).
142 Mac Giolla Coinnig to CS, 29 July 1922 (NAI, DT, S5750/16).
143 Mayne to Cosgrave, 12 Jan. 1923 (NAI, DT, S5750/2; NAI, NEBB, 1/1/12).
144 Frank Crummey to Frank O'Duffy, 25 Jan. 1923 (NAI, DT, S5750/2); Seán Sheehan to Mulcahy, 14 Jan. 1923 (NAI, NEBB, 1/1/12).
145 Activity reports for week ending July 8th, 10 July 1922 (UCDAD, O'Malley papers, P17/B/77/41).
146 Cabinet conclusions, 2 June 1922 (TNA, CAB 23/30).
147 Ó Duibhir, *Donegal & the Civil War*, p. 127.
148 Cabinet conclusions, 1 June 1922 (TNA, CAB 23/30).
149 Churchill to Collins, via Cope telegram, 29 June 1922 (TNA, CAB 23/39).
150 Churchill to Craig, 7 July 1922 (PRONI, CAB 6/75).
151 Report by Gen. Ricardo, June 1922 (TNA, CO 906/27).
152 Farrell, *Arming the Protestants*, pp 153, 283.
153 Report by Ricardo, June 1922 (TNA, CO 906/27).
154 CI Tyrone, 26 Sept. 1922 (PRONI, HA/32/1/290).
155 Summary of outrages in NI, Feb.–Apr. 1923 (PRONI, HA/5/701).
156 DI Cookstown, 27 June 1923 (PRONI, HA/5/2342); Bridget Donnelly to Michael Donnelly, 15 June 1923 (PRONI, HA/5/2132).
157 Internment file, Joseph Campbell, 1923 (PRONI, HA/5/2434).
158 Ricardo, June 1922 (TNA, CO 906/27).
159 Report of intelligence division, Jan. 1924 (NAI, NEBB, 1/1/12); Free State intelligence division, 1924 (IMA, MS 334); Adjt. 4th ND IRA to CS GHQ, Apr. 1924 (UCDAD, Moss Twomey papers, P69/35/115).
160 Bew et al., *Northern Ireland*, p. 16.
161 Paul Murray, *The Irish Boundary Commission and its origins, 1886–1925* (Dublin, 2011), p. 314.
162 Tom Jones and Lionel Curtis, 18 Mar. 1922 (TNA, CAB 24/134); Cabinet memorandum, 15 July 1922 (TNA, CAB 24/138); Robert S. Horne, 'Financial relations with NI', 9 June 1922 (TNA, CAB 24/137).
163 Cabinet conclusions, 7 Sept. 1921 (TNA, CAB 23/27).
164 GOC Ireland, 5 Sept. 1922 (TNA, CAB 24/138).
165 Hopkinson, *Green against green*, pp 105–6.

CHAPTER NINE *Continuity and change*

1 Éamon Phoenix, 'Northern Ireland: from the birth-pangs to disintegration' in Ciaran Brady, Mary O'Dowd & Brian Walker (eds), *Ulster: an illustrated history* (Belfast, 1989), p. 196.

2 *Hansard N.L (Commons)*, xvi, 1091–5 (24 Apr. 1934); T.P. Daly, 'James Craig and Orangeism, 1903–10', *IHS*, 34:136 (2005), 431–48.

3 Knights of Columbanus, Dungannon, Co. Tyrone, 1922–3 (PRONI, HA/32/1/322).

4 Joseph Stewart to Healy, 13 Feb. 1938 (PRONI, Cahir Healy papers, D2991/B/33/71).

5 Alice to William Donnelly, 21 Oct. 1924 (PRONI, HA/32/1/92).

6 Election results, Laffan, *Resurrection*, p. 439.

7 Mitchel, *Revolutionary government*, p. 62.

8 Daly to Tom Daly, OMN (UCDAD, O'Malley notebooks, P17b/132/27).

9 Cabinet conclusions, 30 May 1922 (TNA, CAB 23/30).

10 McCartan to McGarrity, 7 Apr. 1909 (NLI, McGarrity papers, P8186); Garvin, *Evolution*, pp 105–10.

11 Regan, *Counter-revolution*, p. 259.   12 Frank Callanan, *T.M. Healy* (Cork, 1996), p. 298.

13 J.J. Lee, *Ireland, 1912–85: politics and society* (Cambridge, 1989), p. 105.

14 O/C Free State *Argenta* to Cosgrave, 24 Jan. 1923 (NAI, DT, S5750/16).

15 Brian Gallagher to Cosgrave, 15 Feb. 1923 (NAI, DT, S5750/16); internment file of James Gallagher Dromore, Co. Tyrone, 1922–4 (PRONI, HA/5/1735); Bernard McCusker, Daniel Mac Póilín, John Bradley and James Gallagher to T.J. O'Connell T.D., 24 Sept. 1923 (PRONI, HA/5/1735).

16 Denise Kleinrichert, *Republican internment and the prison ship Argenta, 1922* (Dublin, 2001), p. 300.

17 Mayne to Cosgrave, 12 Jan. 1923 (NAI, DT, S5750/2); Frank Crummey to Frank O'Duffy, 25 Jan. 1923 (NAI, DT, S5750/2). The teachers in question were Frank Gallagher, Eugene Gallagher, Tyrone, Pat Mullarkey, Tempo, Fermanagh Army men and Mr Williams and Mr Gallagher; Edward Rice of Augher was a republican and refused.

18 Seán Sheehan to Mulcahy, 14 Jan. 1923 (NAI, NEBB, 1/1/12); Sheehan secured his release in February 1923 and got a job with the Free State government (Cosgrave to Mulcahy, 8 Feb. 1923, NAI, DT, S5750/16); Frank Crummey to Frank O'Duffy, 25 Jan. 1923 (NAI, DT, S5750/2).

19 Francis Gallagher to Blythe, 16 May 1923 (NAI, DT, S5750/16); Seán Mac Eoin to CS, 2 May 1923 (NAI, DT, S5750/16; NEBB, 1/1/12).

20 O'Shiel to Cosgrave, 20 Feb. 1923 (NAI, DT, S5750/16).

21 *IN*, 25 May 1923; Mark Sturgis to Tallents, 13 Dec. 1922 (TNA, HO 45/24814); *IN*, 8 Dec. 1922.

22 Tyrone North, Frank Quinn Drumquin; John O'Donnell, Jim O'Neill Dreggish, Newtownstweart; Brian McKee, Main Street, Strabane (sec.); Mid–Tyrone Sean Corr, Sluggan, Carrickmore; Mick McCartan, VS Campsie, Omagh (sec.); East Tyrone; Liam Donnelly, Loy Hill, Cookstown, South Tyrone: John Shields, Benburb; Frank Dooris, Clogher.

23 P. Thornbury to Moss Twomey, 29 June 1923 (UCDAD, Twomey papers, P69/191/1–2).

24 O'Shiel report on *Argenta*, 11 July 1923 (NAI, DT, S5750/5).

25 O'Shiel to Cosgrave, 16 July 1923 (NAI, DT, S5750/16).

26 Cosgrave to Mulcahy, 19 Oct. 1923 (ibid.).

27 Healy to O'Shiel, 10 Nov. 1923 (UCDAD, Blythe papers, P24/204); O'Shiel to executive council, 17 Nov. 1923 (UCDAD, Blythe papers, P24/204/68).

28 *IN*, 29 Oct. 1923.   29 Ibid., 2 Nov. 1923.

30 *Northern Whig*, 3 Nov. 1923.

31 Mayne to James Doyle, 8 May 1924 (PRONI, HA/5/2118).

32 Mrs John Gallagher to Cosgrave, 21 June 1923; Cosgrave to Mrs Gallagher, 16 July 1923 (NAI, DT, S5750/16).

33 Murray, *Boundary Commission*, p. 309.
34 Cosgrave to Kennedy, 5 July 1924 (UCDAD, Kennedy papers, P4/415).
35 *An Phoblacht*, 11 Dec. 1925.
36 Regan, *Counter-revolution*, p. 251.
37 Patrick Buckland, *The factory of grievances: devolved government in Northern Ireland, 1921–39* (Dublin, 1979), p. 228.
38 Healy to *The Statesman*, Dec. 1926 (PRONI, Healy papers, D2991/A/10).
39 Harbison to Healy, 19 Aug. 1927 (ibid., D2991/A/30).
40 Hepburn, *Catholic Belfast*, p. 257.   41 Laffan, *Resurrection*, p. 295.
42 Fanning, *Fatal path*, p. 352.
43 Jackson, *Home rule*, pp 153–4.
44 Milner to Carson, 21 July 1914 (PRONI, Irish papers, D1507/A/6/40).
45 Murray, *Boundary Commission*, p. 31.
46 Ronald Storrs, *The memoirs of Sir Ronald Storrs* (London, 2008), p. 364.
47 Montgomery to Stronge, 6 Apr. 1920 (PRONI, Montgomery papers, D627/435/21); Montgomery to Leo Maxse, 7 May 1920 (ibid., D627/435/75).
48 Montgomery to W.M. Jellett, 19 Feb. 1918 (ibid., D627/432/11).
49 Cabinet conclusions, 30 May 1922 (TNA, CAB 23/30).
50 Clive Pointing, *Winston Churchill* (London, 1994), p. 132.
51 Phoenix, *Northern nationalism*, p. 225.
52 Londonderry to [?] McKeown, 9 Sept. 1922 (PRONI, Londonderry papers, D3099/2/7/43).
53 Conference with the officers of the Irish Government, 23 July 1920 (TNA, CAB 23/27).
54 Londonderry to Kennedy, 5 Aug. 1922 (UCDAD, Kennedy papers, P4/381/3–4).
55 Murray, *Boundary Commission*, p. 305.
56 Cabinet conclusions, 7 Sept. 1921 (TNA, CAB 23/27).
57 De Valera to Luke Dillon, 7 July 1923 (UCDAD, de Valera papers, P150/1197).

Select bibliography

PRIMARY SOURCES

A. MANUSCRIPTS

Armagh

Cardinal Ó Fiaich Memorial Library & Archive

Cardinal Michael Logue papers.
Cardinal Patrick O'Donnell papers.
Fr Louis O'Kane papers.
Cardinal Joseph MacRory papers.

Belfast

Public Records Office of Northern Ireland

Abercorn papers.
J.B. Armour papers.
Cabinet secretariat.
J.H. Collins papers.
Craigavon political papers.
Crawford papers.
Davies papers.
Falls & Hanna papers.
Arthur Griffith documents.
Cahir Healy papers.
Irish (Carson) papers.
Londonderry (7th Marquess) papers.
Colonel Robert Lowry papers.
Ministry of Finance.
Ministry of Home Affairs.
Ministry of Home Affairs, secret series.
Hugh de Fellenberg Montgomery papers.
Moutray papers.
Newton family papers.
Spender papers and diaries.
Tyrone UVF.
Ulster Unionist Council papers.
Wilson & Simms papers.

Cork

Cork City & County Archives

George Berkeley papers.

Dublin

Dublin Diocesan Archives

Archbishop William Walsh papers.

Military Archives

2nd Northern Division reports, 1921–2.
Bureau of Military History witness statements.
Tyrone Brigade reports, 1919–21.

National Archives of Ireland

Boundary Commission records.
Chief Secretary's Office Registered papers.
Dáil Éireann Local Government records.
Dáil Éireann Tyrone Court records.
Dáil Éireann Ulster sub-committee records.
Department of the Taoiseach general files.
Northeast Boundary Bureau records.

National Library of Ireland

Joseph Brennan papers.
Éamonn Ceannt papers.
Coffey & Chenevix Trench papers.
Michael Collins papers.
George Gavan Duffy papers.
J.J. Horgan papers.
Thomas Johnson papers.
Joseph McGarrity papers.
Maurice Moore papers.
Leon Ó Broin papers.
J.J. O'Connell papers.
Florence O'Donoghue papers.
Kevin O'Shiel, letter book.
Sean O'Mahony papers.
Count Plunkett papers.
John Redmond papers.

Trinity College, Dublin

John Dillon papers.

University College Dublin, Archives Department

Ernest Blythe papers.
Éamon de Valera papers.

Fianna Fáil papers.
Hugh Kennedy papers.
Seán MacEntee papers.
Eoin MacNeill papers.
Richard Mulcahy papers.
Ernie O'Malley papers & notebooks.
Sinn Féin minutes 1919–22.
Moss Twomey papers.

London

House of Lords

Andrew Bonar Law papers.
David Lloyd George papers.

National Archives

Cabinet papers.
Colonial Office papers.
Home Office papers.
War Office papers

B. OFFICIAL RECORDS

Census of Ireland, 1901–11.
Dáil Éireann. Parliamentary debates.
Hansard House of Commons parliamentary debates.
Report of the 1911 census, Province of Ulster, County Tyrone (London, 1911).

C. NEWSPAPERS AND PERIODICALS

An tÉireannach
An Phoblacht
Belfast Newsletter
Dungannon Democrat
Dungannon News and County Tyrone
Advertiser
Donegal News
Freeman's Journal
Gaelic American
Irish Bulletin
Irish Freedom

Irish Independent
Irish News
Irish Times
Irish Volunteer
London Morning Post
Mid-Ulster Mail
Northern Whig
Times
Tyrone Constitution
Tyrone Courier
Ulster Herald

D. PRINTED PRIMARY MATERIAL

Clarke, Thomas J., *Glimpses of an Irish felon's prison life* (Cork, 1922).

Daly, Charlie, 'Call to arms for Ireland's full freedom' in *The story of the Drumboe martyrs – 80th anniversary edition* (Donegal, 2003), pp 30–4.

Hobson, Bulmer, *A short history of the Irish Volunteers* (Dublin, 1918).

Martin, F.X., 'The McCartan documents', *Clogher Record*, 6:1 (1966), 5–65.

O'Brien, William, *An olive branch in Ireland* (London, 1910).

O'Rahilly, *The secret history of the Irish Volunteers* (Dublin, 1915).

SECONDARY SOURCES

E. PUBLISHED WORKS

Augusteijn, Joost, *From public defiance to guerrilla warfare: the experience of ordinary volunters in the Irish War of Independence, 1916–1921* (Dublin, 1996).

Bew, Paul, *Conflict and conciliation in Ireland, 1890–1910: Parnellites and radical agrarians* (Oxford, 1987).

—— *Ideology and the Irish question: Ulster unionism and Irish nationalism, 1912–1916* (Oxford, 1998).

Bew, Paul, Peter Gibbon and Henry Patterson, *Northern Ireland, 1921–2001: political forces and social classes* (London, 2002).

Biagini, Eugenio F., *British democracy and Irish nationalism, 1876–1906* (Cambridge, 2007).

Bowman, Timothy, 'The UVF and the formation of the 36th (Ulster) Division', *IHS*, 32:128 (2001), 498–518.

—— *Irish regiments in the Great War: discipline and morale* (Manchester, 2003).

—— *Carson's army, the Ulster Volunteer Force, 1910–22* (Manchester, 2007).

Breen, Dan, *My fight for Irish freedom* (Tralee, 1978).

Brewer, John D., *The Royal Irish Constabulary: an oral history* (Belfast, 1990).

Brock, Michael and Eleanor (eds), H.H. Asquith, *letters to Venetia Stanley* (Oxford, 1982).

Buckland, Patrick, *Irish unionism, 1885–1923: a documentary history* (Belfast, 1973).

—— *The factory of grievances: devolved government in Northern Ireland, 1921–39* (Dublin, 1979).

Callanan, Frank, *T.M. Healy* (Cork, 1996).

Campbell, Fergus, *Land and revolution: nationalist politics in the west of Ireland, 1891–1921* (Oxford, 2005).

Chambers, Ian, *The Chamberlains, the Churchills and Ireland, 1874–1922* (New York, 2006).

Coleman, Marie, *County Longford and the Irish revolution, 1910–1923* (Dublin, 2003).

Darwin, John, *The empire project: the rise and fall of the British world-system, 1830–1970* (Cambridge, 2009).

Dooley, Terence, 'The organization of unionist opposition to home rule in counties Monaghan, Cavan and Donegal, 1885–1914', *Clogher Record*, 16:1 (1997), 46–70.

Elliott, Sydney, *Northern Ireland parliamentary election results, 1921–1972* (Chichester, 1973).

Fanning, Ronan, 'Anglo-Irish relations: partition and the British dimension in historical perspective', *Irish Studies in International Affairs*, 2:1 (1985), 1–20.

—— *Fatal path: British government and Irish revolution, 1910–1922* (London, 2013).

Farrell, Michael, *Arming the Protestants: the formation of the Ulster Special Constabulary, 1920–27* (London, 1983).

Fitzpatrick, David, 'The geography of Irish nationalism 1910–1921', *Past & Present*, 78 (1978), 113–44.

—— 'Strikes in Ireland 1914–1921', *Saothar*, 6 (1980), 26–39.

—— 'The logic of collective sacrifice: Ireland and the British Army, 1914–18', *Historical Journal*, 38:4 (1995), 1017–30.

—— *Politics and Irish life, 1913–1921: provincial experiences of war and revolution* (2nd ed., Cork, 1998).

—— *The two Irelands: 1912–1939* (Oxford, 1998).

Foy, Michael, 'Ulster unionism and the development of the Ulster Volunteer Force' in Jürgen Elvert (ed.), *Nordirland in Gerschichte und Gegenwart* (Stuttgart, 1994), pp 99–127.

Gailey, Andrew, 'Unionist rhetoric and Irish local government reform, 1895–9', *IHS*, 24:93 (1984), 52–68.

Galtung, Johan, 'A structural theory of imperialism', *Journal of Peace Research*, 8:2 (1971), 81–117.

Garvin, Tom, *Nationalist revolutionaries in Ireland, 1891–1922* (Oxford, 1987).

Hart, Peter, 'The geography of revolution in Ireland, 1917–1923', *Past and Present*, 155 (1997), 142–76.

—— *The IRA at war, 1916–1923* (Oxford, 2003).

Hay, Marnie, *Bulmer Hobson and the nationalist movement in twentieth-century Ireland* (Manchester, 2009).

Hepburn, A.C., *The conflict of nationality in modern Ireland* (London, 1980).

—— *Catholic Belfast and nationalist Ireland in the era of Joe Devlin, 1871–1934* (Oxford, 2008).

Holmes, Janice & Diane Urquhart (eds), *Coming into the light: work, politics and religion of women in Ulster, 1840–1940* (Belfast, 1994).

Hopkinson, Michael, *Green against green: the Irish Civil War* (Dublin, 1988).

—— 'The Craig-Collins pacts of 1922: two attempted reforms of the Northern Ireland government', *IHS*, 27:106 (1990), 145–58.

—— *The Irish War of Independence* (Dublin, 2002).

Jackson, Alvin, *Ireland, 1798–1998: politics and war* (Oxford, 1999).

—— *Home rule: an Irish history, 1800–2000* (London, 2004).

Jalland, Patricia, *The Liberals and Ireland: the Ulster question in British politics to 1914* (Brighton, 1980).

Kelly, Matthew, 'The Irish Volunteers: a Machiavellian moment?' in D. George Boyce & Alan O'Day (eds), *The Ulster crisis, 1885–1921* (Basingstoke, 2005), pp 64–85.

—— *The Fenian ideal and Irish nationalism, 1882–1916* (Woodbridge, 2006).

Kennedy, T.C., 'War, patriotism, and the Ulster Unionist Council, 1914–18', *Éire-Ireland*, 40 (2005), 189–211.

Kleinrichert, Denise, *Republican internment and the prison ship Argenta, 1922* (Dublin, 2004).

Kostick, Conor, *Revolution in Ireland: popular militancy, 1917–1923* (London, 1996).

Kotsonouris, Mary, *Retreat from revolution: the Dáil courts, 1920–24* (Dublin, 1994).

Laffan, Michael, *The partition of Ireland, 1911–1925* (Dundalk, 1983).

—— *The resurrection of Ireland: the Sinn Féin party, 1916–23* (Cambridge, 2005).

Lawlor, Pearse, *1920–1922: the outrages. The IRA and the Ulster Special Constabulary in the border campaign* (Cork, 2011).

Lee, J.J., *Ireland, 1912–85: politics and society* (Cambridge, 1989).

Levenson, Leah & Jerry H. Natterstad, *Hanna Sheehy-Skeffington: Irish feminist* (Syracuse, 1989).

Lucy, Gordon, *The Ulster Covenant: an illustrated history of the 1912 home rule crisis* (Belfast, 2012).

Lynch, Robert, *The northern IRA and the early years of partition, 1920–22* (Dublin, 2006).

Lyons, J.B., 'Tom Kettle, 1880–1916', *Dublin Historical Record*, 43:2 (1990), 85–98.

MacAtasney, Gerald, *Seán Mac Diarmada: the mind of the revolution* (Leitrim, 2004).

Mac Eoin, Uinseann, *Survivors* (Dublin, 1980).

McCarthy, Cal, *Cumann na mBan and the Irish revolution* (Dublin, 2007).

McCluskey, Fergal, *Fenians and Ribbonmen: the development of republican politics in East Tyrone* (Manchester, 2011).

McDowell, R.B., *The Irish Convention, 1917–18* (London, 1970).

McGarry, Fearghal, *Eoin O'Duffy: a self-made hero* (Oxford, 2005).

—— *The Rising: Easter 1916* (Oxford, 2010).

McGee, Owen, *The IRB: the Irish Republican Brotherhood, from the Land League to Sinn Féin* (Dublin, 2005).

McGuire, James & James Quinn (eds), *Dictionary of Irish biography: from the earliest times to the year 2002* (9 vols, Cambridge, 2009).

McKenna, John, *A beleaguered station: the memoir of Head Constable John McKenna* (Belfast, 2009).

McNeill, Ronald, *Ulster's stand for union* (London, 1922).

McVeigh, Mary T., 'Lock Out? Caledon 1919', *Dúiche Néill*, 9 (1990), 94–111.

Mansergh, Nicholas, *The Irish question, 1840–1921: a commentary on Anglo-Irish relations and on social and political forces in Ireland in the age of reform and revolution* (London, 1975).

Martin, F.X., 'The 1916 Rising: A "coup d'état" or a "bloody protest"?', *Studia Hibernica*, 8 (1968), 106–37.

Maume, Patrick, *The long gestation: Irish nationalist life, 1891–1918* (Dublin, 1999).

Mercer, Eric, 'For king, country and a shilling a day: Belfast recruiting patterns in the Great War', *History Ireland*, 11:4 (2003), 29–33.

Miller, D.W., *Church, state and nation in Ireland, 1898–1921* (Dublin, 1973).

—— *Queen's rebels: Ulster loyalism in perspective* (Dublin, 1978).

Mitchell, Arthur, *Revolutionary government in Ireland, Dáil Éireann, 1919–22* (Dublin, 1995).

Murray, Paul, *The Irish Boundary Commission and its origins, 1886–1925* (Dublin, 2011).

Newsinger, John, *Rebel city: Larkin, Connolly and the labour movement* (London, 2004).

Novick, Ben, *Conceiving revolution: Irish nationalist propaganda during the First World War* (Dublin, 2001).

O'Day, Alan, *Irish home rule, 1867–1921* (Manchester, 1998).

Ó Duibhir, Liam, *The Donegal awakening: Donegal and the War of Independence* (Cork, 2009).

—— *Donegal & the Irish Civil War* (Cork, 2011).

Parkinson, Alan F., *Belfast's unholy war: the troubles of the 1920s* (Dublin, 2004).

Pašeta, Senia, *Before the revolution: nationalism, social change and Ireland's Catholic elite, 1879–1922* (Cork, 2004).

Patterson, Henry, *Class conflict and sectarianism: the Protestant working class and the Belfast labour movement, 1868–1920* (Belfast, 1980).

Phoenix, Éamon, 'Northern Ireland: from the birth-pangs to disintegration' in Ciaran Brady, Mary O'Dowd & Brian Walker (eds), *Ulster: an illustrated history* (London, 1989), pp 182–215.

—— *Northern nationalism: nationalist politics, partition and the Catholic minority in Northern Ireland* (Belfast, 1994).

—— 'Nationalism in Tyrone, 1890–1972' in Charles Dillon & Henry A. Jefferies (eds), *Tyrone: history and society* (Dublin, 2000), pp 765–808.

Ponting, Clive, *Winston Churchill* (London, 1994).

Privilege, John, *Michael Logue and the Catholic Church in Ireland, 1879–1925* (Manchester, 2009).

Rafferty, Oliver, *Catholicism in Ulster: an interpretative history* (London, 1994).

Regan, John M., *The Irish counter-revolution, 1921–1936* (Dublin, 2001).

Robinson, Philip, *The plantation of Ulster* (Belfast, 1994).

Savage, D.C., 'The origins of the Ulster Unionist Party, 1885–6', *IHS*, 12:47 (1961), 185–208.

Scholes, Andrew, *The Church of Ireland and the third home rule bill* (Dublin, 2010).

Smith, Jeremy, *The Tories and Ireland, 1910–1914* (Dublin, 2001).

—— 'Federalism, devolution and partition: Sir Edward Carson and the search for a compromise on the third home rule bill, 1913–14', *IHS*, 35:140 (2007), 496–518.

Smyth, Jim, 'Men of no popery: the origins of the Orange Order', *History Ireland*, 3:3 (1995), 48–53.

Staunton, Enda, *The nationalists of Northern Ireland, 1918–1973* (Dublin, 2001).

Storrs, Ronald, *The memoirs of Sir Ronald Storrs* (London, 2008).

Townshend, Charles, *The British campaign in Ireland: 1919–21* (Oxford, 1975).

—— 'The Irish Republican Army and the development of guerrilla warfare, 1916–1921', *English Historical Review*, 94:371 (1979), 318–45.

—— *Political violence in Ireland, government and resistance since 1848* (Oxford, 1983).

—— *Easter 1916: the Irish rebellion* (London, 2006).

—— *The Republic: the fight for Irish independence, 1918–1923* (London, 2013).

Walker, B.M. (ed.), *Parliamentary election results in Ireland, 1801–1922* (Dublin, 1978).

Walker, Graham, 'The Irish Presbyterian anti-home rule convention of 1912', *Studies*, 86:341 (1997), 71–7.

—— *A history of the Ulster Unionist Party: protest, pragmatism and pessimism* (Manchester, 2004).

Wheatley, Michael, *Nationalism and the Irish Party: provincial Ireland, 1910–1916* (Oxford, 2005).
White, J.R., *Misfit* (London, 1930).

F. THESES AND UNPUBLISHED WORK

Dooher, John, 'Tyrone nationalism and the question of partition: 1910–25' (MPhil, University of Ulster, 1986).
Foy, Michael T., 'The Ancient Order of Hibernians: an Irish political-religious pressure group' (MA, Queens University, Belfast, 1976).
Hepburn, A.C. 'Liberal policies and nationalist politics in Ireland' (PhD, University of Kent, 1968).
Ó Corráin, Daithí, 'Resigned to take the bill with its defects: the Catholic Church and the third Home Rule bill', paper to Cork Studies in the Irish Revolution: the home rule crisis, 1912–14 (Oct. 2012).
Woods, Damian, 'Doctor at the masthead: Dr Patrick McCartan and the IRB' (MSc, Queen's University, Belfast, 1998).

G. INTERNET RESOURCES

Ulster Covenant online, PRONI: http://www.proni.go.uk/

Index

Abercorn *see* Hamilton
abstention from parliament, 65, 69, 73, 76, 87, 102, 112, 133
Adair, John, 8, 27, 29
Agar-Robartes, Thomas, 21
Aiken, Frank, 90, 96, 113, 117, 122
Aldrummound, 74, 97
Allen, Fred, 36
All-for-Ireland League (AFIL), 38–9, 131
Allingham, Commander John, 120
ambushes: Altmore, 98; Ballygawley, 94; Benburb, 117; Caledon, 119; Charlemont (Armagh), 117; Dromore, 98; Dunamore (1921), 94; Dunamore (1922) 101; Dungannon, 94; Dungloe (Donegal), 90; Esker, 98; Pomeroy 97; Strabane, 119
amending bill, 43, 50–1
Ancient Order of Hibernians (AOH), 4, 6, 29; conflict with Healyism, 9, 36; moratorium on marches (1912), 42; Irish Volunteers, 33, 45–7; opposition to republicanism, 35, 71–4; IPP, 9, 14, 37, 64, 69; Orange antipathy for, 16, 18, 21–2; National Insurance, 22–3
Anglo-Irish Treaty (1921), 1, 14, 66, 85, 96, 99, 103–7, 109, 130–1; Dáil debates, 113–4, 136; anti-Treaty SF, 114, 116; pro-Treaty SF, 114–15, 117, 133; reaction of Tyrone IRA, 117, 119–20; Treaty negotiations, 110–13, 127, 136; *see also* Irish Civil War (1922–3)
Annaghboe, 112
anti-Treaty IRA (ATIRA), 116–17, 119–20, 121–4
Antrim, 18, 21, 33, 78
Archdale, Edward, 103
Armour, Rev J.B., 19–20, 41
Apprentice Boys of Derry, 13, 24, 42, 54
arbitration courts: *see* Dáil Courts
Ardboe, 24, 33–5, 67, 73, 125
Argenta prison ship, 85, 124, 132–3
Armagh, 21, 112, 115; Diocese, 38, 72; IPP, 69; IRA, 76, 90, 117, 122; IRB, 8, 33–4, 47; Irish Volunteers, 47, 55; Sinn Féin, 71, 82; South Armagh by-election (1918), 72–3; Ulster unionists, 18, 24–5, 54; Ulster Volunteers, 19
Ashbourne, 60
Ashe, Thomas, 60, 68
Asquith, H.H., xv, 1, 43, 49, 131

Aud, 58
Augher, 11, 24
Aughnacloy, 20, 25, 28, 31, 107, 118
Aughnagar, 45
Augusteijn, Joost, 66

Bachelor's Walk killings, 48
Baird, John, 119
Balfour Declaration (1917), 134
Ballinascreen, 108
Ballinderry, 73
Ballygawley, 9, 52, 94
Balmoral, 20
Banbridge, 78, 86, 92
Baronscourt, 10, 27, 28, 30, 46, 75
Bates, Dawson, 54, 75, 83, 86, 88, 92, 100, 107, 118–19, 124–5, 127, 132
Baton Convention (1909), 38
Belcoo, 57
Belfast, 80, 89, 114, 124, 132; Belfast Eugenics Society, 25; Boycott of Belfast goods, 22, 86–7, 91, 106, 114; British Army, 53; Easter Rising, 57–61; female suffrage, 17; government, 61, 64, 83, 88, 96, 102–5, 113, 120, 125–6; industry, 2; IPP, 6; IRA, 107, 121, 132; IRB, 35–6, 49, 55, 90; IPP, 43, 62, 66, 72–3, 76, 102–3; Irish Volunteers, 30, 57–8; labour activity, 83, 85; loyalist violence, 21–2, 78, 86, 92, 108, 118–9, 124, 135–6; Sinn Féin, 116; Ulster Special Constabulary, 121; Ulster unionists, 3, 12, 14, 16, 19, 21, 23, 62, 75, 88, 129, 134; Ulster Volunteers, 27–8, 30–1, 42–3, 61
Belfast Engineers and Dockers' strike (1917–18), 83
Belfast shipyard expulsions (1912), 21–2
Belfast shipyard expulsions (1920), 86
Belleck, 124
Benburb, 42, 79, 90, 117, 118
Beragh, 58, 69, 86
Berkeley, George Fitz Hardinge, 30
Birrell, Augustine, 38–40
Black and Tans: *see* Royal Irish Constabulary (RIC)
Blackwatertown, 46
Blythe, Ernest, 55, 57, 79, 122
Bonar Law, Andrew, 17, 19, 20, 31, 49, 92
Boundary Commission, 77, 111–14, 117, 126–7, 129, 131–3, 136
Bowman, Timothy, 29, 61